914.3155
E45

Berlin Area by Area

Streetsmart

Within each Top 10 list in this book, no hierarchy of quality or popularity is implied. All 10 are, in the editor's opinion, of roughly equal merit.

Front cover and spine *The Reichstag at sunrise*
Back cover *Enjoying the view of the Berliner Dom*
Title page *Unique roof of the Sony Center at Potsdamer Platz*

The information in this DK Eyewitness Top 10 Travel Guide is checked annually. Every effort has been made to ensure that this book is as up-to-date as possible at the time of going to press. Some details, however, such as telephone numbers, opening hours, prices, gallery hanging arrangements and travel information are liable to change. The publishers cannot accept responsibility for any consequences arising from the use of this book, nor for any material on third party websites, and cannot guarantee that any website address in this book will be a suitable source of travel information. We value the views and suggestions of our readers very highly. Please write to: Publisher, DK Eyewitness Travel Guides, Dorling Kindersley, 80 Strand, London WC2R 0RL, Great Britain, or email travelguides@dk.com

Welcome to
Berlin

Few European cities have witnessed as much upheaval and renewal as Berlin. From Prussian powerhouse and Nazi bastion to Cold War zombie and revitalized capital of a reunited Germany – Berlin has seen it all, and then some. With Eyewitness Top 10 Berlin, this fascinating city that is perpetually in a state of becoming is yours to explore.

Even today, the layers of history speak volumes. A stroll along **Unter den Linden** leads you from the classical columns of **Brandenburger Tor** past former Third Reich ministries to the world-class treasures of **Museumsinsel**. Just beyond lies the Socialist architecture of **Alexanderplatz**, compelling in an entirely different way. This kaleidoscope of eras lends charm to Berlin's crooked grin.

For many visitors, the city's star attractions are its exciting arts scene and variety of bars, cafés and nightclubs. The spirit of the Golden Twenties lives on here, and Berlin keeps going around the clock. How much you do depends on your staying power – as any bleary-eyed reveller will tell you, this isn't a city of morning people (the after-parties don't count). But that's not all. For a metropolis, Berlin is surprisingly green, with vast parks such as the **Tiergarten** or **Volkspark Friedrichshain** teeming with lazing couples, families having a barbecue, joggers and cyclists – in a country known for its *autobahns*, people are increasingly trading in their cars for bicycles.

Whether you're visiting for a weekend or a week, our Top 10 guide brings together the best of everything that Berlin has to offer, from the hip cafés of **Prenzlauer Berg** to the gritty nightclubs of **Kreuzberg** and the royal stamping grounds of **Charlottenburg**. There are tips throughout, from seeking out what's free to avoiding the crowds, plus 14 easy-to-follow itineraries, designed to tie together a clutch of sights in a short space of time. Add inspiring photography and detailed maps, and you've got the essential pocket-sized travel companion. **Enjoy the book, and enjoy Berlin.**

Clockwise from top: **Berliner Dom, Sony Center at Potsdamer Platz, Hackescher Markt near Hackesche Höfe, Schloss Charlottenburg, Marx-Engels-Forum, the Philharmonie concert hall**

Exploring Berlin

For a sprawling, historic metropolis whose charms are widely scattered, Berlin is a surprisingly easy place to navigate. There's something for every interest and budget, and excellent public transport whisks you from sight to sight with clockwork efficiency. Here are a few ideas to maximize your fun and minimize your planning.

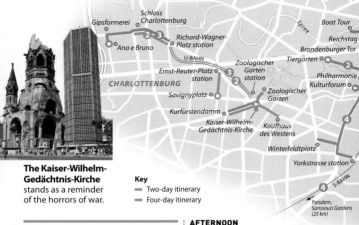

The Kaiser-Wilhelm-Gedächtnis-Kirche stands as a reminder of the horrors of war.

Key
— Two-day itinerary
— Four-day itinerary

Two Days in Berlin

Day ❶
MORNING
Begin at **Alexanderplatz** (see pp102–9) and ascend the **Fernsehturm** (see p104) for an unequalled Berlin panorama. View Babylonian treasures at the **Pergamonmuseum** (see pp24–6).
AFTERNOON
Stroll along historic **Unter den Linden** (see pp16–19). Admire the iconic **Brandenburger Tor** (see pp12–13) and take a guided tour of the **Reichstag** (see pp14–15) before enjoying a classical concert at the **Philharmonie** (see pp38–9).

Day ❷
MORNING
Begin with the ruins of the **Kaiser-Wilhelm-Gedächtnis-Kirche** (see pp32–3) before exploring stores along **Kurfürstendamm** (see pp30–31) and in **Kaufhaus des Westens** (see p76).

AFTERNOON
After lunch, wander through **Schloss Charlottenburg** (see pp34–7) and linger in its Baroque-style gardens. Seek out **Savignyplatz** for cocktails and an evening bite (see p120–21).

Four Days in Berlin

Day ❶
MORNING
Spend time exploring the **Reichstag** and government district (see pp14–15), then take a **boat tour** through Berlin's waterways (see p170). There are piers in the Tiergarten next to the Haus der Kulturen der Welt.
AFTERNOON
Have lunch at **Aigner** (see p93), and visit pretty **Gendarmenmarkt** (see p86). Promenade on **Unter den Linden** (see pp16–17) before admiring the **Brandenburger Tor** (see pp12–13). Catch an evening show at the **Friedrichstadt-Palast** (see p67).

The Reichstag, one of Berlin's most symbolic buildings, is a popular sight.

The Neues Museum contains spectacular treasures, including the bust of Nefertiti.

Potsdamer Platz, untouched for nearly 50 years in rubble, has now been regenerated into a vibrant city hub.

Day ❷
MORNING
Take the lift up to the **Fernsehturm** observation deck (see p104). Peruse the collections of **Museumsinsel** (see pp24–7), particularly the **Neues Museum**, home to the Nefertiti bust, and the **Pergamonmuseum** (see p26).
AFTERNOON
Head to **Potsdamer Platz** (see pp20–23) for daring modern architecture and the Marlene Dietrich exhibit at the **Deutsche Kinamathek** (see p22). Stroll in the **Tiergarten** (see p113).

Day ❸
MORNING
Start at the **Kaiser-Wilhelm-Gedächtnis-Kirche** (see pp32–3), then choose between the **Zoologischer Garten** (see pp42–3) or shopping on **Kurfürstendamm** (see pp30–31).
AFTERNOON
Marvel at Prussian riches at **Schloss Charlottenburg** and wander its beautifully landscaped park (see pp34–7). Stop by the **Gipsformerei** for gift sculptures (see p77). After that, head to **Ana e Bruno** for an excellent Italian meal (see p127).

Day ❹
MORNING
Start the day at the **Kulturforum** (see pp38–41). There are several cultural institutions to be explored in this complex, but a wise use of time is to view the Renaissance masters at the **Gemäldegalerie** (see p40). To enjoy some local specialities for lunch, stop by the last market hall in Berlin, the **Marheineke-Markthalle**, which is full of vibrant stores (see p133).
AFTERNOON
The splendid town of **Potsdam** and the stunning gardens in the palace complex of **Sanssouci** (see pp156–61) are a short trip away from the city by commuter train.

Top 10 Berlin Highlights

The grand auditorium of the Berlin
Staatsoper Unter den Linden

🔟 Berlin Highlights

Berlin is Germany's liveliest city and one of the most fascinating capitals in the world. You'll find no other place where art and culture, museums and theatres, entertainment and nightlife are more diverse and exciting than around the banks of the Spree River. Once reunited, Berlin quickly developed into a cosmopolitan city, and today there is an air of great energy and vibrancy about it.

Brandenburger Tor and Pariser Platz ➊

The Brandenburger Tor stands in Pariser Platz, where the embassies and the famous Hotel Adlon exude a stylish elegance *(see pp12–13)*.

➋ Reichstag

No other building is a more potent symbol of Germany's history than the Reichstag. Its vast egg-shaped dome affords fantastic views across the city *(see pp14–15)*.

MOABIT

KAISERIN-AUGUSTA-ALLEE

BEUSSEL-STRASSE

LEVETZOWSTR

FRANKLINSTR

LESSINGSTR

Schloss-park

Spree

➑ SPANDAUER-DAMM

OTTO-SUHR-ALLEE

KAISER-FRIEDRICH-STR.

HANSAVIERTEL

ALTONAER STRASSE

STRASSE DES 17. JUNI

KAISER-DAMM

BISMARCKSTRASSE

CHARLOTTENBURG

HARDENBERGSTR.

KANTSTRASSE

➓

➐

KURFÜRSTENDAMM

➏

LIETZENBURGER

STRASSE

➌ Unter den Linden

This magnificent, leafy boulevard has always been a central axis along Berlin's most important historic buildings *(see pp16–19)*.

Potsdamer Platz ➍

The new heart of the old city is Potsdamer Platz, where exciting modern structures have been erected *(see pp20–23)*.

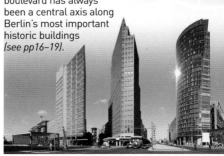

5 Museumsinsel

Among the museums in this complex are the Pergamonmuseum, which houses the Pergamon Altar (see pp24–7), the Altes and the Neues museums.

7 Kaiser-Wilhelm-Gedächtnis-Kirche

The tower ruins of the memorial church, built to commemorate Kaiser Wilhelm I, still stand today as a silent reminder of the horrors of war (see pp32–3).

Kurfürsten-damm 6

Berlin's much visited strolling and shopping avenue is the main thoroughfare in the western part of the city (see pp30–31).

0 kilometres 1
0 miles 1

Schloss Charlottenburg 8

The former Hohenzollern summer residence and its beautiful Baroque gardens offer visitors a slice of Prussian history (see pp34–7).

9 Kulturforum

This complex of museums, which includes the Gemäldegalerie, the Kunstgewerbemuseum and the Neue Nationalgalerie, yields a unique cultural experience (see pp38–41).

Zoologischer Garten 10

Germany's oldest and most famous zoo and aquarium, in the centre of the city, boasts over 19,000 animals and nearly 1,500 different species (see pp42–3).

TOP 10 ⭐ Brandenburger Tor and Pariser Platz

The best known of Berlin's symbols, the Brandenburg Gate stands proudly in the middle of Pariser Platz, asserting itself against the modern embassy buildings that now surround it. Crowned by its triumphant Quadriga sculpture, the famous gate has long been a focal point in Berlin's history: rulers and statesmen, military parades and demonstrations – all have felt compelled to march through the Brandenburger Tor.

Brandenburger Tor ①
Built by Carl G Langhans in 1789–91 and modelled on the temple porticoes of ancient Athens, the Brandenburg Gate **(right)** is the undisputed symbol of Berlin. Since the 19th century, this iconic landmark has been the backdrop for many events in the city's turbulent history.

② Quadriga
The 6-m (20-ft) high sculpture **(below)** was created in 1794 as a symbol of peace by Johann Gottfried Schadow. As the model for the goddess of peace, he used his niece, who subsequently became famous throughout Berlin.

③ Hotel Adlon Berlin
Favoured by visiting dignitaries, the city's most elegant hotel **(below)** is a reconstruction. The legendary original, destroyed in World War II, hosted celebrities that included Greta Garbo, Thomas Mann and Charlie Chaplin.

④ DZ Bank
This modern building, designed by the American architect Frank Owen Gehry, combines the clean lines of Prussian architecture with some daring elements inside (see p57).

⑤ Akademie der Künste
Built in 2000–2005 and designed by Günter Behnisch and Manfred Sabatke, the Academy of Arts incorporates, behind a vast expanse of windows, the ruins of the old art academy, which was destroyed in World War II.

⑥ French Embassy
Christian de Portzamparc built this elegant building in 2001 on the site of the old embassy, which was ruined in World War II. Its colonnades and windows are a homage to the original.

7 Palais am Pariser Platz

This complex **(left)** by Bernhard Winking is a successful modern interpretation of Neo-Classical architecture. Inside you will find a café, a restaurant and a souvenir shop around a pleasantly shaded courtyard.

NEED TO KNOW

MAP K3 ■ Pariser Platz

Tourist information centre: Brandenburger Tor southern gatehouse ■ (030) 25 00 25 ■ www.visitberlin.de

Open Apr–Oct: 9:30am–7pm daily; Nov–Mar: 9:30am–6pm daily

■ One of the best spots for coffee in Pariser Platz is bistro Theodor Tucher *(see p94)*.

■ You can trace the course of the Wall along the former border patrol road, following the green-and-white Berliner Mauerweg signs. Historic interest and natural beauty alternate along the trail.

8 Haus Liebermann

Josef P Kleihues built this in 1996–8, faithfully recreating the original that stood on the same site. The house is named after the artist Max Liebermann, who lived here. In 1933, watching Nazi SA troops march through the gate, he famously said: "I cannot possibly eat as much as I would like to puke."

9 American Embassy

The last gap around Pariser Platz was finally closed in 2008 **(above)**. A dispute had delayed building for years: the US wanted a whole street moved for reasons of security, but had to concede the point in the end.

10 Eugen-Gutmann-Haus

With its clean lines, the Dresdner Bank **(right)**, built in 1997 by gmp, recalls the style of the New Sobriety movement of the 1920s. In front of it is Pariser Platz's famous original street sign.

ᴛᴏᴘ10 ★ Reichstag

Of all the buildings in Berlin, the Reichstag, seat of the Bundestag (parliament), is probably one of the most symbolic. The mighty structure, erected in 1884–94 by Paul Wallot as the proud manifestation of the power of the German Reich, was destroyed by arson in 1933 and bombed during World War II. In 1995, the artist Christo wrapped up the Reichstag and, in 1999, the British architect Lord Norman Foster transformed it into one of the most modern parliamentary buildings in the world.

The Dome ①

The Reichstag dome by Lord Norman Foster affords breathtaking views of Berlin. It is open at the top to air the building and – a symbolic touch – to allow for the free and open dissemination of debates throughout the country. A ramp winds its way up to the top **(right)**.

② Plenary Hall

The plenary hall **(above)** is the seat of the Deutscher Bundestag – the German parliament – which has convened here again since 20 April 1999. Technologically, the hall is one of the most advanced parliament buildings in the world. The federal eagle caused a row: considered too "fat", it had to be slimmed down.

③ Portico "Dem deutschen Volke"

The dedication "To the German People" was designed in 1916, against the will of Wilhelm II.

④ Restored Façade

Despite extensive renovations, small World War II bullet holes are still visible in the building's façade.

THE REICHSTAG FIRE

When the Reichstag went up in flames on 27 February 1933, the Dutch Communist van der Lubbe was arrested for arson. It is, however, likely that the Nazis started the fire themselves. Hitler used it as an excuse to get the "Enabling Act" passed, which let him dispose off his opponents and marked the start of a 12-year reign of terror.

Restaurant Käfer ⑤

This popular luxury restaurant **(right)** on the Reichstag's roof offers an excellent view of the historical centre of Unter den Linden (see p117).

8 The German Flag

The giant German flag (left) was first raised on the occasion of the official national celebrations of German reunification on 3 October 1990.

9 Weiße Kreuze Memorial

Opposite the southern side of the Reichstag, a memorial recalls the Wall, which stood only a few steps away. The white crosses commemorate the people who died at the Wall while trying to escape to West Berlin.

10 Memorial by Dieter Appelt

Unveiled in 1992, the memorial (below) in front of the Reichstag commemorates 97 Social Democratic and Communist delegates who were murdered under the Third Reich.

6 Platz der Republik

Celebrations often take place on the lawn in front of the Reichstag, as in 2006, when Germany hosted the Football World Cup (below).

7 Installation "Der Bevölkerung"

Hans Haacke's work of art "To the People" is a counterpoint to the portico inscription opposite and uses the same style of lettering.

NEED TO KNOW

MAP K2 ▪ Platz der Republik 1
▪ Dome: (030) 22 73 21 52; Käfer: (030) 22 62 99 35 ▪ www.bundestag.de

Open Dome: 8am–midnight (last entry 10pm); Käfer: 9am–4:30pm, 6:30pm–midnight daily

To visit the Reichstag dome you must register at www.bundestag.de 2–3 days in advance. You can try for same-day admission at the Visitors' Service Centre (Nov–Mar: 8am–6pm daily; Apr–Oct: 8am–8pm daily) next to the Berlin Pavilion on Scheidemannstraße. You will require your passport/identity card.

▪ If a meal at Käfer exceeds your budget, many stalls near the Reichstag sell tempting *Bratwurst* (sausages).

🔟⭐ Unter den Linden

"As long as the lime trees still blossom in Unter den Linden, Berlin will always be Berlin," sang Marlene Dietrich about this magnificent avenue. The lime trees blossom more beautifully than ever and the street's old buildings have been extensively restored. The Linden, once a royal bridle path linking the king's town residence (the Stadtschloss) and Tiergarten, became Berlin's most fashionable street in the 18th century, and was synonymous with the city that was then the capital of Prussia.

Deutsches Historisches Museum

Germany's largest history museum **(right)** offers an overview of more than 1,000 years of German history. Housed in the Zeughaus, it is the oldest and architecturally the most interesting building on Unter den Linden *(see p18)*.

2 Staatsoper Unter den Linden

The richly ornamented State Opera House **(above)** is one of Germany's most attractive. Neo-Classical in style, it was built by architect Georg Wenzeslaus von Knobelsdorff between 1741–3 as Europe's first free-standing opera house, to plans devised by Frederick the Great himself *(see p85)*.

3 St Hedwigskathedrale

Designed by von Knobelsdorff in 1740–2 and modelled on the Pantheon in Rome, this is the seat of Berlin's Catholic archdiocese **(below)**. It was commissioned by Frederick the Great to appease Berlin Catholics after the conquest of Silesia *(see p58)*.

4 Humboldt-Universität

Berlin's oldest and most highly regarded university **(above)** was founded in 1890, on the initiative of Wilhelm von Humboldt. Twenty-nine Nobel Prize winners were educated here, including Albert Einstein.

(8) Kronprinzenpalais

Originally created in 1669 as a private residence by Johann Arnold Nering, the building was remodelled in 1732–3 into a Neo-Classical palace by Philip Gerlach and was a residence for several Hohenzollern heirs. After World War I it became an art museum, before the East German government housed state visitors there. The German reunification agreement was signed here in August 1990. It now holds cultural events and exhibitions.

(5) Neue Wache

The central German memorial **(above)** for all victims of war was created in 1816–8 by Karl Friedrich Schinkel. A reproduction of Käthe Kollwitz's moving *Pietà* stands here.

(9) Bebelplatz

Originally named Opernplatz, this wide open space was designed by Georg W von Knobelsdorff as the focal point of his Forum Fridericianum. The elegant square was meant to introduce some of the splendour and glory of ancient Rome to the Prussian capital. In May 1933, it became the scene of the infamous Nazi book burning.

NEED TO KNOW

MAP K5 ■ Deutsches Historisches Museum: Zeughaus, Unter den Linden 2 ■ (030) 20 30 40 ■ www.dhm.de

Open 10am–6pm daily Admission charge

MAP K4 ■ Staatsoper: Unter den Linden 7 ■ (030) 20 35 45 55 ■ www.staatsoper-berlin.de

Closed for renovation; until then, performances take place at the Schillertheater, Bismarckstr. 110

■ Take a break at the Café im Deutschen Historischen Museum (in the Zeughaus) which can be accessed directly from the street.

(6) Opernpalais

The charming building next to the Staatsoper, built in 1733–7, was also known as the Kronprinzessinnenpalais and once served as a palace for the daughters of Friedrich Wilhelm III.

(7) Russische Botschaft

The gigantic Russian Embassy, built in Stalinist "wedding-cake style", was the first building to be erected on Unter den Linden after World War II.

(10) Frederick the Great's Statue

One of Christian Daniel Rauch's grandest sculptures, this equestrian statue **(above)** shows "Old Fritz" (13.5 m/44 ft high) in his tricorn and coronation mantle *(see p85)*.

Deutsches Historisches Museum

1 The Dying Warriors
The 22 reliefs by Andreas Schlüter, displayed on the walls of the courtyard rather than in one of the museum's exhibitions, portray the horrors of war in an unusually immediate way.

2 Europe and Asia
This group of 18th century Meissen porcelain figures reflects the fascinating relationship between the two continents.

3 Steam Engine
A full-sized steam engine from the year 1847 marks the entrance to the exhibition on the Industrial Revolution.

4 Clothes from the Camps
Among the many exhibits here that illustrate the years under Nazi rule is the jacket of a concentration camp inmate – a chilling reminder of the Third Reich.

5 Martin Luther
Luther's portrait, by Lucas Cranach the Elder, is the focal point of exhibition rooms devoted to the Reformation and Martin Luther.

Gloria Victis **by Antonin Mercié**

6 Gloria Victis
The moving allegorical figure of Gloria Victis, created by the French sculptor Antonin Mercié, bears witness to the death of his friend during the final days of the Franco-Prussian War of 1870–71.

7 Soldiers Plundering a House
This painting by Sebastian Vrancx, dating from around 1600, depicts a scene from the wars of religion that tore the Netherlands apart during the 16th century.

8 Saddle
A valuable saddle, dating from the middle of the 15th century, is decorated with elaborately carved plaques made of ivory.

9 The Berlin Wall
An original section of the Berlin Wall, together with the banners of a peaceful pro-unification demonstration in 1989, commemorates the fall of the Wall.

10 V2 Rocket
Exhibited in the section on Nazi Germany is a V2 rocket engine next to an 88-mm flak gun. The V2 missile was one of the *Wunderwaffen* ("wonder weapons") used by German troops at the end of World War II.

Martin Luther **by Lucas Cranach**

ZEUGHAUS UNTER DEN LINDEN

Originally the royal arsenal, the Zeughaus was built in 1706 in the Baroque style according to plans by Johann Arnold Nering. It is an impressive structure, with the building surrounding a historical central courtyard that is protected by a modern glass cupola roof. Especially memorable are Baroque sculptor Andreas Schlüter's figures of 22 dying warriors, lined up along the arcades in the courtyard. They portray vividly the horrors of war. Behind the main building stands a cone-shaped glass annex designed by the Chinese-born architect Ieoh Ming Pei in 2001 for special exhibitions and temporary shows. The permanent exhibition in the main historical building includes a collection entitled "Images and Testimonials of German History". Highlighting the most significant periods and events in the history of the country, the displays include a surprising variety of exhibits dating back to the days of the early Medieval German Empire through the period of the Reformation and the Thirty Years' War as well as the wars of Liberation and the failed Revolution of 1848, right up to the two World Wars and more recent events of the 20th century up to 1994.

Entry of Napoleon into Berlin, 27 October 1806
(1810) by Charles Meynier shows the victorious French at the Brandenburg Gate, Unter den Linden.

TOP 10
UNTER DEN LINDEN EVENTS

1 1573 Elector Johann Georg has a bridle path built, linking the royal Stadtschloss and the Tiergarten

2 1647 During the reign of the Great Elector, the road is planted with *Linden* (lime trees)

3 From 1740 Frederick the Great has grand buildings erected

4 1806 Napoleon and his troops march along Unter den Linden

5 1820 The road turns into a grand boulevard

6 1928 Unter den Linden and Friedrichstraße epitomize the world city

7 1933 Troops celebrate Hitler's victory

8 1945 The avenue is razed to the ground

9 1948–53 Revival of the boulevard

10 October 1989 Demonstrations lead to the fall of the East German regime

🔟⭐ Potsdamer Platz

The heart of the new metropolis of Berlin beats on Potsdamer Platz. This square, where Berliners and tourists alike now flock to cinemas, restaurants and shops, was a hub of urban life in the 1920s. After World War II, it became a desolate wasteland, but since the fall of the Wall, Potsdamer Platz – for a while Europe's largest building site – has become a city within the city, surrounded by imposing edifices that began to appear in the 1990s, and are still being added to today.

Sony Center ①
The Sony Center **(right)** is the most ambitious, successful and architecturally interesting building in the new Berlin. The cupola structure, designed by Helmut Jahn, is the European headquarters of the Sony company, and with its cinemas and restaurants it is also a social magnet.

② Deutsche Kinemathek
This museum **(below)** takes visitors backstage at Babelsberg and Hollywood with Marlene Dietrich's costumes and other exhibits *(see p22)*.

Weinhaus Huth ④
The only building on Potsdamer Platz to have survived World War II, the restored Weinhaus **(right)** today accommodates restaurants and the excellent Daimler Contemporary, which showcases modern art.

③ Café Josty
Café Josty harkens back to its legendary predecessor, a regular haunt of artists and intellectuals in the 19th century. Today's Josty is partially housed in the historic Kaisersaal (Emperor's Hall) of the former Grand Hotel Esplanade.

⑤ Boulevard der Stars
Berlin's walk of fame features stars such as Marlene Dietrich, Werner Herzog, Fritz Lang, Hans Zimmer, Christoph Waltz, Diane Kruger and Romy Schneider **(left)**. The coloured asphalt evokes the red carpet.

ROMY SCHNEIDER

Plan of Potsdamer Platz

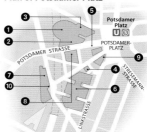

6 Potsdamer Platz Arkaden

The arcades **(above)** draw visitors with three floors hosting 130 shops, exclusive boutiques and restaurants. The lower ground floor is a food court serving a range of meals and snacks.

7 Spielbank Berlin

Berlin's casino invites visitors to *faites vos jeux*. Apart from roulette, Black Jack is also played, and an entire floor is given over to gambling machines.

NEED TO KNOW

MAP L2 ▪ Deutsche Kinemathek: Potsdamer Str. 2 ▪ www.deutsche-kinemathek.de

Open 10am–6pm Tue–Sun (to 8pm Thu)

Admission charge

MAP F4 ▪ Spielbank Berlin: Marlene-Dietrich-Platz 1 ▪ www.spielbank-berlin.de

Open 11–3am daily

Admission charge

MAP F4 ▪ Theater am Potsdamer Platz: Marlene-Dietrich-Platz 1 ▪ (030) 259 244 555

MAP L2 ▪ CinemaxX: Potsdamer Str. 5 ▪ (01805) 24 63 62 99

MAP L2 ▪ Sony Center Potsdamer Platz ▪ www.sonycenter.de/en/

▪ Apart from visiting the famous Café Josty, try Café Möhring in Weinhaus Huth.

---

8 CinemaxX

The CinemaxX with its 17 screens is one of Berlin's largest cinemas. The bigger screens show current Hollywood blockbusters, while the three smallest are for low-budget arthouse and German films.

9 Quartier Potsdamer Platz

Leading architects such as Hans Kollhoff and Renzo Piano designed these skyscrapers. One landmark is the terracotta and glass Atrium Tower.

10 Theater am Potsdamer Platz

Berlin's largest show stage, this venue **(right)** has shown hits such as *Dirty Dancing* and *Mamma Mia!*. The 1,300-seat theatre is often sold out.

Deutsche Kinemathek Exhibitions

Costumes of Marlene Dietrich

film, everyday cinema and the industry's victims: some film stars allowed themselves to be used by the Nazis, others refused to cooperate. The life and work of the actor Kurt Gerron, who was persecuted and murdered, is documented as an exemplary case.

1 Marlene Dietrich

This exhibition of the film star's estate includes costumes from her films, her touring luggage, film clips, posters, photographs, letters and notes.

2 Metropolis

This iconic film, directed by Fritz Lang in 1927, has an alarming vision of a futuristic urban dystopian world as its subject. Models and props from the film are on display.

3 Caligari

The best known German film of the 1920s, *The Cabinet of Dr Caligari* (1920), was an influential masterpiece of Expressionist filmmaking by Robert Wiene.

4 Weimar Republic

The exhibits here are dedicated to the works of the legendary directors of German cinema's golden age from 1918 to 1933.

5 Olympia

This exhibition reveals the technical tricks used in the Nazi propaganda film *Olympia,* a staged documentary by Leni Riefenstahl made in 1936–8 after the Olympics.

6 National Socialism

This exhibition has documents relating to the propaganda uses of

7 Post-War Cinema

The story of films and filmmaking in East and West Germany is shown with props and costumes of popular stars of post-war German cinema such as Hanna Schygulla, Romy Schneider, Heinz Rühmann and Mario Adorf.

8 Transatlantic

This exhibition of documents, letters, keepsakes and souvenirs retraces the careers of German film stars in Hollywood, both of the silent era and from films with sound that followed after 1928.

Exhibits, Transatlantic section

9 Pioneers and Divas

The infant days of cinema are featured here, as well as stars of the silent era such as Henny Porten and the Danish Asta Nielsen.

10 Exile

Documents in this exhibition relate the difficulties encountered by German filmmakers when making a new start in the USA in 1933–45.

THE NEW CENTRE OF BERLIN

In the 1920s, Potsdamer Platz was Europe's busiest square, boasting the first automatic traffic lights in Berlin. During World War II this social hub was razed to the ground. Ignored for almost 50 years, the empty square shifted back into the centre of Berlin when the Wall came down. During the 1990s, it was Europe's largest building site. New skyscrapers were built, old structures were restored – some preserved rooms of the ruined historic Grand Hotel Esplanade were even physically moved into the Sony Center. Millions of people came to follow progress from the famous Red Info Box, which was removed in 2001. Altogether, around €17 billion was invested to create the present square.

TOP 10
POTSDAMER PLATZ ARCHITECTS

1 Helmut Jahn
Sony Center

2 Renzo Piano and Christian Kohlbecker
Atrium Tower, Spielbank Berlin, Musical-Theater, Spielbank, Weinhaus Huth

3 José Rafael Moneo
Hotel Grand Hyatt, Mercedes-Benz Headquarters

4 Hans Kollhoff
Daimler

5 Giorgio Grassi
Park Colonnades

6 Ulrike Lauber and Wolfram Wöhr
Grimm-Haus, CinemaxX

7 Sir Richard Rogers
Office Block Linkstraße

8 Steffen Lehmann and Arata Isozaki
Office and Retail House Linkstraße

9 Heidenreich & Michel
Weinhaus Huth

10 Bruno Doedens and Maike van Stiphout
Tilla-Durieux-Park

Grand Hotel Esplanade remnants, Sony Center

Skyscrapers at dusk on Potsdamer Platz

🔟⭐ Museumsinsel

Formed by the two arms of the Spree River, the Museumsinsel is home to the world's most diverse yet coherent museum complex. Built between 1830 and 1930, the museums, which hold the Prussian royal collections of art and archaeology, were turned into a public foundation in 1918. Heavily damaged in World War II, the complex has since been restored and was declared a UNESCO World Heritage Site in 1999. From 2017, a conceptual path will link the individual museums on the island.

Bode-Museum ①
Located at the northern tip of Museumsinsel, the Bode-Museum is a stately structure dominated by a cupola **(right)**. The building holds the Sculpture Collection, the Museum of Byzantine Art and the Numismatic Collection, made up of a diverse collection of over 500,000 objects.

② Pergamonmuseum
Built in 1909–30, this is one of the world's most important museums of ancient art and architecture, with a vast collection of antiquities *(see p26)*. The huge Ishtar gate **(above)** dates from the 6th century BC.

③ Neues Museum
Spectacularly revamped by British architect David Chipperfield, the building itself is as fascinating as the exhibits. As well as the Museum of Pre- and Early History, the Ägyptisches Museum is also housed here.

④ Ägyptisches Museum
Housed within the Neues Museum, this museum features portraits of Egyptian royals and monumental architecture *(see p50)*.

⑤ Alte Nationalgalerie
First opened in 1876, the Old National Gallery was beautifully restored in the 1990s **(right)** and now holds 19th-century sculptures and paintings, including works by Max Liebermann and Schadow *(see p52)*.

MISSING TREASURES

During World War II, many of the island's exhibits were hidden in underground bunkers. Some pieces of "Priam's Gold", excavated from the site of ancient Troy, were taken by the Red Army as war booty and remain in Moscow. The Neues Museum points out where there are gaps in the collection.

Plan of the Museumsinsel

6 Altes Museum

The first building to be completed on Museumsinsel in 1830, the Altes Museum resembles a Greek temple *(see p55)*. Originally meant to hold paintings, it now houses the collection of Classical antiquities **(right)**.

7 James Simon Gallery

Named in honour of James Simon (1851–1932), a patron of the Berlin State Museums, this will open in 2018 and be the central entrance and visitor centre.

8 Colonnade Courtyard

This columned courtyard between the Alte Nationalgalerie and Neues Museum frames and connects the museums and provides an atmospheric venue for open-air concerts.

9 Lustgarten

This "pleasure park", with a fountain in its centre, is located in front of the Altes Museum. The lawns are popular with tired visitors *(see p55)*.

10 Berliner Dom

Easily the island's most overwhelming structure, this Baroque-style cathedral **(above)** is unusually ornate for a protestant church. Organ concerts and services can be enjoyed in this exquisitely restored church *(see p58)*.

NEED TO KNOW

MAP J5 ▪ (030) 266 424 242 ▪ www.smb.museum

Open 10am–6pm daily, until 8pm Thu (most museums); sections of the Pergamonmuseum may be closed due to a phased remodelling until 2025

Admission charge: €10–12 per museum; Museumsinsel day pass €18; 3-day Berlin Museum Pass €24; extra fee for some exhibitions; free for under-18s

▪ Some of the museums have cafés, but the café at the Altes Museum is convenient as it is a little closer than the others to Karl-Liebknecht-Straße, the island's main road.

▪ It's best to set aside a whole day for the extraordinary collections of the Museumsinsel. There are several parks nearby in which you can take breaks. Sundays can be very busy with long queues and large groups.

Pergamonmuseum

Detail, frieze from Darius's palace

5 Frieze from the Palace of Darius

A frieze dating to around 510 BC from the palace of Darius in Susa (Iran) is made of exquisitely coloured glazed brick and depicts a row of Persian warriors holding lances and carrying bows and quivers.

6 Giant Sculpture of a Bird of Prey

The nearly 2-m- (7-ft-) high Riesensonnenvogel (huge sun bird) was discovered during excavations in Tell Halaf, Syria, the centre of the ancient Aramaic city-state of Guzana.

1 Pergamon Altar

The colossal Pergamon Altar from the ancient eponymous Greek city (in modern Turkey) dates from 160 BC and is the largest and most significant treasure in the collections of the Berlin museums. This hall is closed for reconstruction until 2019.

2 Ishtar Gate

The imposing Ishtar Gate and the Processional Way that led to it are fully preserved. The gate was built under Nebuchadnezar II in the 6th century BC in Babylon. Original faïence tiles depict the sacred lions.

3 Market Gate of Miletus

This vast gate (AD 100) is over 16 m (52 ft) high. To the right of the entrance, a hairdresser has carved an advertisement for his shop into the stone.

4 Assyrian Palace Room

The reconstructed room of the Assyrian kings' palace (9th century BC) boasts impressive door figures and 13th-century BC wall paintings.

7 Aleppo Room

Taken from a Christian merchant's house in Syria and dating from the early 17th century, this small room features magnificent wooden cladding and is a beautiful example of Ottoman architecture.

8 Mosaic of Orpheus

This delightful mosaic floor, depicting Orpheus playing his lyre amid animals enchanted by his skill, comes from the dining room of a private home in Asia Minor (AD 200).

9 The Mshatta Façade

A gift from Ottoman Sultan Abdul Hamid II to Kaiser Wilhelm II, this stone façade elaborately carved with arabesque and animal forms was the south face of a desert fort built in AD 744 in Mshatta, Jordan.

10 Victory Stele of Esarhaddon

This monumental stele, excavated in 1888 in Zincirli, commemorates Esarhaddon's victory over Pharoah Taharqa (671 BC).

Market Gate of Miletus

SAVING THE MUSEUMSINSEL

Visitors at the spectacular Neues Museum

The island of museums is a treasury of antique architecture, but until recently it had been slowly decaying. Since 1992, however, €1.8 billion has been spent on the renovation and modernization of Museumsinsel. A master plan created by renowned architects that include David Chipperfield and O M Ungers will transform the complex into a unique museum landscape – just as it was first conceived in the 19th century by Friedrich Wilhelm IV, when he established the "free institution for art and the sciences". Once completed, an "architectural promenade", will serve as a conceptual and structural link between various individual museums, except the old National Gallery. This promenade will consist of a variety of rooms, courtyards and vaults, as well as exhibition halls. The core of the complex will be a new central entrance building. The museums are gradually reopening after extensive individual renovations – the Pergamonmuseum will be completed by 2025.

TOP 10 MUSEUMSINSEL EVENTS

1 1810 Plan for a public art collection created

2 1830 The Altes Museum, Prussia's first public museum, opens

3 1859 Completion of the Neues Museum

4 1876 Opening of the Alte Nationalgalerie

5 1904 Completion of the Kaiser-Friedrich-Museum (Bode-Museum)

6 1930 Opening of the Pergamonmuseum

7 1943 Bombs destroy most of the museums

8 1958 Most museums reopen after renovation

9 1999 Museumsinsel declared a UNESCO World Heritage Site

10 2009 The Neues Museum reopens

The Altes Museum with the green Lustgarten in front

🔟 ⭐ Kurfürstendamm

After years of decline, the Kurfürstendamm, or Ku'damm for short, has once again become a fashionable hot spot. Breathtaking architecture, elegant boutiques and a lively street artist scene around Breitscheidplatz have made this shopping boulevard one of Berlin's most attractive and – at 3.8 km (2.5 miles) – also its longest avenue for strolling.

Breitscheidplatz ①
Here, in the heart of the western city, artists, Berliners and visitors swarm around J Schmettan's globe fountain **(right)**, known by locals as "Wasserklops" (water meatball).

② Kaiser-Wilhelm-Gedächtnis-Kirche
The church tower (the church itself was destroyed during World War II) stands in the centre of the square **(left)**, serving as both memorial and stark reminder of the terrors of war *(see pp32–3)*.

③ Europa-Center
The oldest shopping centre in West Berlin, opened in 1962, is still worth a visit. Here you will find fashion boutiques, a comedy theatre and an official Berlin Tourist Info centre.

④ Neues Kranzler Eck
This glass and steel skyscraper **(above)** was built in 2000 by architect Helmut Jahn. The legendary Café Kranzler was retained as a bar in front of the office block. There is an official Berlin Tourist Info centre here.

> **WHEN KU'DAMM WAS NO MORE THAN A LOG ROAD**
>
> In 1542, today's magnificent boulevard was just a humble "Knüppeldamm", or log road. It served the Electors as a bridle path, linking their town residence (Stadtschloss) and their hunting lodge (Jagdschloss). It was not until 1871 that the area around the Ku'damm developed into a fashionable "new west end". Chancellor Otto von Bismarck had the boulevard modelled on the Champs Elysées in Paris, and requested that his statue be erected in the street as a thank you. So far, however, the Berliners have failed to oblige him.

⑤ Ku'damm-Eck
This hotel/business complex has a large video screen outside showing news and commercials.

Previous pages The Reichstag and the Paul Löbe legislative building reflected in the Spree

8 Lehniner Platz
The square is home to the Schaubühne theatre **(left)**, built as Universum cinema in 1928 by Erich Mendelsohn and converted in 1978.

9 Fasanenstraße
A small street off Ku'damm, Fasanenstraße **(below)**, with its galleries, expensive shops and restaurants, is one of Charlottenburg's most elegant areas *(see pp120–21)*.

10 Traffic Turret
On the corner of Joachimstaler Straße stands an old-fashioned traffic turret or *Verkehrskanzel*, the last one in the city and now a heritage monument. A policeman sat in the raised glass cabin to control traffic lights manually from 1955 to 1962, when the signals went automatic.

6 RT&W Galerie
The Neo-Classical building housing this gallery gives visitors a glimpse of Ku'damm's erstwhile splendour.

7 Iduna-Haus
The turreted building at No. 59 at the Leibnitzstraße corner is one of the few surviving bourgeois houses from the late 19th century. The ornamented Jugendstil (Art Nouveau) façade has been lavishly restored **(left)**.

NEED TO KNOW

MAP P5 ■ Europa-Center: Tauentzienstr. 9 ■ (030) 348 00 80 ■ www.24EC.de

Open 24 hours (shops and Berlin Tourist Info: 10am–8pm Mon–Sat)

MAP P4 ■ Neues Kranzler Eck (official Berlin Tourist Info): Kurfürstendamm 21 ■ (030) 25 00 25

Open 10am–8pm Mon–Sat, 10am–6pm Sun

■ The Story of Berlin at Kurfürstendamm 207–8 is a multimedia tour of 800 years of Berlin's history from the Great Elector to the fall of the Wall. The exhibition may move locations in 2015; check their website before visiting (www. story-of-berlin.de).

■ Few original cafés in the Kurfürstendamm area have survived: the most charming is the Café Wintergarten in the Literaturhaus on Fasanenstraße *(see p126)*.

■ Avoid Ku'damm on Saturday mornings when it is teeming with locals and tourists out on shopping trips.

🔟 ⭐ Kaiser-Wilhelm-Gedächtnis-Kirche

This ruined Neo-Romanesque church is one of Berlin's most haunting symbols. It was consecrated in 1895 and named Kaiser Wilhelm Memorial Church in honour of Wilhelm I. Following severe damage by the 1943 bombing raids, the ruins of the tower were left standing as a memorial. Egon Eiermann built a new church next to it in 1957–63.

Tower Ruins

Only the church tower **(right)** survived the Allied bombing raids that razed much of the city to the ground in 1943. Today only 71 m (233 ft) high, the tower once rose to 113 m (370 ft). The rough hole in its roof has given rise to its nickname "the Hollow Tooth".

New Bell Tower ②

The hexagonal bell tower **(right)** rises 53 m (174 ft) high next to the tower ruins on the site of the old church's main nave.

A CHURCH WITH TWO LIVES

The Kaiser-Wilhelm-Gedächtnis-Kirche has the Berliners to thank for its preservation: in 1947, the Senate had planned to demolish the tower ruins for safety reasons. In a referendum only about 10 years later, however, one in two Berliners voted for its preservation. And so the idea came about to build a new church next to the ruin and to preserve the vestibule of the old church as a striking memorial hall to the horrors of war.

③ Kaiser's Mosaic

One of the preserved mosaics shows Heinrich I on his throne, with imperial orb and sceptre **(right)**. Originally decorated with scenes from German imperial history, the interior was meant to place the Hohenzollerns within that tradition.

8 Coventry Crucifix

This small crucifix was forged from old nails that were found in the ruins of Coventry Cathedral in England. It commemorates the bombing of Coventry by the German Luftwaffe in 1940.

9 Tower Clock

The tower bears a clock based on a Classical design, with Roman numerals. At night, it is lit in blue by modern light-emitting diodes to match the lighting inside the new church.

4 Main Altar

The golden figure of Christ **(above)** created by Karl Hemmeter is suspended above the main altar in the modern church. In the evening light, the windows behind the altar glow an overwhelming dark blue.

10 Russian Orthodox Cross

This gift from the bishops of Volokolomsk and Yuruyev was given in memory of the victims of Nazism.

5 Mosaic of the Hohenzollerns

The vividly coloured mosaic **(above)** of the Hohenzollerns adorns the vestibule of the church ruins. It depicts Emperor Wilhelm I together with Queen Luise of Prussia and her entourage.

NEED TO KNOW

MAP N4 ◪ Breitscheidplatz
☎ (030) 218 50 23 ◪ www.gedaechtnis kirche.com

Open Church: 9am–7pm daily; memorial hall: 10am–6pm Mon–Fri, 10am–5:30pm Sat, noon–5:30pm Sun; services 10am and 6pm Sun

Free guided tours at 1:15pm, 2pm, 3pm daily and 10:15am, 11am, noon Mon, Fri, Sat (donations welcome); group tours in English available for a small fee

◾ Visit the new church on a sunny day around lunchtime, when the blue glass window is at its most impressive.

◾ There are fantastic views of the church from the Mövenpick Café in the Europa-Center opposite.

Original Mosaics 6

Glittering Jugendstil-style mosaics showing Prussian dukes and princes are preserved on the walls and ceilings along the stairways **(right)**.

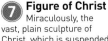

7 Figure of Christ

Miraculously, the vast, plain sculpture of Christ, which is suspended from the ceiling, survived the bombing of the church.

🔟 ⭐ Schloss Charlottenburg

The construction of Schloss Charlottenburg, designed as a summer residence for Sophie Charlotte, wife of the Elector Friedrich III, began in 1695. The Orangerie was extended and a cupola was added by Johann Friedrich Eosander between 1701 and 1713. The palace is being renovated in stages and is expected to be ready in 2017.

1 Altes Schloss
The Baroque tower of the oldest part of the palace (dating to 1695) by Johann Arnold Nering is crowned by Richard Scheibe's golden statue of Fortuna **(above)**.

2 Porzellankabinett
This small, exquisite mirrored gallery **(below)** has been faithfully restored to its original glory. Among the exhibits on display are valuable porcelain items from China and Japan.

3 Schlosskapelle
The luxurious splendour of the palace chapel recalls the once magnificent interior design of the palace, before it was destroyed in World War II. However, apart from the original altar, the entire chapel – including the king's box – is a costly reconstruction.

4 Monument to the Great Elector

The equestrian statue of the Great Elector Friedrich Wilhelm **(right)** is thought to be one of his most dignified portraits. Made by Schlüter in 1696–1703, it stood on the Rathausbrücke originally, near the destroyed Stadtschloss.

5 Neuer Flügel

Built between 1740 and 1747 by Georg W von Knobelsdorff, the new wing contains Frederick the Great's private quarters, as well as a large collection of 18th-century French paintings.

6 Schlosspark

The palace has a lovely Baroque garden, beyond which lies a vast park, redesigned by Peter Joseph Lenné in 1818–1828 in the English style with rivers, artificial lakes and small follies.

7 Belvedere

Friedrich Wilhelm II liked to escape to the romantic Belvedere **(below)**, a summer residence built in 1788 by Carl Gotthard Langhans, which served as a tea pavilion. Today it houses a collection of precious Berlin porcelain objects.

Plan of Schloss Charlottenburg

8 Neuer Pavillon

This Italianate villa, designed by Schinkel for Friedrich Wilhelm III in 1825, was inspired by the Villa Reale del Chiatamone in Naples and clearly shows the Hohenzollerns' love of the Italian style.

9 Mausoleum

Slightly hidden, this Neo-Classical building **(below)** by Schinkel is the final resting place of many of the Hohenzollerns.

10 Museum Berggruen

Situated in the Western Stüler Building opposite the Charlottenburg palace, this modern art gallery houses the permanent exhibition "Picasso and his Time", featuring more than 100 works that span the artist's career. Other highlights of the collection include works by Matisse, Klee and Giacometti *(see p52)*.

NEED TO KNOW

MAP A/B3 ■ Spandauer Damm ■ (030) 32 09 10 ■ www.spsg.de

Altes Schloss: Apr–Oct: 10am–6pm Tue–Sun (to 5pm Nov–Mar)

Neuer Flügel: Apr–Oct: 10am–6pm Wed–Mon (to 5pm Nov–Mar)

Belvedere: Apr–Oct: 10am–6pm Tue–Sun (the Belvedere is closed in the winter Nov–Mar)

Neuer Pavillon: Apr–Oct: 10am–6pm Tue–Sun (to 5pm Nov–Mar)

Mausoleum: Apr–Oct: 10am–6pm Tue–Sun (to 5pm Nov–Mar)

Museum Berggruen: Schlossstr. 1 ■ www.smb. museum ■ 10am– 6pm Tue–Sun

Admission charge (for all)

■ The Orangery Café has an attractive garden.

■ Try a romantic midweek evening stroll to avoid the crowds (park: 6am–dusk).

Schloss Charlottenburg Rooms

Goldene Galerie in the Neuer Flügel

1 Goldene Galerie
The festival salon in the Neuer Flügel, 42 m (138 ft) long, was designed in Rococo style by Frederick the Great's favourite architect von Knobelsdorff. The richly ornamented room has a cheerful appearance.

2 Eichengalerie
The wooden panelling of the Oak Gallery is carved with expensively gilded portraits of Hohenzollern ancestors.

3 Gris-de-Lin-Kammer
This small chamber in Friedrich's second palace apartment is decorated with paintings, including some by his favourite artist, Antoine Watteau. The room was named after its wall coverings in violet-coloured damask (*gris-de-lin* in French).

4 Schlafzimmer Königin Luise
Queen Luise's bedchamber, designed in 1810 by Karl Friedrich Schinkel, features the clear lines typical of the Neo-Classical style. The walls are clad in silk fabrics and wallpaper.

5 Winterkammern
Friedrich Wilhelm II's early Neo-Classical rooms contain fine paintings, tapestries and furniture.

6 Bibliothek
Frederick the Great's small library has outstanding elegant bookcases and a vibrant, light green colour scheme.

7 Konzertkammer
Furniture and gilded panelling in the concert hall have been faithfully recreated as during Frederick the Great's time. Antoine Watteau's *Gersaint's Shop Sign*, considered to be one of his most significant works, hangs here; the king bought the work directly from the artist.

8 Grünes Zimmer
The green room in Queen Elisabeth's quarters is an excellent example of royal chambers furnished in 19th-century Biedermeier style.

Queen Elisabeth's Grünes Zimmer

9 Rote Kammer
The elegant chamber, decorated entirely in red and gold, is adorned by portraits of King Friedrich I and Sophie Charlotte.

10 Friedrich I's Audienzkammer
The ceiling paintings and Belgian tapestries depict allegorical figures symbolizing the fine arts and the sciences. There are also magnificent lacquered cabinets, modelled on Asian originals.

THE HOHENZOLLERNS AND BERLIN

Friedrich Wilhelm, the Great Elector

In 1412, Burggraf Friedrich of the Hohenzollern dynasty of Nuremberg was asked by Sigismund of Luxemburg to support him in the princely feuding before the imperial election for the throne. When Sigismund became king, he gave Friedrich, in 1415, the titles of Margrave and Prince-Elector of Brandenburg as a reward for his services – this is where the histories of the Hohenzollerns and Berlin first became entwined, a relationship that was to last for 500 years. From the start, the family tried to limit the powers of the town and of the Brandenburg nobility. Culture, however, flourished under the new rulers, especially the Great Elector 200 years later, who invited 20,000 Huguenot craftsmen to Berlin and founded an art gallery and several schools. His grandson Friedrich Wilhelm I, father of Frederick the Great, transformed the city into a military camp, with garrisons and parade grounds, and scoured the town for tall men to join his bodyguard. In the 19th century, however, relations between Berlin and the Hohenzollerns became decidedly less cordial.

TOP 10 HOHENZOLLERN RULERS

1 Friedrich Wilhelm the Great Elector (1620–88)

2 Friedrich I (1657–1713)

3 Friedrich Wilhelm I (1688–1740)

4 Friedrich II the Great (1712–86)

5 Friedrich Wilhelm II (1744–97)

6 Friedrich Wilhelm III (1770–1840)

7 Friedrich Wilhelm IV (1795–1861)

8 Wilhelm I (1797–1888)

9 Friedrich III (1831–88)

10 Wilhelm II (1859–1941)

The Great Elector Receiving Huguenot Refugees, **18th-century etching by Daniel Chodowiecki**

🔟 ⭐ Kulturforum

The Kulturforum is a unique complex of museums, concert halls and libraries west of Potsdamer Platz. Here, some of the most outstanding European art museums, as well as the famous concert hall of the Berlin Philharmonic Orchestra, attract millions of visitors interested in culture and music. The complex, based in the former West Berlin, has been growing steadily since 1956 as a counterpoint to the Museumsinsel in the former East Berlin. The Kulturforum also contains some of Berlin's best examples of modern architecture.

Gemäldegaleri ①
Berlin's largest art museum **(right)** holds masterpieces of European art. They are displayed in the modern Neubau, built in 1998 by Heinz Hilmer and Christoph Sattler. The collection includes Bosch, Holbein, Dürer, Gossaert, Vermeer, Brueghel the Elder, Titian, Caravaggio and Rembrandt.

② Neue Nationalgalerie
Based in a building by Mies van der Rohe **(above)**, this holds mainly 20th-century art, with an emphasis on German Expressionism. Collection highlights are on show elsewhere during the renovation *(see p56)*.

Philharmonie ③
This tent-like building **(right)** was the first new structure to be built in the Kulturforum in 1960–3. Considered one of the best concert halls in the world, it is the home of the Berlin Philharmonic Orchestra. Sir Simon Rattle will continue to conduct until 2017 *(see p66)*.

④ Kunstgewerbe-museum
Craft objects from across Europe from the Middle Ages to the present day are on show at this museum **(left)**, including valuable items like the Guelphs' treasure, Lüneburg's silver and Renaissance faïence *(see p51)*.

5 Musikinstrumenten-museum

Concealed behind the Philharmonie is this fascinating little museum of musical instruments. More than 800 exhibits are on show here, particularly early instruments such as harpsichords **(right)** as well as a 1929 Wurlitzer *(see p51)*.

KULTURFORUM
Staatliche Museen zu Berlin

Kulturforum

NEED TO KNOW

MAP L1/2 ◼ West of Potsdamer Platz ◼ (030) 266 424 242 ◼ www.smb.museum

Gemäldegalerie: Matthäikirchplatz 4/6

Open 10am–6pm Tue–Sun (to 8pm Thu)

Kupferstichkabinett: Matthäikirchplatz 8

Open 10am–6pm Tue–Sun

A day pass for all museums is €12; the Neue Nationalgalerie is closed until 2019 for remodelling

Kunstbibliothek: Matthäikirchplatz 6

Open 10am–6pm Tue–Sun

St Matthäuskirche: Matthäikirchplatz 1 ◼ (030) 262 12 02

Open 11am–6pm Tue–Sun; organ concert 12:30pm

Admission charge for exhibitions

◼ The Kulturforum restaurant and café is a convenient spot for coffee.

◼ Take a break around the quiet back of the Neue Nationalgalerie.

---

6 Kammermusiksaal

The smaller relative of the larger Philharmonie, this concert hall is one of Germany's most highly regarded chamber music venues *(see p57)*.

7 Kupferstichkabinett

The Gallery of Prints and Drawings holds more than 550,000 prints and 110,000 drawings from all periods and countries, including a portrait of Dürer's mother.

8 St Matthäuskirche

This church **(right)** is the only historical building preserved in the Kulturforum. Built in 1844–6 by Stüler, it is also a venue for art installations and classical music concerts.

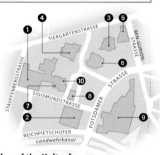

Plan of the Kulturforum

9 Staatsbibliothek

Built in 1978 by Hans Scharoun, the National Library *(see p90)* is one of the world's largest German-language libraries, with five million books, manuscripts and journals.

10 Kunstbibliothek

The Art Library has a collection of advertising and art posters, among other items, and also hosts art and architecture exhibitions and design shows.

Gemäldegalerie

① Portrait of Hieronymus Holzschuher

Albrecht Dürer painted this portrait of the mayor of Nuremburg in 1529.

Holbein's *Portrait of Georg Gisze*

② Portrait of the Merchant Georg Gisze

This 1532 painting by Hans Holbein, showing the Hanseatic League merchant Georg Gisze counting his money, reflects the rise of the rich citizen during the Renaissance.

③ Madonna with Child and Singing Angels

A 1477 painting by Sandro Botticelli depicts the Madonna and Child, surrounded by angels carrying lilies.

④ The Birth of Christ

Martin Schongauer's altar painting (c.1480) is one of only a few religious paintings by the Alsatian artist that have been preserved.

⑤ Victorious Eros

Caravaggio's 1602 painting, after Vergil's model, shows Eros, the god of love, trampling underfoot the symbols of culture, glory, science and power.

Floorplan Key

░ Exhibition area

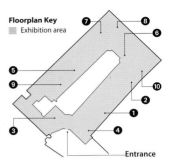

Entrance

⑥ Portrait of Hendrickje Stoffels

In a 1656–7 portrait of his lover Hendrickje Stoffels, Rembrandt's focus is entirely on the subject.

⑦ The French Comedy

This painting by Antoine Watteau belonged to the collection of Frederick the Great.

⑧ The Glass of Wine

This skilfully composed scene by Vermeer (1658–61) shows a couple drinking wine.

⑨ Venus and the Organ Player

This Titian (1550–52) reflects the playful sensuality typical of the Italian Renaissance.

Detail, Botticelli's *Madonna with Child*

⑩ Dutch Proverbs

More than 100 proverbs were incorporated into this 1559 painting by Pieter Brueghel.

Brueghel's *Dutch Proverbs*

ARCHITECTURE IN THE KULTURFORUM

The tent-like roof of the Berlin Philharmonie

The Kulturforum was planned to fill the area between Potsdamer Straße and Leipziger Platz that had been destroyed during the war. The idea for a varied townscape of museums and parks is credited to Berlin architect Hans Scharoun, who had designed plans for this between 1946 and 1957. It was also Scharoun who, with the building of the Philharmonie in 1963, set the character of the Kulturforum: the tent-like, golden roofs of the music hall, the Kammermusiksaal and the national library, designed by him and – after his death – realized by his pupil Edgar Wisniewski, are today among Berlin's top landmarks. All the buildings are characterized by the generous proportions of their rooms, and although controversial when they were built, are today considered classics of modern architecture.

TOP 10 KULTURFORUM ARCHITECTS

1 Hans Scharoun
Philharmonie

2 Mies van der Rohe
Neue Nationalgalerie

3 James Stirling
Wissenschaftszentrum

4 Heinz Hilmer
Gemäldegalerie

5 Christoph Sattler
Gemäldegalerie

6 Friedrich August Stüler St Matthäuskirche

7 Edgar Wisniewski
Kammermusiksaal

8 Rolf Gutbrod
Kunstgewerbemuseum

9 August Busse altes Wissenschaftszentrum

10 Bruno Doedens
Henriette-Herz-Park

The auditorium of the Berlin Philharmonie

🔟⭐ Zoologischer Garten

Berlin's Zoological Garden in the Tiergarten district is the oldest zoo in Germany and, with nearly 1,500 different species, one of the best-stocked in the world. Animals have been kept and bred here since 1844. Today, the zoo hosts about 19,500 animals, ranging from jellyfish to Indian elephants. Many, such as the polar bears and baby gorillas, have become celebrities, while quite a few enclosures are interesting in their own right, making a zoo visit a favourite day out for Berliners and visitors.

1 Penguin House
Playful Antarctic king and rockhopper penguins inhabit this cool haven, complete with realistic cliffs, illuminated "heavens" and a giant skylight. Happier in warmer climes, Humboldt **(above)** and African penguins swim and waddle outside.

2 Monkey House
Monkeys and apes are at home in this house, and here you can watch gorillas, orangutans and chimpanzees playing and swinging from tree to tree. The Eastern Lowland Gorillas are very popular.

3 Polar Bear Feeding
The 10:30am public feeding of the polar bears attracts big crowds. Check all the animal feeding times online or at the entrance on arrival.

4 Giraffe House
The 1872 North-African-style Giraffe House **(below)** is the oldest enclosure. Visitors enjoy watching as the giraffes nibble the leaves of a tree or slowly bend down to drink.

5 Nocturnal Animal House
Located in the Predatory Animal House, this shelters the creatures of the night, including reptiles and birds. Here you can admire striped bandicoots, fruit bats and slender loris **(above)**. Asleep during the day, they have superb hearing and eyes that light up eerily in the dark.

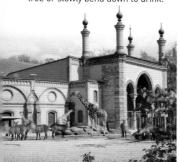
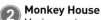

6 Elephant House
These huge, good-natured pachyderms have a healthy appetite: Indian elephants **(left)** devour up to 50 kg (110 lb) of hay a day. Since 1998, 16 elephants have been born here.

7 Aviaries
Nowhere else in the city can you hear such singing, tweeting and whistling – cockatiels, parrots, hornbills and herons **(right)** sound off in the Bird House.

8 Hippo House
Glass domes arch over an aquatic habitat **(left)** at one of the world's most remarkable modern zoo enclosures. An underwater viewing area lets you admire the hippos as they swim with seemingly weightless balletic grace. The animals also have access to an outdoor pool.

9 Aquarium
The greatest draw in the aquarium, where fantastic Caribbean and Amazonian habitats have been re-created, are the green morays and blacktip reef sharks, as well as a jellyfish cylinder allowing 360º views of the shimmering aquatic beauties.

10 Amphibians' Section
Poisonous snakes, bird spiders and reptiles as well as other amphibians crawl and slither around behind glass **(below)** on the second floor of the aquarium. A particularly spectacular event is the feeding of the spiders.

NEED TO KNOW

MAP N5 ■ Hardenbergplatz 8 and Budapester Str. 34 ■ (030) 25 40 10 ■ www.zoo-berlin.de

Open Mid-Mar–Sep: 9am–7pm daily (to 5pm daily in winter)

Admission charge €13; €20 combined entry for zoo and aquarium

■ There is a café and self-service restaurant with a terrace inside the zoo, to the right of the Elephant Gate.

■ A day at the zoo is not complete without a visit to the aquarium. The basins and terraria teem with life, as do the zoo enclosures.

The Top 10
of Everything

Gendarmenmarkt's imposing Deutscher Dom,
with the Konzerthaus entrance in the foreground

Moments in History

The Neues Palais in Potsdam, the town where the 1685 edict was signed

1 1685: Edict of Potsdam

Berlin's history as a cultural capital began in 1685, when the far-sighted Great Elector announced in the Edict of Potsdam that around 20,000 Huguenots would be taken in by Berlin. Many were excellent craftsmen and scientists, who, having fled Catholic France because of their Protestant beliefs, brought a new age of cultural ascendancy to the provincial town.

2 1744: Frederick the Great

Although "Old Fritz", as Frederick the Great was nicknamed, preferred the isolation of Sanssouci to the bustle of Berlin, in 1740 he began to transform the city into a new metropolis. In particular, the "Forum Fridericianum" in Unter den Linden brought new splendours to the town, and masterpieces such as the national opera house helped transform Berlin into one of the most important European cities.

3 Golden Twenties

Between 1919 and 1933, Berlin flourished culturally and became an influential metropolis. Film, theatre, cabaret shows and thousands of restaurants and bars transformed the town into a vibrant international centre of entertainment. Berlin also set new standards in the realms of science and industry, and in architecture and fine art, particularly the Bauhaus movement.

4 1945: Surrender

Signed in Berlin-Karlshorst on 8 May 1945, Germany's unconditional surrender marked more than the end of World War II. The previous Jewish population of 161,000 had virtually disappeared and Berliners called their city "the empire's fields of rubble".

5 1953: Workers' Uprising in East Germany

On 17 June 1953, East Berlin construction workers in Frankfurter Allee demonstrated against an increase in the average rate of production and work quotas. Soviet tanks suppressed the rebellion while, in West Berlin, the uprising was interpreted as a demonstration for German unification.

Soviet tanks during the 1953 uprising

Worker building the Berlin Wall

6 1961: Building of the Berlin Wall

The building of the Berlin Wall, which commenced during the night of 12 August 1961, was a traumatic event for many Berliners. Many families were torn apart by the concrete wall and more than 100 people were to be killed over the following 30 years at the border dividing East and West.

7 1963: "I am a Berliner"

No other politician was as enthusiastically received in Berlin as the US President John F Kennedy. On 17 July 1963, in front of Rathaus Schöneberg, he declared to the cheering crowd: "I am a Berliner". Berliners had forgiven the US for staying silent when the Wall was built. Kennedy confirmed once more that the Western Allies would stand by Berlin and support the town, just as they had done during the blockade of 1948–9, when the US and Britain airlifted food to the "island" of West Berlin.

8 1968: The late Sixties

During the late 1960s, West Berlin students transformed Germany. Rudi Dutschke and others proposed political change and a reappraisal of Germany's Nazi past. The movement came to an untimely end when Dutschke was injured in an assassination attempt by Josef Bachmann in April 1968.

9 1989: Fall of the Wall

The fall of the Berlin Wall on 9 November 1989 heralded a new dawn for the city and the country. For the first time in 30 years, Berliners from both halves of the divided city were able to visit each other. The town celebrated all along Ku'damm and in front of the Brandenburg Gate. When the Wall was built, Willy Brandt, then governing mayor of West Berlin, had promised: "Berlin will survive!" He was right.

10 1991: Berlin becomes the capital of Germany

In June 1991, Berlin was officially declared the capital of the reunified Federal Republic of Germany. Allied Forces left the city during 1994, but it was only when the Bundestag, the German parliament, moved here from Bonn on 19 April 1999 that Berlin became the "real" capital. Today, all the main federal ministries and government authorities, the Bundesrat (upper house), and the Chancellor's and the President's offices are based in Berlin.

People celebrating the fall of the Wall

🔟 Famous Berliners

Actress Marlene Dietrich

1 Marlene Dietrich
The famous filmstar (1901–92), born in Schöneberg, began her career in Berlin in the 1920s. Her breakthrough came with the film *The Blue Angel* (1931). She lies buried in the Friedenau cemetery in Steglitz. Many of her personal possessions are exhibited in the Deutsche Kinemathek *(see p22)*.

2 Albert Einstein
In 1914, Albert Einstein (1879–1955) became the director of the Kaiser Wilhelm-Institute for Physics. He was awarded the Nobel Prize for Physics in 1921 for his explanation of the photoelectric effect, though he is now better known for his Theory of Relativity, first developed in 1905. Einstein mostly lived and worked in Potsdam, but stayed closely connected with Berlin through his lectures and teaching activity. In 1933 Einstein, who was Jewish, emigrated to the USA, where he stayed until his death.

3 Bertolt Brecht
Born in Augsburg, Bavaria, Bertolt Brecht (1898–1956) wrote some of his greatest works, such as the *Threepenny Opera,* in a small apartment in Charlottenburg. During the Third Reich, the playwright emigrated to the US, but he returned to Germany after World War II and founded the Berliner Ensemble in East Berlin in 1949. Until his death, Brecht lived in Chausseestraße in Berlin-Mitte, with his wife, Helene Weigel. His renovated apartment has been turned into a museum.

4 Herbert von Karajan
This famous Austrian conductor (1908–1989) was head of the Berlin Philharmonic Orchestra from 1954 until 1989. During this time he helped create the orchestra's unique sound, which remains legendary until this day. Herbert von Karajan was both revered and feared by his musicians because of his genius and his fiery temperament. Berliners still refer to the Philharmonie as "Circus Karajani".

Conductor Herbert von Karajan

5 Robert Koch
Like few other physicians and microbiologists of his day, Robert Koch (1843–1910) laid the foundations and shaped the face of modern medicine with his pioneering discoveries. The Director of the Institute for Infectious Diseases, Koch also

taught and researched at the Charité Hospital. In 1905 he received the Nobel Prize for Medicine for his pioneering discoveries in the field of tuberculosis research.

6 Theodor Fontane

A Huguenot, Fontane (1819–98) was one of the most influential 19th-century novelists and poets in Germany. He also worked as a journalist and critic for more than 20 years, penning many of his articles and essays in

Theodor Fontane

the Café Josty on Potsdamer Platz. Fontane is particularly well known for his novel *Effi Briest* and five-volume travelogue *Wanderungen durch die Mark Brandenburg (Ramblings through the March of Brandenburg)*, in which he describes the mentality of the people, the historic places, the architecture and the landscapes of the principality of Brandenburg.

7 Käthe Kollwitz

The sculptor and painter Käthe Kollwitz (1867–1945) portrayed the social problems of the poor, and her work provides a powerful, haunting commentary on human suffering. Kollwitz spent a large part of her life in a modest abode in the square that is now named after her, in the Prenzlauer Berg district. A monument recalls how she captured the lives of poor Berlin families, burdened with

large numbers of children, and of social outcasts. An enlarged reproduction of her *Pietà* now adorns the Neue Wache war memorial *(see p17)*.

8 Jacob and Wilhelm Grimm

The brothers Jacob (1785–1863) and Wilhelm (1786–1859) Grimm are known around the world for their collection of classic fairy tales, which include *Little Red Riding Hood*, *Hansel and Gretel* and *Rumpelstiltskin*. Their linguistic output was equally important – their *German Grammar* and *German Dictionary* are standard reference works even today.

9 Georg Wilhelm Hegel

The influential philosopher Hegel (1770–1831) taught at the city's Humboldt University from 1818 until his death.

10 Felix Mendelssohn Bartholdy

The composer (1809–47), a grandson of philosopher Moses Mendelssohn, was also the conductor of the Staatskapelle (state orchestra) at the opera house in Unter den Linden. His grave can be found in the Holy Trinity Cemetery I, located in the city's trendy Kreuzberg district.

Monument to sculptor and painter Käthe Kollwitz by Gustav Seitz

🔟 Museums

Exhibit at the Pergamonmuseum

1 Pergamonmuseum

This impressive museum on the Museuminsel is a vast treasure trove of antiquities *(see p26)*.

2 Ägyptisches Museum

MAP K5 ■ Museumsinsel, Bodestr. 1 ■ (030) 266 424 242 ■ 10am–6pm daily (until 8pm Thu) ■ Adm charge ■ www.smb.museum

The star exhibit in the Egyptian Museum, which is a part of the Neues Museum, is the beautiful bust of Nefertiti, wife of Akhenaton. The long-necked limestone bust, discovered in 1912, was copied all over ancient Egypt. Also worth seeing is the "Berlin Green Head", a small bust from the 4th century BC. The museum also holds numerous mummies, sarcophagi, murals and sculptures *(see pp24–5)*.

3 Deutsches Historisches Museum

Germany's largest history museum uses unique exhibits, documents and films to take the visitor on a journey through German history, from the Middle Ages to the present day. Special exhibitions are devoted to particular themes *(see pp16–19)*.

4 Dahlem Museums

These three museums are a fantastic resource of exotic and historic European cultures *(see p151)*. The Museum of Ethnology is devoted to the cultures of the Pacific, North and South America and Africa. The Museum of Asian Art has exquisite collections from China, Japan, India and Southeast Asia. The Museum of European Cultures explores everyday life within Europe's cultural and historical contexts. Its collections will eventually move to the Humboldt-Forum *(see p89)*.

5 Jüdisches Museum

The Jewish Museum, housed in a spectacular building designed by Daniel Libeskind, documents the German–Jewish relationship through the centuries. There are special exhibitions on the influence of Berlin Jews on the town's cultural life, and on the life of the Enlightenment philosopher Moses Mendelssohn. An empty room commemorates the loss of Jewish culture. There is also an excellent programme of special events *(see p129)*.

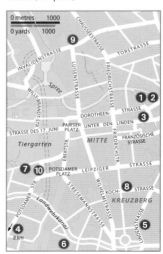

A Junkers Ju 52 plane on display at the Deutsches Technikmuseum

6 Deutsches Technikmuseum

The fascinating German Museum of Technology, built on the site of a former railway goods yard, has some exciting hands-on displays on the history of technology (see p129).

7 Kunstgewerbemuseum

MAP L1/2 ▪ Matthäikirchplatz ▪ (030) 266 424 242 ▪ 10am–6pm Tue–Fri, 11am–6pm Sat–Sun ▪ Admission charge ▪ www.smb. museum

European crafts spanning over five centuries are on display here. Its most valuable exhibits are the treasure of the Guelphs from Braunschweig and the silver treasure of the town council in Lüneburg. The museum also holds Italian tin-glazed earthenware, Renaissance faïence and German Baroque glass and ceramics. Popular displays show Neo-Classical porcelain and furniture, Jugendstil art and Tiffany vases (see pp38–41).

8 Haus am Checkpoint Charlie

The museum at the former Allied checkpoint hosts an exhibition documenting events at the Berlin Wall (see p129).

18th-century hunting horn

9 Museum für Naturkunde

MAP F2 ▪ Invalidenstr. 43 ▪ (030) 20 93 85 91 ▪ 9:30am–6pm Tue–Fri, 10am–6pm Sat–Sun ▪ Admission charge ▪ www. naturkundemuseum-berlin.de

With over 30 million specimens in its collection, the Natural History Museum is one of the largest of its kind in the world. One of the star features is the world's largest dinosaur skeleton, a brachiosaurus found in Tanzania in 1909. There are six more dinosaur skeletons as well as a variety of fossils. Together, they take the visitor back to prehistoric times. It is also worth making a visit to the glittering exhibition of meteorites and minerals (see p96).

10 Musikinstrumenten-museum

MAP L2 ▪ Ben-Gurion-Str. 1 ▪ (030) 25 48 10 ▪ 9am–5pm Tue–Fri (to 8pm Thu), 10am– 5pm Sat–Sun ▪ Admission charge ▪ www.sim.spk-berlin.de

Some 800 musical instruments can be heard in this museum, including Frederick the Great's harpsichord (see p39). Don't miss the silent-film organ which still works (noon, first Saturday of the month).

🔟 Art Galleries

Johannes Vermeer's *The Glass of Wine*

1 Gemäldegalerie

Berlin's best art museum, the Gemäldegalerie holds European art of the 13th–19th centuries, including Vermeer's *The Glass of Wine* and *The Adoration of the Shepherds* by Hugo van der Goes, as well as works by Rembrandt, Dürer, Caravaggio and Rubens *(see pp38–41)*.

2 Brücke-Museum

Bussardsteig 9 ▪ 11am–5pm Wed–Mon ▪ Admission charge ▪ www.bruecke-museum.de

Must-see collection of German Expressionist works by the Brücke (bridge) movement, including Kirchner, Schmidt-Rottluff, Nolde, and Pechstein. Many Brücke works were labelled "degenerate" by the Nazis and destroyed.

3 Alte Nationalgalerie

MAP J5 ▪ Bodestr. 1–3 ▪ 10am–6pm Tue–Sun (to 8pm Thu) ▪ Admission charge ▪ www.smb. museum

The Old National Gallery, built by Friedrich August Stüler in 1866–76, holds a collection of 19th-century, mainly German paintings, including works by Adolf von Menzel, Wilhelm Leibl, Max Liebermann and Arnold Böcklin. It also has sculptures by Schadow, Rauch and Reinhold Begas *(see pp24–25)*.

4 Museum Berggruen

The late Heinz Berggruen, born in Berlin in 1914, emigrated to the US in 1936 but returned to Berlin in 1996. His collection, including works from Picasso's Blue Period, is based in a historic Charlottenburg building by Stüler *(see p35)*.

Museum Berggruen

Warhol's *Mao*, Hamburger Bahnhof

5 Hamburger Bahnhof
MAP F2 ■ Invalidenstr. 50–51 ■ 10am–6pm Tue–Fri (to 8pm Thu), 11am–6pm Sat–Sun ■ Admission charge ■ www.smb.museum

The historic Hamburg Station houses modern paintings, installations and multimedia art. One of its highlights is the Erich Marx Collection, with works by Joseph Beuys. Apart from famous artists like Andy Warhol, Jeff Koons and Robert Rauschenberg, it also owns works by Anselm Kiefer, Sandro Chiao and others *(see p114)*.

6 Bauhaus-Archiv
MAP N6 ■ Klingelhöferstr. 14 ■ 10am–5pm Wed–Mon ■ Admission charge ■ www.bauhaus.de

Few schools have exercised as much influence on 20th-century architecture and design as the Bauhaus, founded in 1919 by Walter Gropius. On display in the museum are furniture, sketches, paintings and everyday objects.

7 C/O Berlin
MAP N4 ■ Amerika-Haus, Hardenbergstr. 22–24 ■ 11am–8pm daily ■ www.co-berlin.org

Located in the former Amerika-Haus, this venue hosts regularly changing exhibitions, lectures and historic and contemporary photography events.

8 Berlinische Galerie
MAP G5 ■ Alte Jakobstr. 124–128 ■ 10am–6pm Wed–Mon ■ Admission charge ■ www.berlinischegalerie.de

Huge collections of mostly German, east European and Russian painters, photographers, graphic designers and architects from the 20th century, such as Baselitz, Grosz and Kirchner.

9 Bröhan-Museum
MAP B3 ■ Schlossstr. 1a ■ 10am–6pm Tue–Sun ■ Admission charge (free 1st Wed of month) ■ www.broehan-museum.de

Jugendstil and Art Deco objects from around Europe, and paintings by Berlin artists, are on display here.

10 Sammlung Scharf-Gerstenberg
MAP B3 ■ Schlossstr. 70 ■ 10am–6pm Tue–Sun ■ Admission charge ■ www.smb.museum

This gallery has rare works by surrealists and their forerunners, such as Goya, Klee, Dalí, Max Ernst and Man Ray.

The Bauhaus-style exterior of Berlin's Bauhaus-Archiv

🔟 Historic Buildings

1 Brandenburger Tor
More than a mere symbol, the Brandenburg Gate is synonymous with Berlin (see pp12–13).

2 Schloss Charlottenburg
This palace boasts Baroque and Rococo splendours and a beautiful park, making it one of the most attractive in Germany (see pp34–7).

Schloss Charlottenburg

3 Schloss Bellevue
MAP E4 ▪ Spreeweg 1
▪ Not open to the public
▪ www.bundespraesident.de/EN/
Built by Philipp Daniel Boumann in 1785–90, this was the residence of the Hohenzollerns until 1861. Since 1994 the stately building with its Neo-Classical façade has been the official residence of the President of the Federal Republic. The modern, egg-shaped Presidential Offices stand next to the old palace.

4 Reichstag
The seat of the Deutscher Bundestag, the German parliament, with its spectacular cupola, is a magnet for visitors (see pp14–15).

5 Berliner Rathaus
MAP K6 ▪ Rathausstraße 15 ▪ 8am–6pm daily
Berlin's Town Hall, also known as "Red Town Hall" because of the red bricks from Brandenburg province with which it is built, harks back to the proud days when Berlin became the capital of the new Empire. Built in 1861–9 according to designs by Hermann Friedrich Waesemann, the town hall was one of Germany's largest and most magnificent buildings, built to promote the splendour of Berlin. The structure was modelled on Italian Renaissance palaces, and the tower is reminiscent of Laon cathedral in France. The exterior was decorated with *Die Steinerne Chronik* (the stone chronicle) in 1879, depicting scenes from the city's history (see p103).

6 Konzerthaus
MAP L4 ▪ Gendarmenmarkt 2 ▪ (030) 203 092 101 ▪ Main hall Apr–Oct: 11am–6pm; tours 3:30pm Mon–Fri, 1pm Sun ▪ en.konzerthaus.de
The Concert Hall, one of Karl Friedrich Schinkel's masterpieces, was formerly known as the *Schauspielhaus* (theatre). The

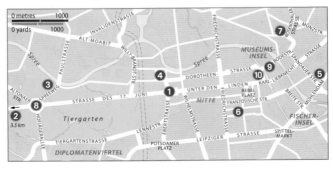

The Neo-Classical exterior of the Konzerthaus

building has a portico with Ionic columns and statues of allegorical and historical personages, some riding lions and panthers, as well as deities, muses and bacchants.

7 Hackesche Höfe
MAP J5 ▪ Rosenthaler Str. 40–41

This complex of 19th-century buildings has eight interlinked courtyards, some of which are decorated in Jugendstil style, originally by August Endell. In the early 1990s the complex was completely renovated. The first courtyard is particularly attractive: coloured glazed tiles with geometric patterns decorate the house from the foundations up to the guttering. In the last courtyard, trees are grouped around an idyllic well. The Hackesche Höfe is one of Berlin's most popular hotspots; restaurants, cafés, a cinema and the Chamäleon musical theatre and variety show *(see p66)* attract visitors from afar.

8 Siegessäule
 The Victory Column in Tiergarten is topped by the statue of Victoria.

Siegessäule

Designed by Heinrich Strack after Prussia's victory in the Danish-Prussian War of 1864, it was refurbished in 2010 *(see p113)*.

9 Altes Museum and Lustgarten

The façade of the Old Museum, possibly one of the most attractive Neo-Classical museum buildings in Europe, is remarkable for the 18 Ionic columns supporting a portico. Built in 1830 to Karl Friedrich Schinkel's design, it was at the time one of the first buildings to be created specifically as a museum. Originally it was to house the royal collection of paintings; today it is home to a collection of antiquities. In front of the museum is a garden designed by Peter Joseph Lenné. Conceived as the king's herb garden, today it is decorated with a 70-ton granite bowl by Gottlieb Christian Cantian, and a fountain *(see p25)*.

10 Zeughaus

Designed by J A Nering as the first Berlin Baroque building, the former Royal Prussian Arsenal is now the Deutsches Historisches Museum *(see pp16–19)*, with a modern addition by I M Pei.

🔟 Modern Buildings

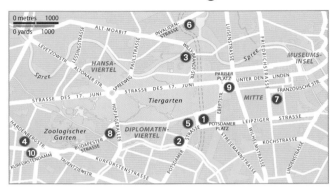

1 Sony Center

The spectacular Sony Center, with its unique roof, is one of Berlin's largest structures *(see p20)*.

Glass membrane roof, Sony Center

2 Neue Nationalgalerie

MAP E4 ■ Potsdamer Str. 50 ■ 10am–6pm Tue–Fri (until 8pm Thu), 11am–6pm Sat–Sun ■ Admission charge ■ Closed until 2019 for remodelling ■ www.smb.museum

This impressive structure was built in 1965–8 by Mies van der Rohe. It was the first building by the pioneering Bauhaus architect after his emigration to the USA. He used his earlier designs for the Havana headquarters of the Bacardi company, which had been abandoned after the Cuban Revolution *(see p38)*.

3 Bundeskanzleramt

MAP J/K2 ■ Willy-Brandt-Str. 1 ■ Not open to the public

Berliners are not too fond of the Chancellor's modern offices, although this is the only government building to have been designed by a Berlin architect. Axel Schultes developed a vast, elongated office complex, which extends north of the Reichstag, in a bend of the Spree, even stretching across the river. In the centre of the hyper-modern building stands a gleaming white cube with round windows, which Berliners quickly nicknamed the "Washing Machine". Critics describe the design as pompous, while civil servants dislike their small offices. The interior of the building is decorated with valuable modern paintings. The Chancellor's office on the 7th floor has a view of the Reichstag building.

Exterior of the Bundeskanzleramt

Ludwig-Erhard-Haus

4 Ludwig-Erhard-Haus
MAP N4 ■ Fasanenstr. 85 ■ 8am–6pm Mon–Fri

The seat of the Berlin Stock Exchange, Ludwig-Erhard-Haus was designed by British architect Nicholas Grimshaw in 1994–8. Locals refer to it as the "armadillo", because the 15 giant metal arches of the domed building recall the animal's armour.

5 Philharmonie and Kammermusiksaal

Two modern concert halls in the Kulturforum were designed by Hans Scharoun in 1961 and 1987 respectively – the Kammermusiksaal (chamber music hall) was completed after Scharoun's death in 1972 according to his plans by his pupil Edgar Wisniewski. Both buildings are renowned for their excellent acoustics as well as for their tent-like roof structures (see pp38–41).

6 Hauptbahnhof
MAP J2 ■ Hauptbahnhof

Europe's largest train station sits on the site of the historic Lehrter Bahnhof. This impressive glass and steel structure doubles as a retail and hospitality hub.

7 Quartiere 205–207 Friedrichstraße

The Galeries Lafayettes and the Friedrichstadtpassagen are based within these three office blocks designed by architects Nouvel, Pei and Ungers (see p87).

8 Nordische Botschaften
MAP N6 ■ Rauchstr. ■ Gallery 10am–7pm Mon–Fri, 11am–4pm Sat–Sun ■ www.nordicembassies.org

No other embassy building has caused as much of a stir as the one housing five embassies of the Nordic countries: its green shutters open and close depending on the available light. Regular art exhibitions are held in the building.

9 DZ Bank on Pariser Platz
MAP K3 ■ Pariser Platz 3 ■ Lobby 10am–6pm Mon–Fri

This elegant building by Frank Owen Gehry combines Prussian and modern architecture. The giant dome inside is remarkable (see p12).

Spectacular interior of the DZ Bank

10 Kant-Dreieck
MAP N4 ■ Kantstr. 155 ■ 9am–6pm Mon–Fri

The enormous "shark fin" on top of the KapHag-Group's headquarters, built by Josef Paul Kleihues in 1992–5, has become a symbol of the new Berlin. The aluminium weather vane is designed to turn in the wind like a sail. Originally, the structure was to be built one-third higher than it is now, but the plans were vetoed by the Berlin Senate.

🔟 Churches and Synagogues

Baroque-style exterior, Berliner Dom

1 Berliner Dom
MAP K5 ▪ Am Lustgarten ▪ (030) 20 26 91 19 ▪ Apr–Sep: 9am–8pm Mon–Sat, noon–8pm Sun; Oct–Mar: 9am–7pm Mon–Sat, noon–7pm Sun ▪ Admission charge ▪ www.berlinerdom.de

Berlin Cathedral, the largest and most lavish church in the city, was reopened in 1993, after almost 40 years of restoration work. Designed by Julius Raschdorf between 1894 and 1905, the building reflects the empire's aspirations to power. In particular, the black marble imperial stairs are a sign of the proximity of the Hohenzollern residence opposite the cathedral. Members of this powerful ruling dynasty are buried in the crypt. The main nave, topped by an 85-m (279-ft) high dome, is remarkable. The church is dominated by a splendid 20th-century Neo-Baroque pulpit and the giant Sauer organ (see p25).

2 St Hedwigskathedrale
MAP K4 ▪ Bebelplatz ▪ 10am–5pm Mon–Sat, 1–5pm Sun ▪ www.hedwigs-kathedrale.de

Berlin's largest Catholic church was built by Frederick the Great in 1747–73 after his conquest of Silesia (see p16).

3 Marienkirche
Work started in 1270 on the Church of St Mary, which nestles at the foot of the Fernsehturm. Gothic and Baroque in style, it has an impressive Neo-Gothic tower, added in 1790 by Carl Gotthard Langhans. The font (1437) and the fresco *Dance of the Dead* (1485) are among the church's oldest treasures. The richly ornamented Baroque pulpit was made by Andreas Schlüter in 1703 (see p104).

4 Nikolaikirche
MAP K6 ▪ Nikolai-kirchplatz ▪ 10am–6pm daily ▪ Admission charge ▪ www.en.stadtmuseum.de

Berlin's oldest sacred building, this was built in 1230 in the Nikolaiviertel quarter. The present church dates to around 1300. It is particularly famous for the portal on the west wall of the main nave, created by Andreas Schlüter. It is adorned with a gilded relief depicting a goldsmith and his wife. The church

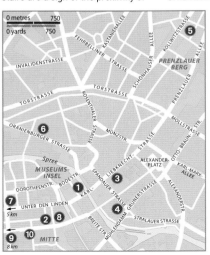

Kaiser-Wilhelm-Gedächtnis-Kirche

7 Kaiser-Wilhelm-Gedächtnis-Kirche

A landmark in West Berlin, the Kaiser Wilhelm Memorial Church successfully combines modern architecture with the ruins of the church tower (see pp32–3).

8 Friedrichswerdersche Kirche

Werderscher Markt ▪ 10am–6pm daily ▪ www.smb.museum
This Neo-Gothic church was built by Karl Friedrich Schinkel in 1824–30. Originally it was meant to serve the German and French communities of the Friedrichswerder district.

was rebuilt in 1987 and completely restored in 2009. It is now a museum exploring the history of the church and the surrounding area. Regular events and concerts are held here.

5 Synagoge Rykestraße

Berlin's largest synagogue, this is one of the few Jewish places of worship in Germany to have survived Kristallnacht. It looks the same today as when it was originally built over 100 years ago (see p139).

6 Neue Synagoge

Once Berlin's largest synagogue, this was built originally in 1859–66. It was demolished in World War II and partially reconstructed in 1988–95. Its magnificent, ornate dome is visible from afar (see p95).

9 Christi-Auferstehungs-Kathedrale

MAP B6 ▪ Hohenzollerndamm 166 ▪ Open only during service 10am & 6pm Sat, 10am Sun
Berlin's largest Russian-Orthodox church, the Church of Christ's Ascension is known for its green onion domes. Services are held in Russian, following Orthodox rituals.

10 Französischer Dom

MAP L4 ▪ Gendarmenmarkt 5 ▪ Noon–5pm Tue–Sun ▪ franzoesische-friedrichstadtkirche.de
At 66 m (216 ft) high, this domed Baroque tower, which dates back to between 1780 and 1789, is a magnificent ornamental addition to the Friedrichstadtkirche serving Berlin's Huguenot community (see p86).

Beautiful dome of the Neue Synagoge

📊 Parks and Gardens

1 Großer Tiergarten
MAP M5/6 ▪ **Tiergarten**

The Tiergarten – the green lungs of Berlin – is the most famous park in the city. Set in the centre of town, the park covers 203 ha (500 acres). Originally designed in 1833–40 by Peter Joseph Lenné as a hunting estate for the Elector, in the latter half of the 19th century the park became a recreation ground for all Berliners. Today it attracts a happy crowd of cyclists, joggers, sun-bathers and families having picnics, especially at weekends *(see p113)*.

2 Schlosspark Charlottenburg
MAP A/B3 ▪ **Schloss Charlottenburg, Spandauer Damm** ▪ **from sunrise to sunset daily** ▪ **www.spsg.de**

The Palace Park is one of the most attractive and charming green spaces in Germany. Immediately behind Schloss Charlottenburg is a small but magnificent Baroque garden, and beyond this extends a vast park, dating back to the early 19th century. It was landscaped in the English style and boasts artificial lake and river landscapes, small hidden buildings and idyllic shaded groves on the banks of ponds and streams. The park is ideal for strolling, and it is also a favourite place for sunseekers *(see pp34–7)*.

The Belvedere, Charlottenburg park

3 Grunewald and Teufelsberg
Grunewald

The Grunewald, or "green forest", is the public woods in the southwest of Berlin (see pp150–55). It is the least built-up area of woodland in the city. Parts of Grunewald are very quiet and isolated indeed, and there are even wild boar in the woods – which can be a nuisance to people who have gardens in the nearby district of Zehlendorf. Grunewald is excellent for hiking and horse-riding.

The folly at Pfaueninsel

4 Pfaueninsel
Peacock Island, an island in the middle of Großer Wannsee that can be reached only by ferry, is probably the most romantic spot in Berlin. In the 19th century, the island served as a love nest for King Friedrich Wilhelm II. His charming folly of a palace ruin was in keeping with the tastes of the time. Today dozens of proud peacocks live in the area around the building *(see p151)*.

5 Botanischer Garten
Königin-Luise-Str. 6–8 (garden and museum) ▪ **(030) 83 85 01 00** ▪ **9am to sunset daily (garden); 10am–6pm daily (museum)** ▪ **Admission charge** ▪ **www.bgbm.org/en**

The 19th-century Botanical Garden is a paradise of flowers and plants in the southwest of the city. The vast area with 15 greenhouses was built in the late 19th century around gentle hills and picturesque ponds. The Great Palm House by Alfred

Koerner has spectacular 26-m (85-ft) high giant bamboo from Southeast Asia. The museum introduces visitors to the world of microbiology.

6 Viktoriapark and Kreuzberg

The old municipal park, originally designed in 1888–94 as a recreation area for local workers, is now one of Berlin's most popular green spaces (see p131). The meadows around Kreuzberg, which rises to 30 m (98 ft), are great for sunbathing. On top of the hill, a monument recalls the Prussian Wars of Liberation.

7 Volkspark Friedrichshain

Berlin's oldest park (1840) is an artificial landscape of lakes and meadows and two wooded mounds, one of which is nicknamed "Mont Klamott", meaning "mount rubble". There is also a fountain with statues of the most popular fairy-tale characters (see p146).

Fountain statue

8 Tierpark Berlin

This second, larger zoo is situated in the idyllic palace park of Friedrichsfelde, and houses some 860 animal species (see p147).

9 Treptower Park

The 19th-century garden on the banks of the Spree has become famous for the Soviet Memorial, which stands next to the graves of 7,000 Red Army soldiers (see p146).

10 Britzer Schloss and Park

Alt-Britz 73 ▪ (030) 60 97 92 30 ▪ 11am–6pm Tue–Sun (palace), 9am to sunset daily (garden) ▪ Admission charge ▪ www.schlossbritz.de

The palace in Britz, dating from 1706 and situated in a lovely park, has been authentically refurbished with historical furniture from the Gründerzeit period after 1871.

TOP 10 LAKES, RIVERS AND CANALS

Boat ride on the Spree River

1 Großer Wannsee
Europe's largest inland beach is beautifully white (see p152).

2 Teufelssee, Grunewald
One of Berlin's cleanest and most relaxed lakes – nudists and dog lovers enjoy the peaceful banks.

3 Großer Müggelsee
Thousands congregate at Berlin's largest lake in summer to swim, row, sail or surf (see p146).

4 Schlachtensee
After Wannsee, this small lake is the second most popular. Avoid the crowds by going during the week.

5 Spree River
MAP J/K 1–6 ▪ Mitte, Tiergarten
Guided boat tours, romantic evening cruises and riverside walks are on offer.

6 Lietzensee
MAP A4 ▪ Am Kaiserdamm
Not suitable for swimming, but the surrounding meadows are idyllic and the lakeside walks popular.

7 Krumme Lanke, Fischerhüttenweg
Although many consider the lake not clean enough for bathing, it seems cleaner (but colder) than Schlachtensee.

8 Landwehrkanal
MAP M/N5 ▪ Lützowplatz
Take a boat trip along the canal to see some of Berlin's most attractive bridges.

9 Tegeler See, Alt-Tegel
The Greenwich Promenade, from Tegeler Hafen (harbour) to Schwarzer Weg, is an attractive walk.

10 Neuer See
MAP M3 ▪ Großer Tiergarten
This tranquil lake is hidden in the vast Großer Tiergarten park. On its banks is the Café am Neuen See (see p117).

🔟 Off the Beaten Track

① Bearpit Karaoke
**MAP G1 ▪ Topsstraße 28
▪ May–Oct: 3pm–5pm Sun ▪ www.
bearpitkaraoke.com**

Sunday afternoon karaoke sessions in the Mauerpark's "bearpit" amphitheatre are extremely popular. The show host, Joe Hatchiban, arrives on a fancy bicycle equipped with loudspeaker and laptop. Crowds of up to 2,000 gather to watch hopefuls take turns belting out oldies.

② Unterwelten Museum
**MAP G1 ▪ Brunnenstraße 105
▪ (030) 49 91 05 18 ▪ English tours
11am & 1pm daily ▪ Admission
charge ▪ www.berliner-
unterwelten.de**

Did you know the Nazis made aircraft underground? Or that Cold War nuclear bunkers were largely futile? Find out on guided tours of bomb shelters, tunnels and vaults going back to the 19th century. Exhibits include an Enigma encryption machine, armaments and atmospheric living quarters.

③ Boros Art Collection
**MAP J3 ▪ Reinhardtstraße 20
▪ English tours at 11am and 1pm
daily ▪ Admission charge ▪ www.
sammlung-boros.de**

This World War II air-raid shelter is now a contemporary art gallery owned by the advertising mogul Christian Boros. Built for the staff of nearby Friedrichstrasse railway station, this concrete behemoth has also served as a prison, a larder for

produce, and a disco. Visits can be made only on 90-minute private tours, which can be booked online.

The Badeschiff in the Spree

④ Badeschiff
**Eichenstraße 4 ▪ (030) 533 20
30 ▪ May–Sep: 8am–midnight daily
▪ Admission charge ▪ www.arena-
berlin.de**

A shimmering island of blue, this old cargo container in the Spree is the city's coolest place for a dip. The pool is reached via a pier from a sandy beach. After sunset DJs spin vinyl and guests migrate to a nightclub boat, *Hoppetosse*, moored alongside.

⑤ Schwerbelastungs-körper
**MAP E6 ▪ General-Pape-Straße ▪ (030)
533 20 30 ▪ Apr–Oct: 2–4pm Tue–
Wed, 10am– 6pm Thu, 1–3pm Sun
▪ www.schwerbelastungskoerper.de**

Hitler and Albert Speer, the Führer's chief architect, planned to transform Berlin into a "world capital" called Welthauptstadt Germania. To test the feasibility of building a huge triumphal arch on the area's soft ground, they commissioned the Schwerbelastungskörper, a concrete

Boros Art Collection

cylinder weighing 12,650 metric tons. The Welthauptstadt was never built but the cylinder houses a historical exhibition.

6 Monsterkabinett

MAP J5 ■ Rosenthaler Straße 39 ■ 0178 80 60 202 ■ 6–10pm Thu, 4–10pm Fri & Sat ■ Admission charge ■ www.monsterkabinett.de

Run by the Dead Chickens art collective, this installation features robots that interact with visitors. The 20-minute tour with heavy metal soundtrack and lightshow ends with a blast of anti-monster spray that blows the head off one creature.

7 Mount Mitte

MAP F2 ■ Caroline-Michaelis-Straße 8 ■ 2pm–sunset Mon–Fri, 10am–sunset Sat–Sun ■ Admission charge ■ www.beachmitte.de

Don a helmet, strap on a security line and wiggle your way through Berlin's oddest high-rope climbing course, tackling wooden barrels, surfboards and old East German Trabant cars suspended in midair.

8 Admiralbrücke

MAP H5 ■ Fraenkelufer 25

This lacy, wrought-iron bridge was built in 1882 in Jugendstil style, spanning one of the prettiest stretches on the Landwehrkanal. On balmy summer nights it fills up with beer-drinking revellers listening to street musicians playing their hearts out.

9 Currywurst Museum

MAP G4 ■ Schützenstraße 70 ■ (030) 88 71 86 30 ■ 10am–6pm daily ■ Admission charge ■ www.currywurstmuseum.de

Curried pork sausage is as much as part of Berlin as the Reichstag. This interactive museum's

Currywurst mascot

displays delve into the 1940s origins of currywurst and the history of fast food. Look out for a wienerwurst-shaped couch, a spice chamber with sniffing stations, a sausage game and a document-ary called Rest of the Wurst.

10 Tieranatomisches Theater

MAP J3 ■ Philippstraße 12 ■ (030) 209 30 ■ 2–6pm Tue–Sat ■ www.kulturtechnik.hu-berlin.de

Nestled in a remote university courtyard, the Veterinary Anatomical Theatre is Berlin's oldest surviving academic building, erected in 1789-90. Wander through the historical exhibition to the circular lecture hall with dissection table and ascending spectator galleries.

Tieranatomisches Theater

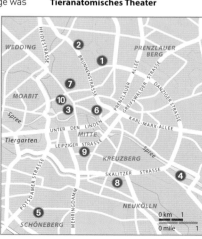

Children's Attractions

Deutsches Technikmuseum

1 Deutsches Technikmuseum

The technology museum is a giant playground for children, excellent for learning through play. There are locomotives to clamber over, windmills to play with and the Science Center Spectrum, where older children can conduct their own physics and technology experiments (see p129).

2 Labyrinth Kindermuseum

Osloer Str. 12 ■ 1–6pm Fri–Sat, 11am–6pm Sun ■ Admission charge ■ www.labyrinth-kindermuseum.de
Berlin's Museum for Children is particularly suitable for children at the preschool stage and in the early school years. Three or four themed exhibitions each year deal with subjects in a child-friendly and entertaining way – for example the "Pots and Pans Orchestra". Every exhibition is interactive, allowing children to join in and experiment. See website for details of special exhibitions and events.

Labyrinth Kindermuseum

3 Grips-Theater

MAP D3 ■ Altonaer Str. 22
■ Phone for performance times
■ Admission charge ■ www.grips-theater.de
This famous Berlin theatre for children has been showing the hit musical *Linie 1* since 1986. The play, which is best suited to older children and adolescents, uses a U-Bahn line running from Kreuzberg to the Ku'damm as a metaphor for life in the big city. All shows are in German.

4 Museum für Naturkunde

Berlin's museum of natural history has the biggest dinosaur skeleton on show anywhere in the world. The collections here are well presented (see p51).

Museum für Naturkunde

5 Zoologischer Garten

If you are visiting Berlin with children you should not miss out on the zoo. Particular favourites are the Monkey House (with baby gorillas and chimpanzees) and the Baby Zoo, where kids are allowed to touch and feed the young animas (see pp42–3).

6 Zeiss-Großplanetarium

Closed until 2016
Artificial stars, planets and nebulae take you to faraway galaxies under the silvery dome of the planetarium (see p140).

LEGO brick models at Legoland

7 Filmpark Babelsberg
Großbeerenstr. 200, Potsdam ▪ Late Mar–early Nov: 10am–6pm daily; check website for park closing days ▪ Admission charge ▪ www. filmpark-babelsberg.de

Exciting shoot-outs, a walk-on film set with a U-boat and a Wild West town are the film park's most popular attractions – and not just with the children. A tour of the former UFA-Film studios takes you behind the scenes: younger visitors can try out costumes or admire the Little Sandman (Sandmännchen), a TV figure popular with children in East Germany since 1959. Everywhere in the park are figures and props from well-known German films. A stunt show features fight scenes, car chases and pyrotechnics like those seen in *Inglourious Basterds*, *Valkyrie* and *Anonymous*, all shot here *(see p159)*.

The Little Sandman

8 Legoland
MAP L2 ▪ Potsdamer Str. 4 ▪ 10am–7pm daily (last entry 5pm) ▪ Admission charge ▪ www.legoland discoverycentre.de

Apart from the 4D cinema and rides at the world's first indoor Legoland, thousands of LEGO bricks are turned into replicas of Berlin sights.

9 Puppentheatermuseum
MAP H6 ▪ Karl-Marx-Str. 135 ▪ (030) 687 81 32 ▪ 9am–3:30pm Mon–Fri, 11am–4pm Sun ▪ Admission charge

At the small but excellent and inspirational Puppet Museum, children are allowed to perform their own puppet shows and have a go at being puppet theatre directors.

10 AquaDom and Sea Life Berlin
MAP K5 ▪ Spandauer Str. 3 ▪ 10am– 7pm daily (last entry 6pm) ▪ Admission charge ▪ www.sealife.de/berlin

Visitors journey from the Spree to the depths of the oceans. A mirror maze and fish feeding add to the fun. The biggest attraction is the lift through the AquaDom, the world's largest cylindrical aquarium *(see p106)*.

TOP10 Performing Arts Venues

1 Staatsoper Unter den Linden
MAP C4 ■ www.staatsoper-berlin.de
Both the theatre troupe and the orchestra of the venerable Berlin Opera enjoy top reputations *(see p16)*. This is the place to see stars of the classical music scene. During refurbishment (until late 2017) performances will take place at Schillertheater, Bismarckstraße 110.

2 Philharmonie
MAP L2 ■ Herbert-von-Karajan-Str. 1 ■ (030) 25 48 89 99 ■ Box Office: 3–6pm Mon–Fri, 11am–2pm Sat–Sun ■ www.berliner-philharmoniker.de
Germany's temple of classical music still presents the best performers in the world. Designed by Scharoun, the concert hall has unique acoustics, much appreciated by artists and audience alike. Concerts by the Berlin Philharmonic Orchestra are very popular and are often sold out for weeks ahead *(see pp38–9)*.

3 Deutsche Oper
MAP B4 & M2 ■ Bismarckstr. 35 ■ (030) 34 38 43 43 ■ www. deutscheoperberlin.de
Berlin's most modern opera house, with its elegant retro design, was built in 1961 on the site of the former Deutsches Opernhaus, which was destroyed during World War II. The

Performance at the Deutsche Oper

controversial 88 slabs of washed-out concrete, chosen by architect Fritz Bornemann for the main façade, replaced the classic columned portico that once stood here, leading critics to describe the building as lacking artistic formation. Concerts and opera and ballet performances are held here, along with an extensive children's programme *(see p124)*.

4 Chamäleon-Varieté
MAP J5 ■ Rosenthaler Str. 40–1, Hackesche Höfe ■ 8pm Tue–Fri, 7pm & 10:15pm Sat, 7pm Sun ■ chamaeleonberlin.com
The lack of technology is more than made up for with much wit and ingenuity by the small, alternative Chamäleon stage. If you are seated in the front row, you are likely to get pulled onto the stage.

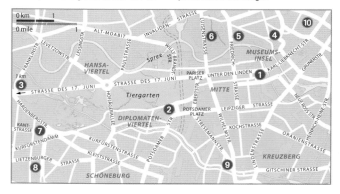

5 Friedrichstadt-Palast
MAP J4 ■ Friedrichstr. 107
■ www.palast.berlin/en

Shiny glass tiles and a white, plumed neon sign adorn the eyecatching façade of the Friedrichstadt-Palast, whose long-legged dancers are as popular today as they were in the 1920s. The legendary original venue was damaged during World War II and replaced in the 1980s with this building. Long celebrated as being among the world's best revues, the performances have become even more spirited and entertaining today.

6 Deutsches Theater
MAP J3 ■ Schumannstr. 13
■ (030) 28 44 12 21 ■ www.
deutschestheater.de/english

Performances at the German Theatre – one of the best – include mainly classic plays in the tradition of Max Reinhardt. Experimental theatre by young playwrights is performed at the DT Baracke (see p98).

7 Theater des Westens
MAP N4 ■ Kantstr. 12 ■ 7:30pm Tue–Fri, 2:30pm & 7:30pm Sat–Sun
■ (01805) 44 44

In addition to producing its own shows, such as *La Cage aux Folles*, this theatre also shows guest productions such as *Blue Man Group* and *Tanz der Vampire (see p124)*.

8 Bar jeder Vernunft
MAP C5 ■
Schaperstr. 24 (car park Freie Volksbühne) ■ Box office: noon–7pm Mon–Sat, 3–7pm Sun & hols
■ www.bar-jeder-vernunft.de/en/

This venue, whose name means "devoid of all reason", is Berlin's most popular comedy theatre. The cabaret offers a humorous and, at times, romantic programme of songs, *chansons*, reviews, cabaret, slapstick

Friedrichstadt-Palast

and comedy, all under an amazing mirror tent dating from the 1920s. Many stars of the international and German cabaret scene can be seen regularly among the performers here, including Tim Fischer, Georgette Dee, the Pfister Sisters and Gayle Tufts, as well as older stars such as Otto Sander.

9 Hebbel am Ufer
MAP F5 ■ Hallesches Ufer 32
■ (030) 25 90 04 27 ■ performances daily ■ english.
hebbel-am-ufer.de

The Hebbel am Ufer has attained cult status in Berlin, thanks to its modern and varied programme of concerts, dance, music and theatre events. Top performers from around the world appear here.

10 Volksbühne
MAP H2 ■ Rosa-Luxemburg-Platz ■ (030) 24 06 57 77 ■ www.
volksbuehne-berlin.de

German theatre director Frank Castorf has transformed this former Socialist stage into a theatre that has become famous for its classy, exciting and at times controversial and experimental performances.

Theater des Westens

🔟 Gay and Lesbian Attractions

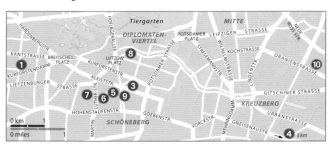

1 Christopher Street Day
MAP P3/4 ■ Kurfürstendamm and Straße des 17. Juni ■ 4th weekend in June

Every summer, Germany's largest gay festival, Christopher Street Day, transforms Berlin into a giant street party, with thousands of gays and lesbians walking in a parade from Kurfürstendamm down the Straße des 17. Juni to Siegessäule *(see p80)*. At night, the party continues in the city's many gay clubs and Kneipen.

Christopher Street Day parade

2 Siegessäule
Free in gay cafés and shops

Berlin's oldest and best-selling gay magazine is named after the Victory Column, Berlin's landmark. This colourful monthly magazine includes all sorts of useful information, a round-up of what's on, small ads and interviews from the city's gay scene.

3 Mann-o-Meter
MAP E5 ■ Bülowstr. 106 ■ (030) 216 80 08 ■ 5–10pm Tue–Fri, 4–8pm Sat–Sun

Berlin's best-known advice centre for gays offers help and advice of all kinds. Apart from psychological support relating to AIDS, safe sex and coming out, its counsellors offer help in finding accommodation, give support to those in troubled relationships and provide legal advice. Mann-o-Meter is also a good starting point for gay visitors to Berlin who wish to find out about the gay scene, and, last but not least, the café is also a good place to meet people.

4 SchwuZ
Rollbergstr. 26 ■ (030) 629 08 80 ■ Open from 11pm Wed, Fri and Sat ■ Admission charge ■ www.schwuz.de

Located in a handsome ex-brewery in Neukölln, this is one of the best venues for gay parties in Berlin, drawing a young, lively crowd for dancing, drinking, seeing and being seen. The parties are often themed – details can be found in gay magazines such as *Siegessäule* or *Sergej*, or on the club's Facebook page.

5 Tom's Bar
MAP D5 ■ Motzstr. 19 ■ (030) 213 45 70 ■ Open from 10pm daily ■ www.tomsbar.de

One of the traditional pubs in Berlin, in the centre of the city's gay heart in Motzstraße, this is not for those who are shy and timid – Tom's is a well-known pick-up joint. Below the (rather dark and dingy) Kneipe is a darkroom.

6 Prinz-Eisenherz-Buchhandlung

MAP D5 ■ Motzstr. 23
■ (030) 313 99 36 ■ 10am–8pm Mon–Sat

Germany's oldest openly gay bookstore stocks the entire range of German and international gay and lesbian publications. Its knowledgeable bookshop assistants will track down rare or out-of-stock titles at your request. The bookshop also hosts frequent literary readings.

7 Connection

MAP D5 ■ Fuggerstr. 33 ■ (030) 218 14 32 ■ Open from 8pm Thu, from 11pm Fri–Sat ■ Adm charge

It may not be the best, but this is certainly one of the most popular gay discos in Berlin. Late at night, this is where gays – mainly scenesters – meet and dance to house and techno rhythms. In the basement under the club is a labyrinth of darkrooms.

8 Schwules Museum

MAP E4 ■ Lützowstr. 73 ■ (030) 69 59 90 50 ■ 2–6pm Mon, Wed–Fri, Sun, 2–7pm Sat ■ Admission charge
■ www.schwulesmuseum.de

Situated in Tiergarten, this small Gay Museum documents, through temporary exhibitions, the high and low points of gay and lesbian life since the 19th century. Next to the museum is an archive, a small library and a venue for cultural events.

9 Café Berio

MAP E5 ■ Maaßenstr. 7 ■ (030) 216 19 46 ■ 8am–1am Fri–Sat, 7am–midnight Sun–Thu

A long-time favourite among Berlin's scene, Café Berio is an old-fashioned café that has been turned totally gay. In the summer its terrace is a great place to have breakfast while people-watching, or to relax over a great meal or afternoon coffee and cake.

Band flyers and posters, SO36

10 SO36

MAP H5 ■ Oranienstr. 190
■ (030) 61 40 13 06 ■ check website for current programmes and opening hours ■ www.so36.de

This famous – and infamous – dance venue for young gays has been very popular for many years. The Sunday night club "Café Fatal", when old German chart hits and dance tunes are played, is legendary *(see p134)*.

Galleries at the small Schwules Museum

Best Places to Eat

The stylish interiors of Reinstoff

sleek and modern fusion of Asian and international dishes, with an emphasis on Japanese (sushi) dishes and French-Italian fare. In summer, reserve one of the tables on the terrace outside. Open for breakfast, too.

① Reinstoff
MAP F2 ■ Schlegelstr. 26C
■ 7pm–midnight Tue–Sun ■ €€€

This gourmet temple earned two Michelin stars after just two years in business. Reinstoff serves fine regional specialities with a molecular twist: try the Brandenburg rabbit with celery and liquorice.

② Vox
MAP F4 ■ Marlene-Dietrich-Platz 2 ■ (030) 25 53 17 72 ■ 6:30–10:30am, 6:30pm–midnight daily; noon–2:30pm Mon–Fri ■ €€

The exquisite food in this elegant restaurant at the Grand Hyatt is a

③ Hugos
MAP N5 ■
Budapester Str. 2 ■
(030) 26 02 12 63 ■
6–10:30pm Tue–Sat
■ €€

The Michelin-starred Hugos at Hotel Intercontinental Berlin (see p172) is the city's most affable gourmet restaurant, with impeccable service and stunning views. Wood panelling and plush leather set the tone, while the international cuisine reveals the light touch of German chef Thomas Kammeier. The wine list is extensive, and there are private dining rooms.

④ Bocca di Bacco
MAP K4 ■ Friedrichstr. 167–8
■ (030) 20 67 28 28 ■ noon–midnight Mon–Sat, 6pm–midnight Sun ■ €€

Berlin's hippest Italian restaurant offers fresh fish and exceptional meat creations such as *bresaola di*

cavallo (cured horse meat served with salad and nuts). Excellent *enoteca* with a good wine list.

5 Borchardt
MAP K4 ▪ Französische Str. 47
▪ (030) 81 88 62 62 ▪ 11:30am–midnight daily ▪ €€

Everyone of importance, including German chancellors, dines at Borchardt. The historic room is furnished in Wilhelminian style (featuring tall columns, wall mosaics and tile flooring) – a stunning setting for the modern French cooking and schnitzel served here. Without a reservation, however, even celebrities can't get a table.

The simple interiors of Borchardt

6 Weinbar Rutz
MAP F2 ▪ Chausseestr. 8
▪ (030) 24 62 87 60 ▪ Open from 6:30pm Tue–Sat (wine bar 4–11pm Tue–Sat) ▪ €€€

This rising star in Berlin's gourmet scene has slowly worked towards its first, well-deserved Michelin star by offering consistently high-quality fish and hearty meat dishes based on local recipes, but served with a creative twist. The Rutz is cosy and informal, with a prodigious wine list containing over 1,000 wines *(see p73)*.

7 Fischers Fritz
MAP K4 ▪ Hotel Regent Berlin, Charlottenstr. 49 ▪ (030) 20 33 63 63
▪ noon–2pm, 6:30–10:30pm daily ▪ €€€

This high-profile establishment is one of five restaurants in Berlin with two Michelin stars. Chef Christian Lohse prepares some of the most inspired and spectacular seafood dishes in the country.

Courtyard dining at Facil

8 Facil
MAP L2 ▪ Potsdamer Str. 3
▪ (030) 590 051 234 ▪ noon–3pm, 7–11pm Mon–Fri ▪ €€€

This Michelin-starred restaurant, in a green oasis in the courtyard of the Mandala Hotel *(see p173)*, is a study in understated elegance. Chef Michael Kempf creates stylish Mediterranean dishes with a French accent.

9 Lutter & Wegner am Gendarmenmarkt
MAP L4 ▪ Charlottenstr. 56 ▪ (030) 202 95 40 ▪ 11am–3pm daily ▪ €€

In this old building, formerly the Berliner Sektkellerei (supposedly the place where sparkling wine, or *sekt*, was invented), Austrian cuisine is the star. Try the best *Wiener schnitzel* in town, accompanied by a classic warm potato salad, at consistently good prices. In the summer, there are tables outdoors.

10 Das Speisezimmer
MAP F2 ▪ Chausseestr. 8, 2nd courtyard ▪ (030) 814 529 430
▪ noon–11pm Mon–Fri, 6–11pm Sat ▪ no credit cards ▪ €€

Hidden in the courtyard of an old locomotive factory, this unpretentious restaurant is run by celebrity TV-chef Sarah Wiener. The philosophy is "fresh and local", and the light and affordable cuisine mixes influences from Austria and Italy. Pleasant outdoor dining on a green terrace.

For a key to restaurant price ranges see p93 ←

🔟 Kneipen (Pubs) and Bars

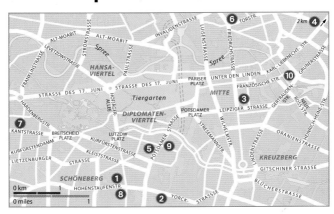

1 Green Door
MAP E5 ◼ Winterfeldstr. 50
◼ (030) 215 25 15 ◼ 6pm–3am Sun–
Thu, 6pm–4am Fri–Sat

This Berlin classic never goes out of style. A young urban crowd enjoys some of the best drinks and cocktails money can buy in Germany, mingling at the minimalist retro-style bar and along the curved, green walls. At weekends, the place is packed to bursting. There's an outdoor bell, but the door policy is pretty liberal as long as you look sober.

2 E & M Leydicke
MAP E6 ◼ Mansteinstr. 4 ◼
(030) 216 29 73 ◼ 7pm–1am daily

This slightly dated winery is still a big hit with tourists as well as groups of pupils and students. Try the sweetish strawberry and raspberry wines.

3 Newton Bar
MAP L4 ◼ Charlottenstr. 57 ◼
(030) 20 29 54 21 ◼ 10am–3am daily

To see and be seen is the name of the game at this elegant venue. Service is charming and the fastest in town, and in summer there's even a fold-down bar on the pavement outside. Heavy leather armchairs make for comfortable sitting, and the walls are adorned with enlarged photographs of nudes by Helmut Newton, after whom the bar is named. Don't miss out on the superb Caribbean and Latin-American cocktails (see p92).

The atmospheric Beckett's Kopf

4 Beckett's Kopf
MAP H1 ◼ Pappelallee 64 ◼
8pm–3am daily ◼ (0162) 237 94 18

One of Berlin's finest cocktail bars, Beckett's Kopf has a portrait of writer Samuel Beckett in its window. Its dark interior is hung with heavy velvet curtains, as if to keep the secret recipes from prying eyes. The superb concoctions include the "Mother-in-Law", with fruity notes, and the "Prince of Wales", said to be a favourite indulgence of King Edward VII.

The retro ambience of Berlin's Victoria Bar

(5) Victoria Bar

MAP E5 ■ Potsdamer Str. 102
■ (030) 25 75 99 77 ■ 6:30pm–4am
Fri–Sat, 6:30pm–3am Sun–Thu

This cosy bar, with its understated 1960s ambience, subdued lighting and sophisticated lounge music is a great place for a relaxing drink and has become a firm favourite among the well-to-do artsy crowd. The cocktails are mixed by the renowned barman Stefan Weber.

(6) Weinbar Rutz

MAP F2 ■ Chausseestr. 8 ■
(030) 24 62 87 60 ■ 4–11pm Tue–Sat

Berlin's best (but pricey) wine bar and shop is found downstairs from the award-winning restaurant of the same name (see p71). It offers over 1,000 wines, but Sommelier Billy Wagner is on hand to assist you. Excellent selection of food.

(7) Zwiebelfisch

MAP N3 ■ Savignyplatz 7–8 ■
(030) 312 73 63 ■ noon–6am daily

A classic of the somewhat ageing Charlottenburg scene, where the last survivors of the 1968 student revolt generation come to reminisce. The artists in the photographs on the walls are former patrons. In the summer, there are tables outdoors.

(8) Café M

MAP E5 ■ Goltzstr. 33 ■ (030) 216 70 92 ■ 8am–late daily (from 9am Sat–Sun)

Noisy yet laid-back, the Café M Kneipe in Schöneberg is (in)famous. If you find the rock music too loud, try the tables outside.

(9) Kumpelnest 3000

MAP E5 ■ Lützowstr. 23
■ (030) 261 69 18 ■ 7pm–5am daily

A very popular venue in a former brothel, complete with chintz wallpaper. They serve a delicious Caipirinha, but for most of the clientele its real attraction is as a great place for people-watching.

(10) Zum Nußbaum

MAP K6 ■ Am Nußbaum 3
■ (030) 242 30 95 ■ noon–midnight

One of only a few traditional kneipen in the historic Nikolaiviertel quarter worth checking out, the Nußbaum serves draught beer and traditional Berlin food (see p108).

The traditional Zum Nußbaum pub

🔟 Lounges and Clubs

① Tresor Club
MAP H4 ▪ Köpenicker Str. 70 ▪ (030) 62 90 87 50 ▪ from midnight Wed, Fri & Sat

Berlin's first techno club, this opened in 1991 in the vaults of the former Wertheim department store. Today, Tresor is sited in the basement and industrial halls of a giant former power station and continues to deliver the latest in electronic music with a full programme of visiting musicians and DJ sets.

② 40 Seconds
MAP E5 ▪ Potsdamer Str. 58 ▪ (030) 890 64 20 ▪ from 11pm Fri–Sat

The stunning, sweeping view of the skyline is the defining feature of this classy club, restaurant and bar. Welcoming a hip "in" crowd in their late 20s to mid-30s, 40 Seconds has less attitude than comparable lounges and offers amazingly good, light food and sublime drinks.

③ Weekend
MAP J6 ▪ (030) 24 63 16 76 ▪ Alexanderstr. 7 ▪ from 11pm Thu–Sat

This rooftop club in an old Soviet block with great views of the glittering high-rises on Alexanderplatz is a young, trendy and surprisingly down-to-earth house, techno and electro pop club, frequented by a young, fashionable and music-oriented crowd.

④ Felix
MAP K3 ▪ Hotel Adlon, Behrenstr. 72 ▪ (030) 301 117 152 ▪ kitchen 6–11pm Mon–Sat, club from 9pm Thu, from 11pm Mon, Fri & Sat

Welcoming the city's hippest crowd, the Felix is the jewel in the crown of Berlin's nightlife. Getting in is as hard as finding a quiet spot in the stylish dance club, but on special weeknights quieter jazz programmes are offered. During international events in Berlin, the Felix is a sure thing for spotting celebrities.

⑤ Spindler & Klatt
Köpenicker Str. 16 ▪ (030) 319 881 860 ▪ kitchen from 8pm daily, club from 11pm Fri–Sat

This event space doubles as a regular lounge with restaurant, but it is famous for special events, mainly dance nights and funky parties.

⑥ Sage Club
MAP H4 ▪ Brückenstr. 1 ▪ (030) 278 98 30 ▪ from 7pm Thu, from 11pm Sat–Sun (Kit Kat Club)

As one of the city's oldest and most successful clubs, the Sage Club (which on weekends hosts the

The fabulous rooftop location of Weekend

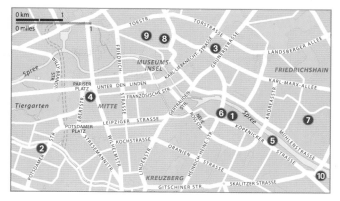

notorious, all-nude Kit Kat Club events) is a sure bet for a thrilling night out. It has a stylish interior and an impressive state-of- the-art sound system.

7 Berghain
Am Wriezener Bahnhof ■ **(030) 29 36 02 10** ■ **8pm–6am Thu, midnight–open end Fri–Sat, 3pm–6am Sun**

Housed in a Communist-era power station, this is Berlin's hottest bastion of electronic music. Some of the world's top DJs spin to spectacular light shows, and the bouncers are notoriously picky. Party animals have been known to spend entire weekends here with no sleep. The top-floor Panorama Bar affords a fantastic view over the Spree River, while anything goes in the men-only cellar sex club Lab.Oratory (see p148).

8 Sophienclub
MAP J5 ■ **Sophienstr. 6** ■ **(030) 282 45 52** ■ **from 11pm daily**

One of the oldest of the East Berlin clubs, the Sophienclub is tucked away next to the Hackesche Höfe complex (see p95). It attracts an enthusiastic and upbeat alternative and indie rock and pop crowd, as well as being popular with students. It also hosts special nights with music ranging from swing to ballroom and is undoubtedly one of the liveliest clubs in the city.

9 Clärchen's Ballhaus
MAP G2 ■ **Auguststr. 24** ■ **(030) 282 92 95** ■ **from noon daily**

The Ballhaus is the last survivor of the 1920s "Tanzcafés" where classic society dances are still fashionable. Apart from its many long-time, mostly working-class clientele, the Ballhaus also attracts a younger hip crowd who enjoy the quirky atmosphere and old-fashioned hits.

Dancing at Clärchen's Ballhaus

10 Watergate
Falckensteinstr. 49 ■ **(030) 61 28 03 95** ■ **from midnight Wed, Fri & Sat**

Located on the Spree River with beautiful views of the illuminated Warschauer Brücke, the Watergate, with its stunning LED dance floor, is one of Berlin's cutting-edge clubs, featuring the latest in house, techno and drum 'n' bass styles.

Shops and Markets

Kaufhaus des Westens

of buying something splendid. With its street artists and buskers, the market is an ideal weekend spot for a bit of browsing, dawdling and people-watching.

③ Galeries Lafayette

Located within Quartier 207, this small branch of the luxury French department store specializes in classic womens- and menswear on one level, and young fashion upstairs. French delicacies are sold in the food department (see p91).

④ Department Store Quartier 206

MAP L4 ▪ Friedrichstr. 71 ▪ (030) 20 94 62 40 ▪ 10:30am–7:30pm Mon–Fri, 10am–6pm Sat

This fashion store is one of the most exclusive in town. Here, men can purchase Gucci or DKNY ties, while women can try on Versace or Calvin Klein. The three-floor store in the Friedrichstadtpassagen also offers luxury homeware and lifestyle products (see p91).

① Kaufhaus des Westens (KaDeWe)

MAP P5 ▪ Tauentzienstr. 21–24 ▪ (030) 212 10 ▪ 10am–8pm Mon–Thu, 10am–9pm Fri, 9:30am–8pm Sat

Whatever you are looking for, you will find it here, in Europe's largest temple of consumption. Over its eight floors, the venerable Kaufhaus des Westens ("department store of the West"), affectionately called KaDeWe, offers more than three million products. On its gourmet floor, West Berlin's former "shop window", you can choose from 1,800 cheeses, 1,400 breads and pastries and 2,000 cold meats. The window displays and inner courtyards are also worth a visit in themselves (see p170).

② Antik- und Flohmarkt Straße des 17. Juni

MAP M4 ▪ Str. des 17. Juni ▪ 10am–5pm Sat–Sun

Berlin's largest art and antiques market specializes in antique furnishings and fittings, cutlery and porcelain, books, paintings, clothing and jewellery. The traders are professionals and demand high prices, but in return you are assured

Department Store Quartier 206

5 Stilwerk

MAP C4 ■ Kantstr. 17 ■ (030) 31 51 50 ■ 10am–8pm Mon–Fri, 10am–6pm Sat

Style is writ large in this trendy shopping centre catering to Charlottenburg's well-to-do residents. Stilwerk specializes in designer furniture, lamps and fittings – basically anything good and expensive (see p125).

6 Gipsformerei Staatliche Museen

MAP A3 ■ Sophie-Charlotten-Str. 17–18 ■ (030) 326 76 90 ■ 9am–4pm Mon–Fri, to 6pm Wed

If you fancy a Schinkel statue for your home or an elegant Prussian sculpture from the Charlottenburg Palace gardens, you'll find moulded plaster reproduction here.

7 Königliche Porzellan-Manufaktur (KPM)

MAP M4 ■ Wegelystr. 1 ■ (030) 39 00 90 ■ 10am–6pm Mon–Sat

Prussia's glory and splendour to take away – traditional KPM porcelain for your dining table at home. Apart from elegant porcelain dinner services, figures and accessories made in the Berlin factory are also on sale here.

8 Winterfeldtmarkt

The trendiest and also the most attractive weekly food and clothing market in Berlin has

Shoppers at Winterfeldtmarkt

developed into something of a hotspot with the Schöneberg crowd. This is the place for meeting up on Saturday mornings (see p133).

9 Türkenmarkt am Maybachufer

MAP H5 ■ Maybachufer ■ 11am–6:30pm Tue & Fri

Berlin's largest weekday Turkish market lures visitors with its smells and dishes from *A Thousand and One Nights* and sells everything from unleavened bread to goat's cheese Bartering is expected (see p133).

10 Berliner Antik- und Flohmarkt

MAP J4 ■ Am Kupfergraben 1 ■ (030) 208 26 45 ■ 11am–6pm Wed–Mon

Numerous stalls for antiques and souvenirs are scattered along the Kupfergraben in front of the Bodemuseum. Much of it is over-priced, but occasionally browsers will find a bargain.

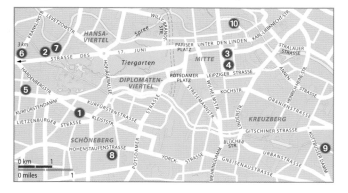

Berlin for Free

View from the Reichstag dome

1 Reichstag

Berlin's biggest freebie happens to be a must-see attraction. There's no topping the fabulous 360° view of the city skyline that you get from Lord Foster's beautiful modern dome. Guided tours take in the plenary hall and graffiti left by Russian soldiers in 1945. You have to register in advance and will need your passport to enter (see pp14–15).

2 Tempelhofer Park
MAP G6 ▪ Tempelhofer Damm 1 ▪ (030) 901 661 500 ▪ Open 24 hours ▪ www.tempelhoferfreiheit.de

A powerful symbol of the new Berlin, the grounds of this historic airport (see p132) have been turned into a green space for the people. You will find lolling couples, urban gardeners, cyclists, in-line skaters, go-karters, and people barbequeing, doing T'ai Chi, flying kites and playing baseball.

3 Open Door Days
May–Sep ▪ www.visitberlin.de

Beautiful private gardens, interiors of historic monuments, and the hallowed halls of government ministries are opened to the public for a few days every year. Chancellor Angela Merkel shakes hands with visitors to her office.

4 Free Concerts
MAP L2 ▪ Herbert-von-Karajan-Str. 1 ▪ (030) 25 48 89 99 ▪ Sep–Jun ▪ www.berliner-philharmoniker.de

Churches, universities and even renowned classical orchestras give free concerts. The Berliner Philharmoniker's gratis lunchtime concerts, usually with small ensembles, are held every Tuesday at 1pm (see pp38–9).

5 East Side Gallery
MAP H4 ▪ Mühlenstraße ▪ (030) 251 71 59 ▪ Open 24 hours ▪ www.eastsidegallery-berlin.de

The biggest remaining stretch of Berlin Wall is now an artistic statement on Germany's division from 1961 to 1989. Famous murals include a Trabant busting through the masonry, Heads with Big Lips by Thierry Noir, and Brezhnev and Honecker kissing (see p146).

Mural on the Berlin Wall

6 Gedenkstätte Berliner Mauer
MAP 2F ▪ Bernauer Str. 111 ▪ (030) 46 79 86 66 ▪ Centre 9:30am–7pm Tue–Sun ▪ www.berliner-mauer-gedenkstaette.de

The Berlin Wall Memorial is well worth a visit for its recreated "death strip", excellent documentary centre and dramatic stories of how East Germans escaped over (or under) the hated barrier. Listening stations and displays are spread along the former border.

7 Free Walking Tours

Daily, year-round ■ **see websites for times and departure points** ■ **www.alternativeberlin.com, www.brewersberlintours.com, www.newberlintours.com**

Join a guided walking tour of the city run by Alternative Berlin Tours, Brewer's Berlin Tours and New Berlin Tours. They're free of charge, although tips are encouraged.

8 Museums

Many museums and galleries, including the Alliiertenmuseum *(see p152)* and Knoblauchhaus *(see p104)* have no admission charge. Some of Berlin's most prestigious museums, such as Gemäldegalerie *(see pp38–40)*, the Pergamonmuseum *(see p24–6)* and Alte Nationalgalerie *(see p52)* are free to visitors under 18.

9 Holocaust-Denkmal

Designed by New York architect Peter Eisenman, the Memorial to the Murdered Jews of Europe consists of 2,711 concrete pillars, many of them off-kilter and placed on undulating ground *(see p87)*. The underground Information Centre offers a moving introduction to the horrors of the Holocaust.

10 Schlosspark Sanssouci

Fancy a stroll through a Romantic landscape painting? Just a half-hour from Berlin by commuter train, these gardens in Potsdam are strewn with ponds and whimsical follies, including an Orangerie, Roman Baths modelled on an Italian villa and a Rococo-style Chinese house *(see p158)*.

The charming Schlosspark Sanssouci

TOP 10 MONEY-SAVING TIPS

Bode-Museum, Museumsinsel

1 The city's public museums, including the comprehensive complex on the Museumsinsel, are covered by the popular Berlin Museum Pass (€24). This offers free entry at participating institutions on 3 consecutive days.

2 The berlinScheckheft (€7.50 at newsagents) contains vouchers that offer steep discounts on restaurants, museums, theatres, music events and other attractions.

3 Theatres and opera houses sell reduced tickets at the door on the day of the performance.

4 Go gallery-hopping in the arty Mitte district. Here, Auguststrasse and Linienstrasse teem with collections open to the public.

5 Visit berlin.eintritt-frei.org for an up-to-date list of free events taking place in the city.

6 Buy discounted public transport tickets (such as a 4-pack or a day pass) or hire a bicycle to get around and see the city like a local.

7 Bus lines 100 and 200 take in many of Berlin's best sights for the price of a single fare.

8 Take advantage of the good-value set meals in cafés and restaurants, particularly at lunchtime.

9 Comb through the vast Mauerpark flea market for unique vintage and retro finds. The market runs all day on Sundays *(see p140)*.

10 If you are a visitor from outside the EU and are leaving the EU with purchased goods, remember to get a refund from Germany's 19 per cent sales tax. Ask sales staff at stores for an *Ausfuhrbescheinigung* (export papers).

🔟 Festivals and Fairs

Crowds at the Berliner Filmfestspiele

① Berliner Filmfestspiele
MAP L2 ■ Filmhaus Potsdamer Platz ■ 2nd & 3rd week in Feb ■ www.berlinale.de

The Berlinale is the top German film festival, and is attended by Hollywood and German stars alike. Until 1999, the film festival took place around the Zoo-Palast cinema; today the area around Potsdamer Platz takes centre stage for the festivities.

② Pop-Kultur
Various venues ■ End Aug ■ www.pop-kultur.berlin

As a successor of the Berlin Music Week, this new festival for bands, musicians, artists, producers, labels as well as audiences is held in and around the Berghain Club (see p75).

③ Internationale Funkausstellung (IFA)
MAP A5 ■ CityCube Berlin ■ (030) 30 38 30 00 ■ every year in Aug or early Sep ■ Admission charge

The latest in high-tech toys and entertainment technology are on show from over 1,500 global exhibitors at the IFA (International Broadcasting Exhibition).

④ Christopher Street Day
MAP P3/4 ■ Kurfürstendamm and Straße des 17. Juni ■ (030) 23 62 86 32 ■ 3rd or 4th weekend in Jun

This colourful gay parade on Christopher Street Day celebrates sexual diversity. Up to 500,000 gays and lesbians from all around the world boisterously dance, drink and celebrate in the streets of Central Berlin (see p68).

⑤ Festival of Lights
Various venues ■ Oct ■ www.festival-of-lights.de

For 10 days, dozens of Berlin's most popular landmarks are illuminated in spectacular ways

Berliner Dom illuminated by light art during the Festival of Lights

and light art and creative installations set up around the city. A mecca for photographers and lovers of optical illusions.

6 Lange Nacht der Museen

Berlin museums ▪ (030) 24 74 98 88 ▪ last weekend Mar & Aug ▪ www. lange-nacht-der-museen.de ▪ Admission charge

For one night, one ticket gives access to all the city's museums until well after midnight, offering visitors an unusual experience. Many institutions also put on special events, and street artists and sellers entertain the patiently queueing public.

7 Grüne Woche

MAP A5 ▪ CityCube Berlin ▪ (030) 30 38 30 00 ▪ 2nd half of Jan ▪ Admission charge

The largest gourmet feast in the world, Green Week is a tasty agricultural and gastronomical fair for everyone. Nowhere else can you enjoy a culinary journey around the world in such a condensed space.

8 Fashion Week

Various venues ▪ Jan & Jul ▪ www.fashion-week-berlin.com/en ▪ Admission charge

Top designers and local talent present their new collections.

9 Karneval der Kulturen

MAP G/H5/6 ▪ Kreuzberg ▪ Whitsun (varying date in Jun)

Multicultural Berlin celebrates for three days in the colourful Kreuzberg district in a cheerful street carnival parade.

10 Internationale Tourismus Börse (ITB)

MAP A5 ▪ CityCube Berlin ▪ (030) 30 38 30 00 ▪ Mar ▪ Admission charge

The world's largest tourism fair offers up-to-date travel information to the general public, often at elaborately designed stalls. The night-time shows put on by many of the exhibiting countries are especially popular.

TOP 10 SPORTS HIGHLIGHTS

Runners at the Berlin Marathon

1 Berlin Marathon
Str. des 17. Juni ▪ 3rd/4th Sun in Sep
The most exuberant marathon in the world attracts thousands of runners.

2 Skate by Night
Str. des 17. Juni ▪ Jun–Aug: Sun evening
In-line skaters from around the world meet for night-time "blading".

3 Sechstagerennen
Velodrom ▪ 2nd half of Jan
The Six-Day Race is one of Berlin's most venerable sports events.

4 Tempelhofer Park
MAP F6 ▪ www.tempelhofer-park.de
This former airport has become the city's largest sports ground (see p78).

5 Berliner Neujahrslauf
MAP K3 ▪ Brandenburger Tor ▪ 1st Jan
This New Year's Day Run is for those who are fit and not afraid of the cold.

6 Internationales Stadionfest (ISTAF)
Olympiastadion ▪ Summer
Germany's biggest athletics festival.

7 DFB-Pokalfinale
Olympiastadion
Germany's second-most important soccer cup final is played here.

8 Deutsches Traberderby
Trabrennbahn Mariendorf ▪ 1st week in Aug
The derby for professional trotter races.

9 Berlin Triathlon
Treptower Park ▪ early Jun ▪ triathlon-service.de
Amateurs can register online for this.

10 Berliner Motorradtage
Kurfürstendamm ▪ end Mar
The international meeting of bikers is a noisy event.

Berlin
Area by Area

Nikolaiviertel and Rotes Rathaus with the Berliner
Dom and Fernsehturm in the background

🔟 Central Berlin: Unter den Linden

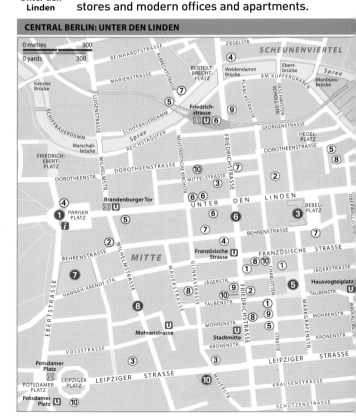

The magnificent boulevard of Unter den Linden is the heart of historic Mitte. Many of Berlin's sights are clustered along this grand avenue and around Bebelplatz, creating an impressive picture of Prussian and German history from the early 18th century onwards. To the south lies the Neo-Classical Gendarmenmarkt, one of Europe's most attractive squares; around it are elegant restaurants and cafés. Not far away, chic Friedrichstraße is lined with luxury stores and modern offices and apartments.

Statue, Unter den Linden

CENTRAL BERLIN: UNTER DEN LINDEN

1 Brandenburger Tor
MAP K3 ■ Pariser Platz

Berlin's best-known landmark on Pariser Platz leads through to Unter den Linden *(see pp12–13)*.

2 Humboldt-Box
MAP K5 ■ Schlossplatz 5
■ 10am–8pm daily ■ Admission charge ■ www.humboldt-box.com/en

This colourful structure on the Museumsinsel provides information on the reconstruction of the Berliner Schloss and is a multimedia introduction to the Humboldt-Forum *(see p89)*. Upon completion of the Forum (scheduled for 2019), the temporary Humboldt-Box will be dismantled. Until then, it will host science, art,

The futuristic Humboldt-Box

culture and architecture exhibitions. It also has a sky-lounge restaurant and viewing platform.

3 Forum Fridericianum
MAP K4 ■ Unter den Linden and Bebelplatz

The historic structures of this complex are among the city's finest. From 1740, Frederick the Great commissioned the prestigious Neo-Classical buildings for the area around today's Bebelplatz and personally influenced their design: Deutsche Staatsoper, the Catholic St Hedwigskathedrale, Alte Bibliothek and Prinz-Heinrich-Palais, later the Humboldt University. A memorial set into the ground at Bebelplatz recalls its dark past – in 1933, it was the site of the Nazi book burning. Frederick's successors commissioned the Altes Palais and a statue of "Old Fritz", surrounded by "his" buildings. Christian Daniel Rauch created the bronze figure in 1840, portraying Frederick wearing his trademark tricorn hat and coronation mantle. The statue has always faced west but wags claim that the East German government mistakenly placed the figure the wrong way around.

FREDERICK AS ARCHITECT

Forum Fridericianum was not only Frederick the Great's memorial to himself, it also ensured that Unter den Linden became one of the greatest boulevards in Europe. The king, who favoured a Neo-Classical style, himself drew up plans for the buildings, and Knobelsdorff executed his ideas.

Museumsinsel's Bode-Museum, with the Fernsehturm in the background

4 Museumsinsel

MAP J5 ▪ Pergamonmuseum,
Bodestr. 1–3 ▪ (030) 266 424 242
▪ 10am–6pm daily, to 8pm Thu ▪
Admission charge ▪ Alte
Nationalgalerie, Bodestr. 1–3 ▪ (030)
266 424 242 ▪ 10am–6pm Tue–Sun,
to 8pm Thu ▪ Admission charge ▪
www.smb.museum

Museum Island, a UNESCO World
Heritage Site, is one of the most
significant complexes of museums
in the world, holding major arts
collections and imposing, full-scale
ancient structures. Based here are
the Pergamonmuseum, the Alte
Nationalgalerie, the Bode-Museum
and the Altes and Neues Museums,
including the famous Ägyptisches
Museum (see pp24–27).

5 Gendarmenmarkt

MAP L4 ▪ Mitte

This square, whose strict layout
is reminiscent of an Italian
Renaissance piazza, is probably the
most beautiful in Berlin. Named
after a regiment of *gens d'armes*
stationed nearby, Gendarmenmarkt
was built at the end of the 17th
century as a market square. The
Schauspielhaus (theatre) on the
west side of the square, built by
Schinkel in 1818–21, was used as
a theatre until 1945. Damaged in
World War II, it was reopened as
Konzerthaus (concert hall) in 1984
(see p54). A statue of the playwright
Friedrich Schiller stands in front of
the building. To the left and right of
the Konzerthaus stand the twin
towers of the Deutscher and
Französischer Doms (German and
French cathedrals), dating back to
the late 18th century. Französischer
Dom, to its north, is a prestigious
late Baroque building (see p59);
concealed behind it is the French
Friedrichstadtkirche, a church
serving Berlin's Huguenot
community. The Deutscher Dom
opposite, built in 1708 on the south
side of the square for the Reformed
Protestant Church, did not receive its
first tower until 1785. Today it has an
exhibition on democracy in Germany.

THE HUGUENOTS IN BERLIN

In 1685, the Great Elector issued the
famous Edict of Potsdam, granting
asylum in Berlin to around 20,000
Huguenots, who were persecuted in
their native France because of their
Protestant faith. Skilled academics and
craftsmen, they moulded Berlin's social
and cultural life and enriched it with
the French art of living. Today, the
city's French community still worships
at the Friedrichstadtkirche, part of the
Französischer Dom complex (**below**).

6 Friedrichstraße
MAP J–L4 ▪ Mitte

Friedrichstraße has regained some of the glamour and vibrancy it possessed before World War II. Today, Berlin's Fifth Avenue once again boasts elegant shops and upmarket restaurants and cafés. Especially worth visiting are the three Quartiers 205, 206 and 207 (the latter designed by architect Jean Nouvel) within the Friedrichstadtpassagen, containing the Galeries Lafayette store and Department Store Quartier 206 (see p91). At the northern end of the street is the famous Dussmann store (books, music, events), S-Bahn station Friedrichstraße and the former entertainment district, which includes the Friedrichstadt-Palast (see p67) and the impressive Admiralspalast (see p90).

Concrete steles, Holocaust-Denkmal

7 Holocaust-Denkmal
MAP L3 ▪ Ebertstr.
▪ Information Centre: 10am–8pm Tue–Sun (Oct–Mar: to 7pm)

The Memorial to the Murdered Jews of Europe serves as Germany's national Holocaust memorial (see p79). After years of debate, US star architect Peter Eisenman completed the monument in 2005. It consists of a large field with dark grey steles of varying heights up to 2 m (6 ft) high, which symbolize the six million Jews and others murdered by the Nazis in their concentration camps between 1933 and 1945. Below the memorial, an information centre explains the causes and history of the genocide.

HISTORIC MITTE WALK

▶ MORNING

Turn back the clock on **Wilhelmstraße** (see p88), Berlin's political nerve centre until 1945. Starting at Hotel Adlon, head south past the bold modern British Embassy. Turn right at Behrensstraße to visit the **Holocaust-Denkmal**, then carry on along Wilhelmstraße, where signs point out the old ministries. The Prussian State Council was in the Neo-Classical building at No. 54; its last president was Konrad Adenauer, who became West Germany's first chancellor. At the corner of Vossstraße were Hitler's main offices in the Neue Reichskanzlei. Continue down to No. 97 on the right, the giant structure of the former Ministry of Aviation. Today the Federal Ministry of Finance is based here. Retrace your steps north, turn right into Mohrenstraße then left into **Friedrichstraße**. Head to **Galeries Lafayette** (see p91), whose gourmet food department is perfect for a snack lunch.

AFTERNOON

After lunch, indulge in a spot of shopping at Galeries Lafayette and at **Department Store Quartier 206** just down the street (see p91). Then head to the beautiful **Gendarmenmarkt** square nearby. Take some time to admire its Konzerthaus and the imposing Deutscher and Französischer Dome. The latter holds regular classical music concerts – check its website for the schedule. Round off your day with a meal at the gourmet Italian restaurant **Malatesta** (see p93) nearby on Charlottenstraße.

See map on pp84–5

British Embassy, Wilhelmstraße

8 Wilhelmstraße

MAP K/L3 ■ **Between Unter den Linden and Leipziger Str.**

In imperial Berlin, the centre of the German Empire's governmental power was based in Wilhelmstraße. Around 100 years later, nothing remains of the prestigious historic buildings which represented the equivalent of No. 10 Downing Street in London or Quai d'Orsay in Paris. All political decisions were made at Wilhelmstraße: both Chancellor (at No. 77) and President (No. 73) of the German Reich lived here in old town houses. Their gardens became known as "ministerial gardens". Adolf Hitler had the street system-atically developed into the nerve centre of Nazi power. The Neue

Reichskanzlei (the Chancellor's office) was built in 1937–9 to plans by Albert Speer, at the corner of Vossstraße and Wilhelmstraße. It was blown up in 1945. Behind the Reichskanzlei was the so-called "Führerbunker" where Adolf Hitler committed suicide on 30 April 1945. Today it is a car park. Of the historic buildings, only the former Ministry of Aviation (Reichsluftfahrtministerium) remains. Today, Wilhelmstraße is lined by modern residential and office buildings; the British Embassy, built in 2000 by Michael Wilford, creates a link with the international importance of this street.

9 Schlossplatz
MAP K5 ■ **Mitte**

Today Schlossplatz seems deserted, but once the Stadtschloss (town residence) of the Hohenzollerns stood here. It was blown up by the East German government in 1950–51, and today just a few historic fragments of the original can be seen. Remains include the façade of the doorway where Karl Liebknecht supposedly proclaimed the Socialist Republic in 1918. The portal has been incorporated into the former Staatsratsgebäude (State Council Building) on the south side of the square. On its eastern side, the square used to be bordered by the Palast der Republik (Palace of the Republic), the former seat of the East German parliament demolished

NAZI ARCHITECTURE

One of few surviving examples of the monumental architectural style favoured by the Nazis is the former Reichsluftfahrtministerium (Ministry of Aviation), commissioned by Hermann Göring in 1935–6 from Ernst Sagebiel. The sandstone office block was the world's largest and most modern, strengthened by steel girders against attack. After reunification, the Treuhandanstalt (privatisation agency) was based here; today it houses the Federal Ministry of Finance (**right**).

in 2008. The Humboldt-Forum cultural centre will be complete in 2019. It will have a façade reminiscent of the old Hohenzollern Palace, a library and the non-European collections of the Dahlem Museums *(see p151)*. Until then, the Humboldt-Box *(see p85)* will provide information on the Forum's development.

Staatsratsgebäude, Schlossplatz

⑩ Museum für Kommunikation

MAP L4 ▪ Leipziger Str. 16 ▪ (030) 20 29 40 ▪ 9am–5pm Tue–Fri (to 8pm Tue), 10am–6pm Sat–Sun ▪ Admission charge ▪ www.mfk-berlin.de

The world's largest Post Office Museum opened in 1872. Its excellent displays document the history of communication from the first postage stamps of the Middle Ages to today's satellite technology. Particularly worth seeing are a blue and a red stamp from Mauritius, one of the first telephone installations (dating back to 1863) and three talking robots who interact with the visitors. Younger visitors always enjoy the Computer-galerie, where they can learn and gain new insights while playing.

Historic letterbox

A DAY OF CULTURE

▶ MORNING

Start your stroll on Unter den Linden, which begins in front of the **Brandenburger Tor** on **Pariser Platz** *(see pp12–13)*. This was Berlin's prestigious royal avenue, and the rich and famous still promenade here today. For breakfast, pop into **Café Einstein** *(see p92)*. Afterwards continue east along the boulevard; you will pass the **KunstHalle**, a gallery of contemporary art run by Deutsche Bank. From here you can already see the 13.5-m (44-ft) high equestrian statue of Frederick the Great at **Forum Fridericianum** *(see p85)*. This area and the nearby Bebelplatz are right in the centre of old Berlin, with the Staatsoper, Altes Palais, St Hedwigskathedrale and Humboldt-Universität around them. Stop for an early lunch at the pleasant museum café of the **Zeughaus** *(see p19)*.

AFTERNOON

In the early afternoon continue east along Unter den Linden. At the end of the street lies the **Museumsinsel** *(see pp24–7)*. Cross over on the Schloßbrücke to explore the wealth of treasures in the island's museums. Then, if you still have the time and energy, visit the **Berliner Dom** *(see p58)*. Opposite the cathedral you will see **Schlossplatz**, with its modern **Humboldt-Box** *(see p85)* information centre. Round off your day in Mitte with a delicious evening meal at the French brasserie **Dressler Unter den Linden** *(see p93)*. To get there, retrace your steps to return along Unter den Linden in a westerly direction.

See map on pp84–5 ←

The Best of the Rest

Trabant at the DDR Museum

1 DDR Museum
MAP K5 ▪ Karl-Liebknecht-Str.
1 ▪ www.ddr-museum.de/en

This museum of everyday life in East Germany recreates socialist-era interiors and displays examples of East German design, including a Trabant car visitors can sit in.

2 Staatsbibliothek Unter den Linden
MAP K4 ▪ Unter den Linden 8 ▪ (030) 26 60 ▪ staatsbibliothek-berlin.de/en/

The lovely reading rooms of this Neo-Baroque library contain many books and manuscripts that are of worldwide importance *(see p39)*.

3 WMF-Haus
MAP L3 ▪ Leipziger Str., corner Mauerstr.

The former headquarters of the porcelain and cutlery manufacturer WMF has remarkable façades decorated with beautiful mosaics.

4 Alte Kommandantur
MAP K5 ▪ Unter den Linden 1

This impressive Classicist building designed by Schinkel houses the Berlin offices of the media con-glomerate Bertelsmann.

5 Maxim-Gorki-Theater
MAP K4 ▪ Am Festungsgraben
2 ▪ english.gorki.de

This renowned theatre was once Berlin's Singakademie, or singing school. Paganini and Liszt, among others, performed here.

6 S-Bahnhof Friedrichstraße
MAP J4 ▪ Friedrichstr.

Remodelled several times, this has always been one of Berlin's most famous stations. Between 1961 and 1989, it was the principal crossing point between East and West.

7 Komische Oper
MAP K4 ▪ Behrenstr. 55–57
▪ english.komische-oper-berlin.de

One of Germany's most magnificent opera houses, dating from 1892, is concealed behind a modern façade. All performances are in German.

8 Palais am Festungsgraben
MAP K4 ▪ Am Festungs-graben 1
▪ (030) 208 40 00

The 1753 Baroque palace has retained its original elegant interior and magnificent ceiling frescoes.

9 Admiralspalast
MAP J4 ▪ Friedrichstr. 101
▪ www.admiralspalast.de

Berlin's most legendary venue, dating from the 1920s, stages musicals and comedy shows.

Façade of the Admiralspalast

10 Dalí Museum
MAP L3 ▪ Leipziger Platz 7
▪ (0700) 32 54 23 75 ▪ www.
daliberlin.de

A rotating exhibition of some 400 works by the 20th-century Surrealist, including drawings, lithographs, etchings, paintings, sculptures and other three-dimensional works.

Shops

1 Galeries Lafayette
MAP L4 ■ Friedrichstr. 76–78 ■
(030) 20 94 80 ■ 10am–8pm Mon–Sat

Located within Quartier 207, this is the only German branch of the luxury French store *(see p76)*. Here you will find elegant fashion, and gourmet foods on the lower level.

2 Quartier 206
MAP L4 ■ Friedrichstr. 71

This is where stylish Berliners shop for up-to-the-minute and luxury designer clothes. Shops include Gucci, DKNY and the Department Store Quartier 206 *(see p76)*.

3 Mall of Berlin
MAP L3 ■ Leipziger Platz 12 ■
(030) 20 62 17 70

A shiny temple of retail commerce, the Mall of Berlin occupies an entire block and connects Leipziger Straße and Wilhelmstraße with a passage. There are 270 shops and restaurants in this shopping centre.

4 Jack Wolfskin
MAP K4 ■ Behrenstr. 23/corner of Friedrichstr. ■ (030) 20 64 80 70

Stock up on apparel, equipment and footwear before setting out on any outdoor activities at this branch of Germany's famous outfitter.

5 Fassbender & Rausch
MAP L4 ■ Charlottenstr. 60 ■ (030) 20 45 84 43

Giant chocolate sculptures of the Reichstag and Brandenburger Tor adorn the windows and tempt visitors into this shop, a chocaholic's paradise. There is a café on the upper floor where you can try some of the store's chocolate creations.

6 Berlin Story
MAP K4 ■ Unter den Linden 40 ■ (030) 20 45 38 42

Almost any book about Berlin, as well as photographs and souvenirs, is available here. There is even a Berlin museum, the Historiale.

Kulturkaufhaus Dussmann

7 Kulturkaufhaus Dussmann
MAP K4 ■ Friedrichstr. 90 ■ (030) 20 25 11 11

A mecca for culture junkies, this store offers books, movies, computer games, sheet music and a large section of classical music. It is open until midnight on weekdays.

8 Ritter Sport Bunte Schokowelt
MAP K4 ■ Französische Str. 24 ■ (030) 20 09 50 80

The chocolate-maker's flagship store has fun merchandise, a chocolate-themed exhibition and workshops.

9 Escada
MAP L4 ■ Friedrichstr. 176–179 ■ (030) 238 64 04

Stylish fashion and accessories label for women, boasting a fantastic selection of luxurious materials.

Mannequins in Escada

10 Bucherer
MAP L4 ■ Friedrichstr. 176–179 ■ (030) 204 10 49

A luxury outlet selling quality watches and jewellery.

See map on pp84–5

Pubs and Bars

1 Newton Bar
MAP L4 ▪ Charlottenstr. 57 ▪
(030) 20 29 54 21 ▪ 10am–3am daily

One of the trendiest bars in town. Sink into the deep leather armchairs and sip your cocktails, surrounded by enlarged photographs of nudes by Helmut Newton (see p72).

2 Sra Bua Bar
MAP K3 ▪ Behrenstr. 72 ▪ (030) 22 61 19 59 ▪ 8pm–2am daily

At the back of Hotel Adlon, this elegant bar specializes in Asian cocktails and creative cuisine by the team of star chef Tim Raue.

3 1a Lauschgift
MAP J5 ▪ Kleine Präsidentenstr. 3 ▪ (030) 66 76 67 27 ▪ From 8pm Thu–Sat

A 20-something crowd sips reasonably priced cocktails in this stylish retro bar with good DJs. The venue is sometimes rented out for private parties, so be sure to call and check in advance.

4 Theodor Tucher
MAP K3 ▪ Pariser Platz 6A ▪ (030) 22 48 94 64 ▪ 7am–11pm daily

This lovely restaurant/bistro next to the Brandenburg Gate also hosts readings and art events.

5 Café LebensArt
MAP K4 ▪ Unter den Linden 69A ▪ (030) 44 72 19 30 ▪ 9am– midnight Sun–Thu, 9am–1am Fri–Sat

A café rather than a bar, offering breakfast and afternoon cakes, this is one of the few places open at night on Unter den Linden.

6 Café Einstein
MAP K4 ▪ Unter den Linden 42 ▪ 7am–10pm daily ▪ (030) 204 36 32

This small and cosy branch of the café serves excellent wines and Austrian specialities.

7 Ständige Vertretung
MAP J3 ▪ Schiffbauerdamm 8 ▪ (030) 282 39 65 ▪ 11am–1am daily

The name harks back to the permanent West German repre-sentation in East Berlin. The pub is famous for its Rhine specialities, such as Kölsch beer.

8 Oh, Angie!
MAP L4 ▪ Friedrichstr. 67 ▪ (030) 20 64 41 64 ▪ 9am–10pm Mon–Sat

An elegant lobby bar in the basement of Q205 shopping centre, perfect for a quick healthy lunch or a snack. Definitely try the delicious focaccias and carrot cake.

9 Brauhaus Lemke
MAP J5 ▪ Dircksenstr. S-Bahn arch No. 143 ▪ (030) 24 72 87 27 ▪ noon–midnight daily

An atmospheric pub located under the S-Bahn arches with a small courtyard.

10 Windhorst
MAP K3 ▪ Dorotheenstr. 65 ▪ (030) 20 45 00 70 ▪ from 6pm Mon– Fri, from 9pm Sat

Sophisticated jazz bar with bartenders whipping up your cocktail of choice.

Pleasant interiors of Theodor Tucher

Restaurants

Atmospheric interiors of Refugium

(1) Refugium
MAP L4 ■ Gendarmenmarkt 5 ■ (030) 229 16 61 ■ noon–11pm daily (winter: from 5pm Mon–Fri) ■ €€

A cosy cellar restaurant next to the French cathedral. International and German dishes.

(2) Chipps
MAP L5 ■ Jägerstr. 35 ■ (030) 36 44 45 88 ■ 9am–late Mon–Sat (to 5pm Sun) ■ €€

Possibly the best vegetarian/vegan restaurant in Berlin. Organic dishes focus on variations of Asian *chipps* (potato pancakes) and rice rolls.

(3) Vapiano
MAP K4 ■ Mittelstr. 51 ■ (030) 501 541 00 ■ 10am–midnight daily ■ €

Quality Italian food made in front of you at this self-service restaurant.

(4) Grill Royal
MAP J4 ■ Friedrichstr. 105b ■ (030) 28 87 92 88 ■ 6pm–midnight daily ■ €€

Steak-lovers can choose from a range of cuts from around the world.

(5) Tausend Cantina
MAP J3 ■ Schiffbauerdamm 11 ■ (030) 27 58 20 70 ■ 7:30pm–late Tue–Sat ■ €€

Top-notch Asian and Ibero-American cuisine by celebrated chef Duc Ngo, a Berliner with Vietnamese roots.

(6) Dressler Unter den Linden
MAP K3 ■ Unter den Linden 39 ■ (030) 204 44 22 ■ 8am–1am daily ■ €€

In season, this French brasserie, decorated in Art Deco style, is excellent for oysters. Their inexpensive three-course set menu is recommended.

(7) Opera Court
MAP K4 ■ Hotel de Rome, Behrenstr. 37 ■ (030) 46 06 09 12 60 ■ 2–6pm Fri–Sun ■ €€

Petit fours, scones, sandwiches and tea are served beneath the gilded skylights at this historic café that boasts marble columns and an original glazed ceiling.

(8) Café Nö
MAP L3 ■ Glinkastr. 23 ■ (030) 201 08 71 ■ noon–1am Mon–Fri, 7pm–1am Sat ■ €

Mediterranean flavours meet German classics at this wine bar and restaurant.

(9) Malatesta
MAP L4 ■ Charlottenstr. 59 ■ (030) 20 94 50 71 ■ 10am–midnight daily ■ €€

Gourmet Italian food served in stylish, minimalist surroundings.

(10) Aigner
MAP K4 ■ Französische Str. 25 ■ (030) 203 751 850 ■ noon–2am daily ■ €€

Original Viennese restaurant serving typically Austrian food.

PRICE CATEGORIES

For a three-course meal for one with half a bottle of wine (or equivalent meal), taxes and charges included.

....

€ under €30 €€ €30–60 €€€ over €60

See map on pp84–5

TOP10 Central Berlin: Scheunenviertel

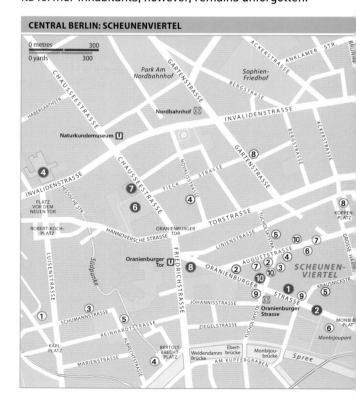

Richly decorated Postfuhramt building

From the mid-19th-century onwards, the Scheunenviertel ("barn quarter") was home to thousands of poor Jewish migrants. After World War II the area was entirely neglected and fell into decay. It has experienced a regeneration in recent decades, and today, many historic merchants' yards and narrow side streets have been restored, reviving the quarter's unique and lively character. With its new restaurants, galleries and shops, the district has become fashionable. The tragic history of its former inhabitants, however, remains unforgotten.

CENTRAL BERLIN: SCHEUNENVIERTEL

1 Neue Synagoge

MAP J4/5 ■ Oranienburger Str. 28–30 ■ 10am–8pm Sun–Mon, 10am–6pm Tue–Thu, 10am–5pm Fri ■ Admission charge ■ www.centrumjudaicum.de/en

The New Synagogue was once the largest in Europe. In 1938, it survived Kristallnacht thanks to a brave guard, but it was damaged by bombs during World War II. Behind the Moorish façades are a prayer room and the Centrum Judaicum (see p59).

2 Oranienburger Straße

MAP J4/5 ■ Mitte, between Friedrichstr. and Rosenthaler Str.

In the centre of old Scheunenviertel, Oranienburger Straße symbolizes the rise and fall of Jewish culture in Berlin like no other street. Traces of

Striking dome of the Neue Synagoge

its Jewish past are visible at the Neue Synagoge and several Jewish cafés and restaurants (see p101). Some 18th- and 19th-century buildings attest to the street's former splendour – the Postfuhramt (see p97), for example, or the house at No. 71–72, built in 1789 by Christian Friedrich Becherer for the Grand Lodge of the German Freemasons.

3 Hackesche Höfe

MAP J5 ■ Rosenthaler Str. 40–41

Berlin's largest and most attractive group of restored commercial buildings, Hackesche Höfe extends between Oranienburger and Rosenthaler Straße. The complex, comprising eight interconnecting courtyards, was designed around the turn of the 20th century by August Endell and Kurt Berndt, two leading exponents of the Jugendstil. The first courtyard especially has elements typical of the style: geometric motifs on vibrant glazed tiles cover the building from the foundations to the guttering. The complex has been carefully restored and is now a popular centre of nightlife.

- 1 **Top 10 Sights** see pp95–7
- 1 **Restaurants** see p101
- 1 **The Best of the Rest** see p98
- 1 **Pubs, Bars and Clubs** see p100
- 1 **Old Courtyards** see p99

4 Museum für Naturkunde

The Museum of Natural History – one of the largest of its kind – has the world's largest dinosaur skeleton: a brachiosaurus found in Tanzania. Also displayed are fossils, meteorites and minerals (see p51).

5 Sophienstraße

MAP J5 ▪ Große Hamburger Str. 29

Narrow Sophienstraße has been beautifully restored and looks as it did in the late 18th century. The buildings and courtyards now host shops and arts and crafts workshops. The Baroque Sophienkirche nearby, the first Protestant parish church, was founded by Queen Sophie Luise in 1712. Next to it is a cemetery with some 18th-century tombs (see p98).

6 Dorotheenstädtischer Friedhof

MAP F2 ▪ Chausseestr. 126 ▪ Summer: 8am–8pm daily; winter: 8am–4pm daily

Many celebrities have found their final resting place in this striking cemetery, dating back to 1762. To the

Museum für Naturkunde

left of the entrance are the graves of Heinrich Mann (1871–1950) and Bertolt Brecht (1898–1956); further along are the pillar-like tombstones of Johann Gottlieb Fichte (1762–1814) and Georg Wilhelm Friedrich Hegel (1770–1831). On Birkenallee (left off the main path) you can see the graves of Karl Friedrich Schinkel (1781–1841), Friedrich August Stüler (1800–65) and Johann Gottfried Schadow (1764–1850).

7 Brecht-Weigel-Gedenkstätte

MAP F2 ▪ Chausseestr. 125 ▪ (030) 200 571 844 ▪ 10am–noon, 2–3:30pm Tue; 10–11:30am Wed & Fri; 10am–noon, 5–6:30pm Thu; 10am–3:30pm Sat; 11am–6pm Sun ▪ Admission charge ▪ www.adk.de/en/archive

Bertolt Brecht, one of the greatest playwrights of the 20th century, lived here with his wife, Helene Weigel, between 1953 and 1956. On display are original furnishings, documents and photographs.

8 Tacheles

MAP F3 ▪ Oranienburger Str. 54–56A ▪ (030) 282 61 85

In the 1990s, the ruins of the Wilhelm-Einkaufs-Passagen, an elegant shopping centre from the early 20th century, were taken over

---

JEWISH BERLIN

In the 19th century, Berlin had a population of 200,000 Jews, the largest such community in Germany. Apart from the wealthier Jews who lived in the west of the city, it included many Jewish migrants from Eastern Europe. They settled in Spandauer Vorstadt, primarily in Scheunenviertel, an impoverished part of the district that had the reputation of being a criminal red-light area. Later, Nazi propaganda used that name to denote the whole area to tarnish all Jews by association. Nazi stigmatization of Jews also included the enforced public wearing of a Star of David (below). The Jewish quarter is still known as Scheunenviertel, but very few Jews live here now. Only some 5,000 Jewish Berliners survived the 1933–45 persecution.

by squatters and turned into an alternative arts centre. Recently this listed monument was sold, and will re-emerge as a cultural space with apartments, shops and hotel rooms.

⑨ Gedenkstätte Große Hamburger Straße

MAP J5 ▪ Große Hamburger Str. ▪ www.jg-berlin.org/en.html

Before 1939, this was a thoroughly Jewish street, with Jewish schools, the oldest Jewish cemetery in Berlin and an old people's home. The latter achieved tragic fame during the Nazi period – the SS used it as a detention centre for Berlin Jews before transporting them to the concentration camps. A monument commemorates thousands of Jews who were sent to their death from here. To the left of the home is a Jewish school, on the site of an earlier school founded in 1778 by the Enlightenment philosopher Moses Mendelssohn (1729–86). To the right is the Alter Jüdischer Friedhof (old Jewish cemetery), where some 12,000 Berlin Jews were buried between 1672 and 1827. In 1943, the Nazis almost completely destroyed the cemetery, and in 1945 it was converted into a park. Only a few Baroque tombstones or *masebas* survived; these are now fixed into the original cemetery wall. The spot thought to be Moses Mendelssohn's tomb is marked by a *maseba*.

Moses Mendelssohn

⑩ Postfuhramt

MAP J4 ▪ Oranienburger Straße 35

The richly ornamented Postfuhramt (post office transport department) dates from the 19th century. The building was used as an exhibition space, but it has now been converted into the head office of a medical technology firm.

A DAY IN SCHEUNENVIERTEL

Brecht-Weigel-Gedenkstätte
August-strasse
Schulhof
Oranienburger Strasse
Chaussee-strasse
Keyser Soze
Hackesche Höfe
Reinhardt-strasse
Tacheles
Neue Synagoge
Gedenkstätte Grosse Hamburger strasse
Bertolt-Brecht-Platz
Berliner Ensemble
Friedrichstrasse station

▶ MORNING

Take the S-Bahn to Berlin's former entertainment district at Friedrichstraße and explore this vibrant, glamorous street. Then walk north up to Reinhardstraße, opposite the Friedrichstadt-Palast, and turn left here towards Bertolt-Brecht-Platz. Continue south to Albrechtstraße to the **Berliner Ensemble** *(see p98)*. Admire the theatre where Bertolt Brecht used to work, then make a detour to visit his home, the **Brecht-Weigel-Gedenkstätte**. The best way to get there is on foot – return to Friedrichstraße and walk north to Chausseestraße. Then retrace your steps and turn left into **Oranienburger Straße** *(see p95)* to get to the heart of fashionable Scheunenviertel. About 100 m (330 ft) ahead rises the former arts centre **Tacheles**, and a 5-minute walk down the street will bring the dome of the **Neue Synagoge** into view *(see p95)*.

AFTERNOON

Before exploring further, stop for some refreshments; not far from the synagogue is the **Keyser Soze** café *(see p101)*. Continue along Tucholskystraße, then turn right into Auguststraße. Here you will find some of the most attractive courtyards, such as the old-world **Schulhof** at No. 21. Continue along Auguststraße then turn right for the **Gedenkstätte Große Hamburger Straße** and the **Hackesche Höfe** *(see p95)*. Shop a little, then round off your tour of Scheunenviertel with an evening meal at one of its restaurants.

See map on pp94–5

The Best of the Rest

Exhibit at the Charité museum

1 Charité
MAP J3 ▪ Schumannstr. 20–21 ▪ (030) 450 536 156 ▪ Medizin-historisches Museum 10am–5pm Tue, Thu, Fri, Sun, 10am–7pm Wed & Sat

Many renowned physicians, such as Rudolf Virchow and Robert Koch, worked and taught at this world-famous hospital, founded in 1710. The Museum of Medical History has some 750 remarkable exhibits on display.

2 Alte and Neue Schönhauser Straße
MAP J5 ▪ Hackescher Markt

Alte Schönhauser Straße is one of the oldest streets in Spandauer Vorstadt. The lively road is still characterized by a colourful jumble of traditional and new fashion shops.

3 Deutsches Theater
MAP J3 ▪ Schumannstr. 13A ▪ (030) 28 44 12 25

Once the place of work of stage and screen actor and director Max Reinhardt, this theatre – widely considered the best German-language theatre – shows mainly German classics, often in new interpretations *(see p67)*.

The imposing Baroque Sophienkirche

4 Berliner Ensemble
MAP J3 ▪ Bertolt-Brecht-Platz 1 ▪ (030) 28 40 81 55

This theatre, established in 1891–2 by Heinrich Seeling, was the main venue for Bertolt Brecht's plays.

5 Hochbunker
MAP J3 ▪ Albrechtstr. corner of Reinhardtstr.

One of the last surviving World War II bunkers in Berlin.

6 Monbijoupark
MAP J5 ▪ Oranienburger Str./Spree

A small park, in which once stood the little Monbijou palace. It is now an attractive green space for a break.

7 Auguststraße
MAP G2 ▪ Between Oranienburger and Rosenthaler Str.

The area round this road harks back to old Scheunenviertel, featuring interior courtyards and now brimming with art galleries.

8 Koppenplatz
MAP G2 ▪ Near Auguststr.

In this small square, a monument of a table and upturned chair recall the expulsion of the Jews.

9 Sophienkirche
MAP G3 ▪ Große Hamburger Str. 29

This parish church, built in 1712, has managed to preserve its traditional old Berlin charm. Be sure not to miss the Baroque pulpit.

10 Tucholskystraße
MAP J4

This narrow street is typical of the transformation of Scheunenviertel – trendy shops next to both decaying and beautifully renovated façades.

Old Courtyards

1 Sophie-Gips-Höfe
MAP G3 ▪ Sophienstr. 21–22

Famous for the Hoffman art collection, which is based here, this former sewing machine factory is a popular meeting place.

2 Sophienhöfe
MAP G3 ▪ Sophienstr. 17–18

The 19th-century red-brick artisans' workshops have been transformed into artists' studios and a theatre.

Courtyards of Heckmann-Höfe

3 Heckmann-Höfe
MAP G3 ▪ Between Oranienburger Str. 32 and Auguststraße 9

These lavishly restored yards in a candy factory attract visitors with a restaurant and fashionable shops.

4 Sophienstr. 22 and 22A
MAP G3

Two small inner courtyards, partially planted, are surrounded by yellow and red-brick walls.

5 Rosenthaler Straße 37
MAP J5

This green-tiled courtyard is unique. Once part of the Wertheim department store, it now houses a boutique and tapas bar. The 1775 townhouse through which it is accessed has a beautiful wooden staircase.

6 Schulhof
MAP G2 ▪ Auguststr. 21

Time seems to have stood still around 1900 in this courtyard, which houses an elementary school.

7 Hof Auguststraße 5A
MAP G3

The extensive courtyard of the former Postfuhramt permits a glimpse of the original façade of the building.

8 Rosenthaler Straße 39
MAP J5

Berlin's post-Wall subculture of edgy art collectives is still alive and well in this unrenovated courtyard.

9 Kunsthof
MAP J4/5 ▪ Oranienburger Str. 27

A courtyard full of nooks and crannies, which is today occupied by a number of workshops, offices and cafés. Take a look at the richly ornamented staircases.

10 Kunst-Werke (KW)
MAP G2 ▪ Auguststr. 69

Large-scale installations by the resident artists are regularly on display at this well-known centre for contemporary art; artists-in-residence have included Susan Sontag. The courtyard has a café designed by US artist and curator Dan Graham in the conservatory.

The Kunst-Werke courtyard

See map on pp94–5

Pubs, Bars and Nightclubs

The trendy interiors of Riva

1 Riva
MAP J5 ▪ Dircksenstr., Arch 142 ▪ (030) 24 72 26 88 ▪ 6pm–4am daily
This elegant and trendy bar is named after an Italian football player.

2 Bellini Lounge
MAP J4 ▪ Oranienburger Str. 42 ▪ (030) 97 00 56 18 ▪ 6pm–3am daily
Some of the most authentic tropical cocktails north of the equator.

3 Betty F
MAP G2 ▪ Mulackstr. 13 ▪ (030) 304 717 440 ▪ From 9pm daily
A trashy gay and straight pub paying ironic homage to former US First Lady Betty Ford. Great cocktails.

4 Reingold
MAP F2 ▪ Novalistr. 11 ▪ (030) 28 38 76 76 ▪ From 7pm Tue–Sat
A relaxed, fashionable bar with a 1920s atmosphere. Perfect for a nightcap after dinner in Mitte.

5 Fire Bar
MAP J5 ▪ Krausnickstr. 5 ▪ (030) 28 38 51 19 ▪ From 8pm daily
In this friendly though somewhat dingy bar, a young crowd enjoys reasonably priced drinks and snacks.

6 B-flat
MAP J5 ▪ Rosenthaler Str. 13 ▪ (030) 283 31 23 ▪ From 8pm Sun–Thu, from 9pm Fri–Sat
Live jazz, and occasionally dancing, are on offer at this small venue.

7 CCCP Bar
MAP G2 ▪ Torstr. 58 ▪ (0151) 23 60 76 05 ▪ From 7pm daily
A retro Soviet-style bar, CCCP Bar serves vodka and blinis to a lively crowd. The tiny stage hosts DJ nights and burlesque shows.

8 Yosoy
MAP J5 ▪ Rosenthaler Str. 37 ▪ (030) 28 39 12 13 ▪ from 11am daily
Tasty tapas, good wines and exciting cocktails are served at this attractively furnished Spanish restaurant – which is why it is usually crowded late into the night.

9 Kaffee Burger
MAP G2 ▪ Torstr. 58–60 ▪ (030) 28 04 64 95 ▪ From 8pm daily
Thanks to its quirky record release parties, readings and movie screenings, this pub and music venue is a firm favourite with East Berlin hipsters.

10 Oxymoron
MAP J5 ▪ Rosenthaler Str. 40–41 ▪ (030) 28 39 18 86 ▪ From 9am daily
This small bar, club and restaurant in popular and lively Hackesche Höfe (see p95), features chintz decoration and serves light German and international meals.

Oxymoron restaurant and bar

Restaurants

PRICE CATEGORIES
For a three-course meal for one with half
a bottle of wine (or equivalent meal),
taxes and charges included.

€ under €30   €€ €30–60   €€€ over €60

1 Pan Asia
MAP J5 ■ Rosenthaler Str. 38
■ (030) 27 90 88 11 ■ noon–midnight
daily ■ €
Asian dishes, many with seared fish
and vegetables, are served in vintage
1960s surroundings.

2 Keyser Soze
MAP G3 ■ Tucholskystr. 33
■ (030) 28 59 94 89 ■ 7:30am–3am
daily ■ €
Unpretentious restaurant serving
breakfast until 6pm and hearty
German snacks.

3 Monsieur Vuong
MAP G2 ■ Alte Schönhauser
Str. 46 ■ (030) 99 29 69 24
■ noon–midnight daily ■ €
This tiny Vietnamese snack joint
serves delicious Asian dishes.

4 Pauly Saal
MAP G2 ■ Augustr. 11
■ (030) 33 00 60 70 ■ 3–6pm,
6pm–3am Mon–Sat ■ €€€
Classy Michelin star restaurant in a
former school that also houses art
galleries. Its wine list is extensive.

5 Beth-Café
MAP G2 ■ Tucholskystr. 40
■ (030) 281 31 35 ■ 11am–5pm Fri,
11am–8pm Sun–Thu ■ no credit
cards ■ €
Small Jewish café of the Adass-
Jisroel community, serving Jewish
snacks and kosher wines and beers.

6 Hackescher Hof
MAP J5 ■ Rosenthaler Str.
40–41 ■ (030) 283 52 93 ■ from 8am
Mon–Fri, from 9am Sat–Sun ■ €€
The best restaurant in Hackesche
Höfe serves delicious local produce.

Fondue at Nola's am Weinberg

7 Nola's am Weinberg
MAP G2 ■ Veteranenstr. 9
■ (030) 44 04 07 66 ■ 10am–1am
daily ■ €
The Swiss cuisine served here is
surprisingly inspired. Try one of their
delicious fondues. There is a lovely
outdoor terrace.

8 Alpenstück
MAP G2 ■ Gartenstr. 9
■ (030) 21 75 16 46 ■ 6pm–1am
daily ■ €
The best of the area's homely
restaurants serving traditional,
hearty fare from southern Germany
and Austria in a cosy setting,
decorated in an Alpine style.

9 Kamala
MAP J4 ■ Oranienburger Str. 69
■ (030) 283 27 97 ■ noon–11:30pm
daily ■ €
This hidden gem offers diners
traditional Thai cuisine alongside a
surprisingly impressive wine list.
Good value for money.

10 Barist
MAP J5 ■ Am Zwirngraben
13–14 ■ (030) 24 72 26 13 ■ 10am–
2am Sun–Thu, 10am–3am Fri–Sat
■ €€
A mixture of French, Italian and
Austrian dishes are on offer here.
There is always a good atmosphere
under the S-Bahn arches; live jazz
plays at the weekends.

See map on pp94–5

TOP 10 Central Berlin: Around Alexanderplatz

Berliner Rathaus

The area around Alexanderplatz – "Alex" to locals – is one of the city's oldest parts. It was here that the twin towns of Cölln and Berlin merged in the 13th century. The square defined the heartbeat of the city before World War II; after the ravages of war, it seemed vast and a little forlorn. The vibrancy described by Alfred Döblin in his novel *Berlin Alexanderplatz*, is only slowly returning. A short walk away is the city's oldest coherent quarter – the 18th-century Nikolaiviertel – with its medieval Nikolaikirche.

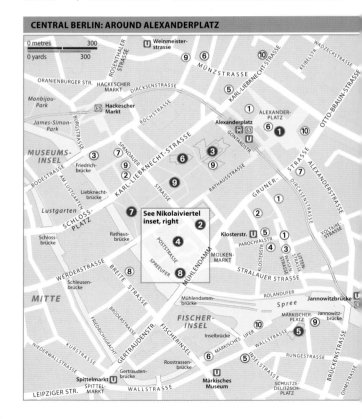

CENTRAL BERLIN: AROUND ALEXANDERPLATZ

Alexanderplatz's Neptunbrunnen with Marienkirche in the background

1 Alexanderplatz
MAP J6 ▪ Mitte

The huge, largely desolate square in the centre of East Berlin, called "Alex" by Berliners, was one of the

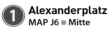

1	**Top 10 Sights** *see pp103–5*
①	**Restaurants** *see p109*
①	**The Best of the Rest** *see p106*
①	**Pubs, Cafés and Beergardens** *see p108*
①	**Shops and Markets** *see p107*

most vibrant places in Berlin before World War II – and no doubt it will be again some day. Alfred Döblin beautifully captured the rhythm of the city in his world-famous novel *Berlin Alexanderplatz* (1929). Not much remains today of the once frenzied atmosphere, although there is plenty of bustle around the Galeria Kaufhof department store *(see p107)*. Alexanderplatz was originally a cattle and wool market. Not many of the prewar buildings have survived – only Berolinahaus and Alexander-haus remain, next to the historic S-Bahn station Alexanderplatz, both dating back to 1929. The square was almost completely laid to waste in World War II, and most of the surrounding soulless tower blocks were built in the 1960s.

2 Berliner Rathaus
MAP K6 ▪ Rathausstr. 15
▪ (030) 902 60 ▪ 9am–6pm Mon–Fri

Berlin's proud town hall, the office of the Governing Mayor, is the political centre of power in Greater Berlin. It was built in 1861–9 to a design by Hermann Friedrich Waesemann on the site of an older town hall. The Rathaus was meant to demonstrate the power and the glory of Berlin, and the architect took his inspiration for the new building from Italian Renaissance *palazzi*. The building is also known as the *Rotes Rathaus* or Red Town Hall – not a reference to its Socialist past, but to the red bricks from Brandenburg province with which it is built *(see also p54)*.

③ Berliner Fernsehturm
MAP J6 ▪ Panoramastr. 1a
▪ **(030) 242 33 33** ▪ **Mar–Oct: 9am–midnight; Nov–Feb: 10am–midnight** ▪ **Admission charge** ▪ **www.tv-turm.de/en/**

The 368-m (1,207-ft) high TV tower is the tallest building in Berlin, affording views of up to 40 km (25 miles). There is a viewing platform at 203 m (666 ft). The Sphere restaurant above rotates once around its own axis every 30 minutes. The tower, visible from afar, was erected in 1965–9 by the East German government to signify the triumph of their capital East Berlin.

④ Nikolaiviertel
MAP K6 ▪ Mitte ▪ Knoblauchhaus: Poststr. 23 ▪ **(030) 240 020 171** ▪ **10am–6pm Tue & Thu–Sun, noon–8pm Wed** ▪ **Admission charge** ▪ **www.en.stadtmuseum.de**

Centred around the medieval Nikolaikirche *(see p58)*, the small Nikolaiviertel quarter with its nooks and crannies, old Berlin restaurants and souvenir shops is one of the most charming parts of the city. The area extending between the banks of the Spree River and Mühlendamm was razed to the ground in World War II. East Germany restored it

Märkisches Museum

after the war, unfortunately not always successfully: some houses were covered in prefabricated façades. Knoblauchhaus was one of few to escape wartime destruction. Dating from 1835, it was the former home of the Knoblauch family (Neue Synagoge was designed by architect Eduard Knoblauch). Today it houses a museum depicting everyday life in Berlin, and includes a fully furnished apartment in the Biedermeier style.

⑤ Märkisches Museum
MAP L6 ▪ Am Köllnischen Park 5 ▪ (030) 24 00 21 62 ▪ **10am–6pm Tue–Sun** ▪ **Admission charge** ▪ **www.en.stadtmuseum.de**

Berlin's municipal museum holds artefacts relating to the city's culture and history, including architectural treasures such as doorways and the head of one of the horses from the top of the Brandenburg Gate. There is also a Gothic Chapel room with a collection of medieval sculptures.

⑥ Marienkirche
MAP J6 ▪ Karl-Liebknecht-Str. 8 ▪ **(030) 242 44 67** ▪ **10am–6pm Mon–Sat, noon–6pm Sun**

Originally built in 1270, Marienkirche was extensively remodelled in the 15th century. Thanks to its Baroque church tower, it is one of Berlin's loveliest churches. Inside, the alabaster pulpit by Andreas Schlüter (1703) and the main altar (1762) are highlights. The 15th-century Gothic font and a 22-m (72-ft) long fresco from 1485, *Der Totentanz* (The Dance of Death), are its two oldest treasures. The church is now the only reminder of the once densely built-up historic city core here *(see p58)*.

⑦ Marx-Engels-Forum
MAP K5

Shortly after German reunification in 1989, the words "Next time it will all be different" were scrawled onto this

Buildings in the Nikolaiviertel

monument to Friedrich Engels and Karl Marx, the fathers of Socialism. Bronze statues created by Ludwig Engelhart in 1986 adorn the square.

 Ephraim-Palais
MAP K6 ∎ Poststr. 16 ∎ (030) 24 00 21 62 ∎ 10am–6pm Tue & Thu–Sun, noon–8pm Wed ∎ Admission charge ∎ www.en.stadtmuseum.de

This Rococo palace, built in 1766 for the merchant, court jeweller and mint master Nathan Veitel Heinrich Ephraim, was once regarded as the city's most beautiful spot. Rebuilt using original elements after the old palace was demolished, it houses a museum on Berlin art history.

Neptunbrunnen
MAP K6 ∎ Am Rathaus

The green Neo-Baroque fountain, dating from 1895, depicts the sea god Neptune. He is surrounded by four female figures, symbolizing Prussia's main rivers at the time: the Rhine, Weichsel, Oder and Elbe.

Neptunbrunnen, Alexanderplatz

 Karl-Marx-Allee and Frankfurter Allee
MAP H3 ∎ Mitte/Friedrichshain

This avenue, lined by Soviet-style buildings, was built as a showpiece for Socialism in 1949–55. Known then as "Stalinallee", it provided ultra-modern apartments that are again in high demand today.

A DAY AROUND ALEXANDERPLATZ

▶ **MORNING**

Start your day at Strausberger Platz where you can admire the products of Socialist architecture lining **Frankfurter Allee**. Then take the U-Bahn (or continue on foot) to the vast **Alexanderplatz** *(see p103)* where you can indulge in a bit of people-watching or do a spot of shopping before heading to the beautiful **Marienkirche**. Step back outside to admire the lovely **Neptunbrunnen** fountain a few steps away, then walk to the **Berliner Fernsehturm** and – if the weather is nice – take the lift up to the viewing platform. After that, cross the square to the **Berliner Rathaus** *(see p103)*. The town hall's basement restaurant, or Ratskeller, is an excellent place for lunch, or you could stroll past the statues of Marx and Engels in the **Marx-Engels-Forum** to the nearby historic Nikolaiviertel and enjoy the rustic fare at **Reinhard's** *(see p109)*.

AFTERNOON

After lunch, experience the historic ambience of the old **Nikolaiviertel** quarter by exploring its narrow alleyways and hidden nooks on foot. The **Knoblauchhaus** museum and the Nikolaikirche are especially worth a visit. Then walk down Grunerstraße to reach the opposite bank of the Spree River, where you can immerse yourself in Berlin's culture and history at the **Märkisches Museum**. Round off your day with a meal at the stylish **Zur Gerichtslaube** *(see p109)*.

See map on pp102–3

The Best of the Rest

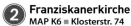

Lacy balustrades at the Stadtgericht

1 Stadtgericht
MAP K6 ▪ Littenstr. 13–15
▪ 8am–6pm Mon–Fri

The imposing municipal courts building boasts extravagant stairs in the lobby area, with curved balustrades and elegant columns.

2 Franziskanerkirche
MAP K6 ▪ Klosterstr. 74

Remnants of a 13th-century Franciscan abbey, these ruins are surrounded by lawns, making this a picturesque spot for a break in the city centre.

3 Stadtmauer
MAP K6 ▪ Waisenstr.

A fragment of the 13th–14th-century town wall that once surrounded the twin towns of Berlin and Cölln.

4 Parochialkirche
MAP K6
▪ Klosterstr. 67

This church, by Johann Arnold Nering and Martin Grünberg, was one of Berlin's most charming Baroque churches, but the magnificent interior was destroyed in World War II, and the bell tower collapsed. It is now a venue for contemporary music concerts.

Detail, Parochialkirche

5 Palais Podewil
MAP K6 ▪ Klosterstr. 68 ▪ (030) 24 74 96 ▪ 11am–10pm Mon–Sat

The light yellow Baroque palace, built in 1701–4, has been transformed into Podewil, a cultural centre, and a subsidiary of the Grips-Theater *(see p64)*.

6 Märkisches Ufer
MAP L6

This picturesque riverside promenade gives a good impression of the city in the late 18th century. Look out for No. 12, a typical Berlin Baroque house that was originally built on Fischerinsel in 1740 and transplanted here in 1969.

7 Heiliggeistkapelle
MAP J5 ▪ Spandauer Str. 1

A beautiful example of Gothic brick architecture, this hospital church was built around 1300.

8 Ribbeckhaus
MAP K5 ▪ Breite Str. 36

The only Renaissance house in central Berlin, with a remarkable, lavishly ornamented façade.

9 AquaDom and Sea Life Berlin

Discover a host of species living in rivers, lakes and seas, and see amazing corals and tropical fish at this fascinating centre, which boasts the world's largest cylindrical aquarium *(see p65)*.

10 Historischer Hafen
MAP L6 ▪ Märkisches Ufer ▪ Museum May–Sep: noon–6pm Sun ▪ (0172) 392 67 48

Moored at this port are barges and tugboats that once operated on the Spree River. The *Renate-Angelika* hosts a historical display on inland shipping.

Shops and Markets

Vast interiors of the Galeria Kaufhof

1 Galeria Kaufhof
MAP J6 ▪ Alexanderplatz 9
▪ (030) 24 74 30 ▪ 9:30am–8pm
Mon–Wed, 9:30am–10pm Thu–Sat
The largest department store in
eastern Berlin stocks everything
your heart could desire. Its food
department entices with a range of
international gourmet foods.

2 Die Puppenstube
MAP K6 ▪ Propststr. 4 ▪
(030) 242 39 67 ▪ 10am–6:30pm
Mon–Sat, 11am–6pm Sun
Adorable dolls made from
porcelain and other materials
await, as do mountains of cute
fluffy teddy bears.

3 Teddy's
MAP K6 ▪ Propststr. 4
▪ (030) 247 82 44 ▪ 10am–6pm
daily (from 11am Sat–Sun)
An old-fashioned toy store with
probably the city's best selection
of teddy bears, including brands
like Steiff. They also have bear
clothing and accessories.

4 TeeGschwendner
MAP K6 ▪ Propststr. 3 ▪ (030)
242 32 55 ▪ 10am–7pm Mon–Sat
A charming specialist tea shop
opposite Nikolaikirche, full of delicious scents. They carry more than
300 varieties of tea.

5 Ausberlin
MAP J6 ▪ Karl-Liebknecht Str.
17 ▪ (030) 41 99 78 96 ▪ 10am–8pm
Mon–Sat
Whimsical stock, with a fashion
focus, all created in Berlin. Exclusive
designer items include Breath of
Berlin perfume, bags and T-shirts.

6 U- and S-Bahnhof Alexanderplatz
MAP J6 ▪ Alexanderplatz
This bustling area has a selection
of shops for daily needs, plus late-
opening fast food outlets and
German *imbisse* (food stands).

7 Alexa
MAP K6 ▪ Am Alexanderplatz,
Grunerstr. 20 ▪ (030) 269 34 00
▪ 10am–9pm Mon–Sat
This mall boasts some 180 retail
outlets, such as Build-a-Bear
Workshop, where kids assemble
their own teddy, and LOXX, the
world's largest digitally operated
model train set.

8 Erzgebirgischer Weihnachtsmarkt
MAP K6 ▪ Propststr. 8 ▪ (030)
241 12 29 ▪ 11am–6pm
Mon–Sat
A vast array of stalls laden
with a range of German
handicrafts, including traditional wooden nutcrackers.

Wooden nutcracker

9 Münzstraße
MAP J6
This tiny street, just off
Alexanderplatz, is full of
original fashion boutiques
and designer stores. A real mecca
for fashion aficionados.

10 die mitte
MAP J6 ▪ Alexanderplatz
▪ (030) 263 99 70 ▪ 10am–9pm
Mon–Sat
Visit this large shopping centre for
flagship fashion stores Esprit and
New Yorker, or multimedia at Saturn.

See map on pp102–3

Pubs, Cafés and Beer Gardens

1 Zur letzten Instanz

MAP K6 ▪ Waisenstr. 14–16 ▪ (030) 242 55 28 ▪ noon–1am Mon–Sat

Berlin's oldest pub dates back to 1621, and former guests include Napoleon, Beethoven, the German artist Heinrich Zille, former Soviet leader Mikhael Gorbachev and Angela Merkel.

German pub food at Zur letzten Instanz

2 Zum Nußbaum

A charming historic pub in the Nikolaiviertel quarter serving draught beers and *Berliner Weiße* in summer *(see p73)*.

3 A Tavola Allegretto

MAP K5 ▪ Anna-Louisa-Karsch-Str. 2 ▪ (030) 28 04 23 09 ▪ noon–midnight daily

Sit on the sunny terrace alongside the Spree River, opposite Berliner Dom, and enjoy a lunch or late afternoon coffee with pastry.

4 Brauhaus Georgbräu

MAP K5/6 ▪ Spreeufer 4 ▪ (030) 242 42 44 ▪ summer: 10am–midnight daily; winter: from noon daily

Attracting Bavarians and tourists alike, this beer garden offers a variety of rustic fare and beer from both Berlin and Munich.

Interior, Brauhaus Georgbräu

5 Chefetage

MAP L6 ▪ Inselstr. ▪ (030) 24 72 36 55 ▪ 9am–6pm Mon–Fri, 9am–4pm Sat

This tiny place serves excellent coffee, sandwiches, soups and salads, all cooked fresh from regional ingredients. A varied menu and friendly, speedy service is on offer.

6 Café Oliv

MAP J6 ▪ Münzstr. 8 ▪ (030) 89 20 65 40 ▪ 8:30am–7pm Mon–Fri, 9:30am–7pm Sat, 10am–6pm Sun

Trendy Berliners get their organic sandwiches, flat whites and home-baked cakes from this sleek venue.

7 Café Ephraim's

MAP K6 ▪ Spreeufer 1 ▪ (030) 24 72 59 47 ▪ noon–10pm daily ▪ no credit cards

Hearty German food and excellent coffee and cakes added to the great views of the Spree River attract both locals and tourists.

8 tigertörtchen

MAP K6 ▪ Spandauer Str. 25 ▪ (030) 67 96 90 51 ▪ 11am–6pm Thu–Tue

Come here for inventive cupcake creations such as date and walnut or crab and dill.

9 Marinehaus

MAP L6 ▪ Märkisches Ufer 48-50 ▪ (030) 279 32 46 ▪ noon–late daily ▪ €

Traditional pub with maritime decor, serving German food.

10 Der Alte Fritz

MAP J6 ▪ Karl-Liebknecht-Str. 29 ▪ (030) 96 20 06 00 ▪ noon–midnight Mon–Sat, noon–10pm Sun ▪ €€

German dishes such as pork knuckles and roasted duck with green cabbage are served here.

Restaurants

PRICE CATEGORIES
For a three-course meal for one with half a bottle of wine (or equivalent meal), taxes and charges included.

€ under €30   €€ €30–60   €€€ over €60

1 Reinhard's
MAP K6 ▪ Poststr. 28 ▪ (030) 242 52 95 ▪ 9am–midnight daily ▪ €€

One of Mitte's most charming restaurants. Savour the international food, surrounded by photos and paintings of famous contemporaries.

2 HEat
MAP K5 ▪ Karl-Liebknecht-Str. 3 ▪ (030) 238 283 472 ▪ 6am–11pm daily ▪ €€

This ultra-chic fusion restaurant at the SAS Radisson Blu *(see p172)* serves an imaginative blend of Oriental and European tastes.

3 Zur Gerichtslaube
MAP K6 ▪ Poststr. 28 ▪ (030) 241 56 98 ▪ 11:30am–1am daily ▪ €

The former court building is a stylish setting for traditional Berlin specialities such as Prussian sausages.

4 Le Provençal
MAP K6 ▪ Spreeufer 3 ▪ (030) 302 75 67 ▪ noon–midnight ▪ €€

Baked oysters, scallop soup and other seafood delicacies are served in this family-run French restaurant. Try the lavender ice cream.

5 Zum Paddenwirt
MAP K6 ▪ Nikolaikirchplatz 6 ▪ (030) 242 63 82 ▪ noon–midnight daily ▪ no credit cards ▪ €

A mecca for fans of traditional Berlin food, including fried herrings and brawn, and a strong beer.

6 Zillestube
MAP K6 ▪ Propststr. 9 ▪ (030) 242 52 47 ▪ from 11am daily ▪ €

Named after the 19th-century Berlin illustrator and photographer

The simple interior of Zillestube

Heinrich Zille, this tiny pub serves hearty Berlin food and traditional beers in a rustic setting.

7 Marcellino
MAP K6 ▪ Poststr. 28 ▪ (030) 242 73 71 ▪ noon–midnight daily ▪ €

An agreeable Italian restaurant, with a pleasant terrace and a large inviting garden offering shade on a hot summer's day.

8 La Riva
MAP K6 ▪ Spreeufer 2 ▪ (030) 242 51 83 ▪ 11am–11pm daily ▪ €

A more upmarket Italian venue in Nikolaiviertel, offering delicious pasta dishes, which can be enjoyed outside in summer, with a view of the Spree River.

9 Sphere
MAP J6 ▪ Panoramastr. 1a ▪ (030) 247 575 875 ▪ 9am–midnight daily ▪ €€

The menu may be limited, but the fabulous views from this rotating restaurant at the top of the TV tower cannot be beaten.

10 Mutter Hoppe
MAP K6 ▪ Rathausstr. 21 ▪ (030) 241 56 25 ▪ 11:30am–midnight daily ▪ €

Gigantic portions of delicious traditional German food make up for the sometimes brusque service.

See map on pp102–3 ➙

The Tiergarten and Federal District

In 1999, Berlin's green centre became the government district. Around the Tiergarten, Berlin's largest and most popular park, stand the Reichstag, the Bundeskanzleramt and Schloss Bellevue, official residence of the President of the Federal Republic of Germany. The sprawling Tiergarten itself is a great place for strolling and cycling, and it also boasts the Landwehrkanal, the Neuer See, the Spree River and Berlin's zoo. In summer, its lawns are used for soccer games and barbecue parties.

Sowjetisches Ehrenmal

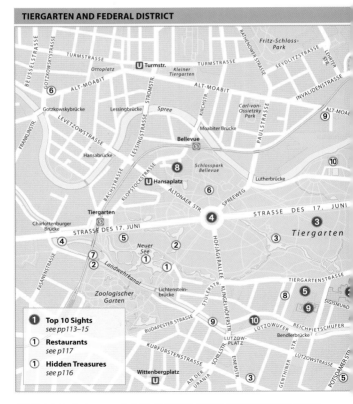

TIERGARTEN AND FEDERAL DISTRICT

1. **Top 10 Sights**
   see pp113–15
1. **Restaurants**
   see p117
1. **Hidden Treasures**
   see p116

Previous pages Early summer in the lovely wooded environs of Berlin's Großer Tiergarten

The majestic Reichstag with its beautiful modern dome

1 Reichstag

More than any of the other landmarks in Berlin, the Reichstag – the seat of the German parliament – has come to symbolize German history *(see pp14–15)*.

2 Kulturforum

This unique complex of modern buildings features the best museums and concert halls in western Berlin *(see pp38–41)*.

3 Großer Tiergarten
MAP M5/6 ◼ Tiergarten

The Großer Tiergarten is Berlin's largest park, straddling an area of 200 hectares (494 acres) between the eastern and western parts of the town. Formerly the Elector's hunting grounds, it was redesigned in the 1830s as a park by Peter Joseph Lenné. At the end of the 19th century, the Siegesallee was established in the east of the park, more than 500 m (1,640 ft) in length, lined by statues of monarchs and politicians. After World War II, the starving and freezing population chopped down nearly all the trees for firewood and dug up the lawns to grow food. Thanks to reforestation since the 1950s, the Tiergarten is today Berlin's favourite green space and the lungs of the city *(see p60)*.

4 Siegessäule
MAP M6 ◼ Großer Stern ◼ Admission charge

In the middle of the Tiergarten stands the 62-m (203-ft) high Victory Column, erected to commemorate Prussian victory against Denmark in the war of 1864. After victory over Austria in 1866 and France 1871, the structure was crowned by a 35-ton gilded statue of the goddess Victoria. There are great views from the viewing platform, 285 steps up *(see p55)*.

PETER JOSEPH LENNÉ

Lenné (1789–1866), one of Germany's most influential landscape architects, was born into a family of gardeners in Bonn. He studied in Paris and joined the Royal Gardens in Potsdam as an apprentice in 1816. There he met Schinkel and together they set out to design the parks of Berlin and Potsdam in the harmonious style of the time.

⑤ Diplomatenviertel
MAP E4 ■ Between Stauffen-bergstr. and Lichtensteinallee as well as along Tiergartenstr.

In the late 19th century, an embassy district sprang up. Most structures were destroyed during World War II, and until German reunification the buildings were left to decay. After the government moved back to Berlin from Bonn in 1999, new life was breathed into the diplomats' quarter and, thanks to its adventurous architecture, it is now one of Berlin's most interesting areas. Especially worth seeing are the Austrian and Indian embassies on Tiergartenstraße, the Nordic embassies (see p57) on Rauchstraße and the Mexican embassy on Klingelhöferstraße.

⑥ Hamburger Bahnhof
This former railway station, now the Museum für Gegenwart (Museum of the Present Day), holds contemporary works of art. Former dispatch warehouses were converted and linked to the old railway building, forming the Rieckhallen, and doubling the exhibition space. One of the highlights is the private collection of Erich Marx, with works by Beuys and others (see p53).

Sowjetisches Ehrenmal

⑦ Sowjetisches Ehrenmal
MAP K2 ■ Str. des 17. Juni

The Soviet Memorial was opened on 7 November 1945, the anniversary of the Russian October Revolution. It is flanked by two tanks, supposedly the first to reach Berlin. The memorial commemorates the 300,000 Red Army soldiers who died during World War II in the fight to liberate Berlin. A legend persists that the large column was made from the marble blocks of Hitler's Reich Chancellery. Designed by Nicolai Sergijevski, the column is crowned by a bronze statue by Lev Kerbel. Behind the memorial, 2,500 Russian soldiers are buried.

⑧ Hansa-Viertel
MAP D3 ■ Tiergarten, Hanseatenweg

The Hansa estate west of Schloss Bellevue was built for the Interbau architecture exhibition in 1957. World War II bombs had flattened the Tiergarten, and 36 residential complexes were erected in the park, designed by distinguished architects from around the world, including Walter Gropius (Händelallee 3–9), Alvar Aalto (Klopstockstr. 30–32) and Oscar Niemeyer (Altonaer Str. 4–14).

Hamburger Bahnhof

⑨ Gedenkstätte Deutscher Widerstand

MAP E4 ■ Stauffenbergstr. 13–14 ■ (030) 26 99 50 00 ■ 9am–6pm Mon–Wed & Fri, 9am–8pm Thu, 10am–6pm Sat–Sun ■ www.gdw-berlin.de/en/

Today known as Bendlerblock, this 1930s complex lies behind the former Prussian Ministry of War. During World War II it served as army headquarters. It was here that a group of officers planned the assassination of Adolf Hitler. When the attempt failed on 20 July 1944, Claus Schenk Count von Stauffenberg and the others involved were arrested here, and many of them were shot in the courtyard during the night. A memorial, created by Richard Scheibe in 1953, commemorates these events. On the upper floor is a small exhibition documenting the German resistance against the Nazi regime. Today, the Bendlerblock has been incorporated into the Berlin branch of the Federal Ministry of Defence.

Gedenkstätte Deutscher Widerstand

⑩ Villa von der Heydt

MAP E4 ■ Von-der-Heydt-Str. 18 ■ www.preussischer-kulturbesitz.de/en

This late Neo-Classical villa, built in 1860–61 by architects Hermann Ende and G A Linke for one of the city's most elegant residential areas at the time, is one of the few extant examples of the architectural villa style typical of the Tiergarten. The Prussian Heritage Foundation now has its headquarters here.

A DAY OUT

▶ MORNING

Start your tour of the Tiergarten near the **Reichstag** *(see pp14–15)*. Explore the government district starting with the Federal Chancellor's Office or the Bundeskanzleramt. Stop at **Restaurant Käfer** *(see p117)* in the Reichstag building for breakfast. Via John-Foster-Dulles-Allee you will pass the **Carillon** *(see p116)* and the Haus der Kulturen der Welt on the way to **Großer Tiergarten** *(see p113)*. Continue along one of the paths into the park, directly opposite the old Kongresshalle, until you reach Straße des 17. Juni. Turn right to go towards **Siegessäule** *(see p113)*. From there continue along Fasanerieallee in a southwesterly direction until you reach **Café am Neuen See** *(see p117)* for lunch.

AFTERNOON

After lunch, take a stroll through the **Diplomatenviertel**. From Neuer See, it is only a few steps east along Lichtensteinallee and Thomas-Dehler-Straße until you get to Rauchstraße with its Scandinavian embassies. On Tiergartenstraße you will pass, among others, the embassies of Japan, Italy, India and Austria. Head back to Klingelhöferstraße and walk south, making a small detour for refreshments at **Café Einstein** *(see p117)*. Head back to the canal and continue along Lützowufer until you reach the **Kulturforum** *(see pp38–41)* via Potsdamer Brücke. A good place for an evening meal would be **Vox** *(see p70)* at the Grand Hyatt.

See map on pp112–13 ←

Hidden Treasures

① Neuer See
MAP M5 ▪ S-Bahn station Tiergarten

Shimmering in a mysterious emerald green, the largest lake in the Tiergarten is perfect for rowing. Afterwards you can recover in the Café am Neuen See.

② Löwenbrücke
MAP M5 ▪ Großer Weg

The Lion Bridge, which leads across a small stream near Neuer See, was built in 1838 and is "suspended" from the sculptures of four lions. This idyllic spot is a favourite meeting point for gays in Berlin.

③ Lortzing-Denkmal
MAP L1 ▪ Östlicher Großer Weg

There are 70 statues of philosophers, poets and statesmen in Tiergarten. The statue of the composer Lortzing, at one end of Neuer See, is one of the most beautiful.

④ Houseboats
MAP M4 ▪ Str. des 17. Juni, Tiergartenufer

Docked on the banks of the Spree River are some of the few remaining houseboats in Berlin – an idyllic haven in the middle of the city's bustle.

⑤ Gaslights in Tiergarten
MAP M5 ▪ At S-Bahn station Tiergarten

With 80 beautiful historic gaslights illuminating the paths, an evening stroll in the Tiergarten can be a romantic affair.

⑥ Englischer Garten
MAP P3 ▪ An der Klopstockstr.

The lovely English-style landscaped garden near Schloss Bellevue is ideal for strolling or relaxing at the Teehaus with coffee and cake.

⑦ Locks
MAP M5 ▪ At the Zoo, S-Bahn station Tiergarten

The two Landwehrkanal locks and the quirky Schleusenkrug beer garden (next to the eponymous lock) are very popular with locals and visitors.

Beer garden on the canal lock

⑧ Estonian Embassy
MAP E4 ▪ Hildebrandstr. 5

In a street next to the ruined Greek Embassy, this building is characteristic of the diplomats' quarter.

⑨ Landwehrkanal
MAP M/N5/6 ▪ Corneliusstr.

The grassy banks of the 11-km (7-mile) long Landwehrkanal are ideal for chilling out.

⑩ Carillon
MAP K1 ▪ John-Foster-Dulles-Allee (Haus der Kulturen der Welt) ▪ Open-air concerts: 3pm Sun May–Sep

The *carillon*, officially dedicated in 1987, is the largest of its kind in Europe. The 68 bells are rung every day at noon and 6pm in the 42-m (138-ft) high black tower.

The *carillon* tower

Restaurants

PRICE CATEGORIES

For a three-course meal for one with half a bottle of wine (or equivalent meal), taxes and charges included.

€ under €30 ■ €€ €30–60 ■ €€€ over €60

1 Café am Neuen See
MAP M5 ■ Tiergarten, Neuer See, Lichtensteinallee 2 ■ (030) 254 49 30 ■ Mar–Oct: 9am–11pm daily; Nov–Feb: 10am–8pm Sat–Sun ■ €

On the shore of the lake, this is a restaurant, café and beer garden. The "Italian breakfast" is delicious.

2 Schleusenkrug
MAP M5 ■ Tiergarten-Schleuse ■ (030) 313 99 09 ■ 10am–1am daily (to 7pm winter) ■ no credit cards ■ €

This small café, right next to a lock, has a rustic beer garden and is very popular with students.

3 Café Einstein
MAP E5 ■ Kurfürstenstr. 58 ■ (030) 26 39 19 18 ■ 8am–1am daily ■ €€

Based in the villa belonging to the film star Henny Porten, this is the ultimate in Viennese style.

4 Käfer im Reichstag
MAP K2 ■ Platz der Republik ■ (030) 22 62 99 35 ■ 9am–midnight ■ €€

An ambitious restaurant, better known for its view than its food.

5 Joseph-Roth-Diele
MAP E5 ■ Potsdamer Str. 75 ■ (030) 26 36 98 84 ■ 10am–midnight Mon–Fri ■ €

Popular restaurant/bar serving home-made traditional German food. Accepts cash payments only.

6 Focaccia, Pasta & Pizza
MAP C3 ■ Alt-Moabit 51 ■ (0176) 26 12 38 23 ■ noon–6pm Mon–Fri ■ no credit cards ■ €

This tiny Italian place is reputed to make the best pizza in town.

Lorenz Adlon Esszimmer

7 Lorenz Adlon Esszimmer
MAP K3 ■ Unter den Linden 77 ■ (030) 22 61 19 60 ■ 7–10:30pm Tue–Sat ■ €€€

Superb European cuisine is on the menu at this restaurant with two Michelin stars in the Hotel Adlon.

8 Brasserie Desbrosses
MAP L2 ■ Potsdamer Platz 3 ■ (030) 337 776 341 ■ 6:30am–11pm daily ■ €€

An appealing, historic French restaurant in the Ritz-Carlton. Its seafood is particularly good.

9 Paris-Moskau
MAP J1 ■ Alt-Moabit 141 ■ (030) 394 20 81 ■ 6pm–midnight daily ■ €€

A classic restaurant serving seasonal dishes with an emphasis on game and seafood.

10 Lutter & Wegner Potsdamer Platz
MAP L2 ■ Bellevuestr. 1 ■ (030) 26 39 03 72 ■ 11am–1am daily ■ €€

This tiny outlet of Lutter & Wegner (see also p71) offers great Berlin and Austrian-French dishes in the historic setting of the Kaisersaal of the 1920s Grand Hotel Esplanade, whose remnants were incorporated into the Sony Center.

See map on pp112–13 ←

TOP 10 Charlottenburg and Spandau

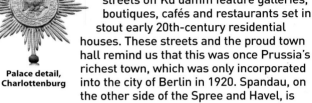

The sophisticated haute bourgeoisie enclave of Charlottenburg was the only Berlin district that did not touch the Wall. The historical streets off Ku'damm feature galleries, boutiques, cafés and restaurants set in stout early 20th-century residential houses. These streets and the proud town hall remind us that this was once Prussia's richest town, which was only incorporated into the city of Berlin in 1920. Spandau, on the other side of the Spree and Havel, is almost rural in comparison, with a Late Medieval core and citadel that make it seem like a small independent town.

Palace detail, Charlottenburg

1 Kurfürstendamm

This famous Berlin boulevard was frequented by writers, directors and painters in the interwar years. Today it is a lively avenue lined with designer stores and elegant cafés (see pp30–31).

2 Schloss Charlottenburg

The Baroque and English-style gardens of this Hohenzollern summer residence are ideal for a stroll. The palace's restored interiors are stunning (see pp34–7).

SPANDAU AND BERLIN

Berliners consider the Spandauers to be rather different sorts of people, provincial and rough, and not as "real" Berliners at all. But the Spandauers can reassure themselves that Spandau is 60 years older than Berlin, and proudly point to their independent history. The mutual mistrust is not just a result of Spandau's geographical location, isolated from the remainder of the city by the Havel and Spree Rivers. It is also due to the fact that Spandau was only incorporated into Berlin in 1920. Spandauers today still say they are going "to Berlin", even though the city centre is only a few U-bahn stops away.

CHARLOTTENBURG AND SPANDAU

0 metres 500
0 yards 500

3 Zitadelle Spandau
Am Juliusturm ▪ 10am–5pm daily ▪ (030) 354 94 40 ▪ Admission charge

Berlin's only surviving fortress, this citadel at the confluence of the Havel and Spree is strategically well sited. The structure, built in 1560 by Francesco Chiaramella da Gandino, was based on Italian forts. It has four bastions – Brandenburg, Kronprinz (crown prince), Königin (queen) and König (king). The Juliusturm, a remnant of a fortress that stood here as early as the 12th century, is a keep that was used as a prison in the 19th century. At the time, Berliners used to say "off to the Julio" when they sent criminals to prison. Later, the reparations paid by France after its defeat in the Franco-Prussian War of 1870–71 were kept here.

The imposing Zitadelle Spandau

4 Zoologischer Garten
Founded in 1844, this is the country's oldest and most prominent zoological garden, combined with an aquarium *(see pp42–3)*.

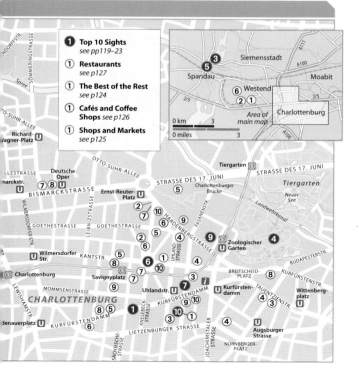

Exterior of the 15th-century Gotisches Haus in Spandau's Altstadt

5 Spandau Old Town
Breite Str., Spandau

When walking around Spandau's pedestrianized Old Town (Altstadt), it is easy to forget that you are still in Berlin. The narrow alleyways and nooks and crannies around the 13th-century Nikolaikirche are lined by Late Medieval houses, a reminder that Spandau was founded in 1197 and is older than Berlin itself. The Gotisches Haus – the oldest house in Berlin, dating back to the late 15th century – stands at Breite Straße 32. It was built of stone at a time when most houses were made of wood. It is now the Visitor Information Centre, and some of its rooms are used to showcase finds from the house and other artefacts of the period.

6 Savignyplatz
MAP N3 ■ **An der Kantstr.**

One of Berlin's most attractive squares is right in the heart of Charlottenburg. Savignyplatz, named after a 19th-century German legal scholar, is the focal point of the neighbourhood's reputation as a district for artists and intellectuals and as a trendy area for dining out and entertainment. The square has two green spaces, either side of Kantstraße. It was built in the 1920s as part of an effort to create parks in the centre of town. Small paths, benches and pergolas make it a pleasant place for a rest. Dotted all around Savignyplatz are street cafés, restaurants and shops, especially in Grolman-, Knesebeck-, and Carmerstraße, all three of which cross the square. Many a reveller has lost his way here after a night out celebrating, which is why the area is jokingly known as the "Savignydreieck" (the Savigny Triangle). North of Savignyplatz it is worth exploring some of the most attractive streets in Charlottenburg, including Knesebeck-, Schlüter- and Goethestraße. This is still a thriving Charlottenburg community; the small shops, numerous bookstores, cafés and specialist retailers are always busy, especially on Saturdays. South of the square, the red-tiled S-Bahn arches also lure visitors with their shops, cafés and bars, particularly the Savignypassage near Bleibtreustraße and the small passageway between Grolman- and Uhlandstraße on the opposite side of the square.

7 Fasanenstraße
MAP N/P4 ■ **Charlottenburg**

This elegant street is the most attractive and trendiest street off Ku'damm. Designer shops, galleries and restaurants are tucked away here, a shoppers' paradise for all those who regard Kurfürstendamm as a mere retail strip catering for the masses. The junction of Ku'damm and Fasanenstraße is one of the liveliest spots in Berlin. One of the best known places is the Kempinski Hotel Bristol Berlin at the northern end of Fasanenstraße. The former bank opposite cleverly combines a historic building with a modern structure. Next to it is the Jüdisches Gemeindehaus, the Jewish community house *(see p124)* and a little farther along, at the junction with Kantstraße, is the Kant-Dreieck *(see p57)*. The Berliner Börse (the stock exchange), based in the ultra-modern Ludwig-Erhard-Haus *(see p57)*, is just above, at the corner of Hardenbergstraße. The southern end of the street is dominated by residential villas, some of which may seem a little pompous, as well as the Literaturhaus, Villa Grisebach, one of the oldest art auction houses in Berlin, and the Käthe-Kollwitz-Museum *(see p123)*, which holds about 200 of the Berlin artist's works, including several self-portraits. There are also some very expensive fashion stores here, as well as a few cosy restaurants. At its southern end, the street leads to picturesque Fasanenplatz, where many artists lived before 1933.

Antiques store on Fasanenstraße

See map on pp118–19

A DAY IN CHARLOTTENBURG

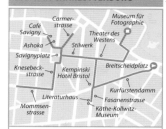

▶ MORNING

Begin your tour of Charlottenburg at Breitscheidplatz and head west along **Kurfürstendamm** *(see pp30–31)*. At **Fasanenstraße** turn left to visit the **Käthe-Kollwitz-Museum** *(see p123)* and the **Literaturhaus**. You could stop for a mid-morning breakfast at the lovely **Café Wintergarten** *(see p126)* in the Literaturhaus, before going back up Fasanenstraße in a northerly direction. You will pass the **Kempinski Hotel Bristol Berlin** on the left, and on the right you can see the **Jüdisches Gemeindehaus** and the **Ludwig-Erhard-Haus**. Diagonally opposite across Kantstraße stands the **Theater des Westens** *(see p67)*. Turn left and head west along Kantstraße until you reach the shopping centre **Stilwerk** *(see pp77)*, a place no one has ever been known to leave without buying something.

AFTERNOON

Carry on west along Kantstraße to **Savignyplatz**. Northwest of the square, at Grolmanstraße 51, the tiny Indian eatery **Ashoka** is a great place for lunch. Explore the small streets around the square, such as Carmer-, Knesebeck- and Mommsenstraße. Browse the small retailers for unique gifts, and visit **Café Savigny** *(see p126)* for coffee and a fruit flan with whipped cream. Head back up Kantstraße and Jebensstraße to end your tour with a visit to the **Museum für Fotografie** *(pp123)* where you can marvel at Helmut Newton's iconic *Big Nudes*.

The Funkturm rising above the old ICC building at the Messegelände

⑧ Funkturm and Messegelände

MAP A4/5 ▪ Messedamm 22 ▪ (030) 303 80 ▪ 10am–8pm Mon, 10am–11pm Tue–Sun (tower) ▪ Admission charge ▪ www.messe-berlin.de/en/

The 150-m (492-ft) high Funkturm (TV tower), reminiscent of the Eiffel Tower in Paris, is one of the landmarks of Berlin that can be seen from afar. Built in 1924 to plans by Heinrich Straumer, it served as an aerial and as an air-traffic control tower. The viewing platform at 125 m (410 ft) provides magnificent views, while the restaurant, situated at 55 m (180 ft), overlooks the oldest part of the complex, the exhibition centre and the surrounding pavillions. The giant building in the east is the Hall of Honour built to designs by Richard Ermisch in 1936, in the colossal Fascist architectural style. On the opposite side rises the shiny silver ICC, the International Congress Centrum, built in 1975–9 by Ralf Schüler and Ursulina Schüler-Witte. Once considered one of the world's most advanced conference centres, it has fallen into a state of disrepair and may be demolished. Nearby is the two-tier CityCube, Berlin's new trade fair and conference facility. The expansive ExpoCenter grounds (160,000 sq m/40 acres) around it host Grüne Woche (Green Week, an agricultural fair), Internationale Tourismus Börse (ITB, a tourism fair) and Internationale Funkausstellung (IFA, the consumer electronics fair).

THE HISTORY OF CHARLOTTENBURG

The magnificent Charlottenburger Rathaus or town hall (left) on Otto-Suhr-Allee is a reminder of the time when this district of 200,000 people was an independent town. The town, named after the eponymous palace, arose in 1705 from the medieval settlement of Lietzow. Towards the end of the 19th century, Charlottenburg – then the wealthiest town in Prussia – enjoyed a meteoric rise following the construction of the Westend colony of villas and of Kurfürstendamm. Thanks to its numerous theatres, the opera and the Technical University, the district developed into Berlin's west end during the 1920s.

(9) Museum für Fotografie

MAP N4 ■ Jebensstr. 2 ■ 10am–6pm Tue–Sun (to 8pm Thu) ■ Admission charge ■ www.smb.museum

Helmut Newton (1931–2004), the world-famous photographer, has finally returned to his home city. This museum presents changing exhibitions of his early fashion and nude photography, as well as his photos of the famous, rich and beautiful, artfully captured since 1947.

Museum für Fotografie

(10) Käthe-Kollwitz-Museum

MAP P4 ■ Fasanenstr. 24 ■ (030) 882 52 10 ■ 11am–6pm daily ■ Admission charge ■ www.kaethe-kollwitz.de

The museum is dedicated to Berlin artist Käthe Kollwitz (1897–1945), who recorded 1920s workers' lives in prints, graphics and sketches. After losing a son and a grandson in World War I, she concentrated on the themes of war and motherhood.

A SPANDAU AND WESTEND WALK

▶ MORNING

Start with a journey on the U-Bahn. From the centre of town, take a U2 train in the direction of Ruhleben, and at Bismarckstraße station change to the U7 train in the direction of Rathaus Spandau. Ten minutes later you will have reached the centre of **Spandau Old Town** (see p120), where you can visit Breite Straße and Nikolaikirche. Before returning to Charlottenburg, visit the **Zitadelle Spandau** (see p119). There, in the **Zitadellenschänke**, you can also enjoy a late breakfast. Return by U-Bahn, getting off at the Wilmersdorfer Straße station, one of the few pedestrianized areas in Berlin. This is a particularly good area for shopaholics and bargain hunters.

AFTERNOON

From Wilmersdorfer Straße a 30-minute walk west along Kantstraße and Neue Kantstraße will take you to the **Funkturm** and the **Messegelände** with the "Ehrenhalle". Have lunch at the **Funkturm-Restaurant** and enjoy the magnificent views. The Haus des Rundfunks (broadcasting house) nearby and the **Georg-Kolbe-Museum** (see p124), a 25-minute walk (or brief S-Bahn ride) away, are worth visiting. Then, if you still have time and energy, take the S-Bahn to the **Olympiastadion**. In the evening, return to Savignyplatz by S75 from S-Olympiastadion. End your day by enjoying inventive, hearty Franconian cooking at the famed **Florian** (see p127).

See map on pp118–19

The Best of the Rest

The Fascist-style architecture of the Olympiastadion

1 Georg-Kolbe-Museum
Sensburger Allee 25 ▪ (030) 304 21 44 ▪ 10am–6pm Tue–Sun ▪ Admission charge

Sculptures by Kolbe (1877–1947) are exhibited in his home and workshop.

2 Le-Corbusier-Haus
Flatowallee 16

This innovative block was built for the 1957 Interbau trade fair. French architect Le Corbusier lived here.

3 Jüdisches Gemeindehaus
MAP P4 ▪ Fasanenstr. 79–80 ▪ (030) 88 02 82 06 ▪ 9am–5pm Mon–Thu, 9am–3pm Fri

The Jewish community house stands on the site of the Charlottenburg synagogue. It was damaged during Reichskristallnacht on 9 November 1938 and mostly destroyed during World War II. Only the portal remains.

4 Theater des Westens
MAP N4 ▪ Kantstr. 12 ▪ (0180) 544 44

Based in an attractive building from 1895–6, this theatre is regarded as one of Germany's best musical theatres *(see p67)*.

5 Technische Universität
MAP M4 ▪ Str. des 17. Juni ▪ (030) 31 40 ▪ 8am–8pm Mon–Fri

Berlin's Technical University was founded in 1879.

6 Olympiastadion
Olympischer Platz ▪ (030) 25 00 23 22 ▪ mid-Mar–Oct: 9am–7pm daily (to 8pm Jun–mid-Sep); Nov–mid-Mar: 10am–4pm daily)

Built for the 1936 Olympic Games, the stadium is an example of Fascist architecture favoured by the Nazis.

7 Deutsche Oper
MAP B4 ▪ Bismarckstr. 34–37 ▪ (030) 34 38 43 43 ▪ Admission charge

The German Opera, opened in 1961, specializes in Italian and German classics *(see p66)*.

8 Denkmal Benno Ohnesorg
MAP B4 ▪ Bismarckstr.

Alfred Hrdlicka's 1971 sculpture commemorates the student Benno Ohnesorg, who was shot dead here during a demonstration in April 1967.

9 Universität der Künste
MAP N4 ▪ Hardenbergstr. 32–33 ▪ (030) 318 50 ▪ 8am–6pm Mon–Fri

The School of Art is one of the best German universities for the fine arts, architecture and design.

10 Renaissance Theater
MAP M3 ▪ Knesebeckstr. 100 ▪ (030) 312 42 02

A jem of Art Deco architecture, this little venue has been run as an actors' theatre since the 1920s.

Shops and Markets

① Stilwerk
MAP N3 ▪ Kantstr. 17
▪ (030) 31 51 50

A shopping centre specializing in stylish designer home furnishings (see p77).

Stilwerk in Charlottenburg

② Manufactum Store
MAP M3 ▪ Hardenbergstr. 4–5,
Hardenberghaus

Unique store with a lovely selection of classic and sustainable textiles, retro design furniture, garden tools, lamps and office supplies.

③ Peek & Cloppenburg
MAP P5 ▪ Tauentzienstr. 19 ▪
(030) 21 29 00 ▪ 10am–8pm Mon–Sat

Offering five floors of men's, women's and children's clothing, this is one of Berlin's most popular department stores.

④ Hallhuber
MAP P5 ▪ Tauentzienstr. 18a
▪ (030) 21 91 32 49

This huge upscale clothing store offers the latest designer labels for both men and women (DKNY, Paul Smith and the like) as well as its own less expensive house label.

⑤ Butter Lindner
MAP N3 ▪ Knesebeckstr. 92
▪ (030) 313 53 75 ▪ 8am–6pm Mon–Fri, 8am–1:30pm Sat

This traditional Berlin store specializes in fresh, home-made foods and delicatessen products. Of its many branches, one of the most attractive ones is in Charlottenburg.

⑥ Jil Sander
MAP P2 ▪ Kurfürstendamm
185 ▪ (030) 886 70 20

Simple, elegant designer fashions for men and women are for sale at this cool boutique.

⑦ Bücherbogen
MAP N3 ▪ Savignyplatz ▪ (030) 31 86 95 11

Berlin's leading arts and photography bookseller is tucked away within three arches under the S-Bahn viaduct.

⑧ Hellmann Mens Wear
MAP P2 ▪ Kurfürstendamm 53 ▪ (030) 882 25 65 ▪ 10am–7pm Mon–Fri, 10am–6pm Sat

Gentlemen's fashions made from the best materials, including Hellmann's own collection and clothes from well-known designers.

⑨ Tee Gschwendner
MAP P4 ▪ Kurfürstendamm 217 ▪ (030) 881 91 81 ▪ 10am–7pm Mon–Fri, 10am–4pm Sat

This tiny store is a haven for tea lovers, and upstairs you can try out a new flavour in their own tea room.

⑩ TITUS Berlin Zoopreme
MAP P4 ▪ Meinekestr. 2 ▪ (030) 32 59 32 39 ▪ 10am–8pm Mon–Sat

The latest must-have labels are stocked at this streetwear store.

Butter Lindner store and deli

See map on pp118–19

Cafés and Coffee Shops

1 Café Wintergarten im Literaturhaus

MAP P4 ▪ Fasanenstr. 23 ▪ (030) 882 54 14 ▪ 9am–midnight daily

One of Berlin's most beautiful cafés is based in the conservatory of an old city mansion. In summer guests can sit outside in the garden.

2 Café Savigny

MAP N3 ▪ Grolmanstr. 53–54 ▪ (030) 32 89 06 61 ▪ 9am–midnight daily

This gay and lesbian café, with traditional 19th-century interior, has a relaxed atmosphere; the tarts are particularly worth trying.

Berliner Kaffeerösterei

3 Berliner Kaffeerösterei

MAP P4 ▪ Uhlandstraße 173 ▪ (030) 88 67 79 20 ▪ 9am–8pm Mon–Sat, 10am–7pm Sun

A cosy mix of traditional café and coffee bar, this place offers coffee beans from around the world, cakes and breakfast snacks.

4 Café Filmbühne am Steinplatz

MAP N4 ▪ Hardenbergstr. 12 ▪ (030) 312 65 89 ▪ 9am–midnight daily

This coffee shop is popular thanks to its student atmosphere.

5 Einstein Coffeeshop

MAP P3 ▪ Kurfürstendamm 50a (off Ku'damm) ▪ (030) 93 93 13 65 ▪ 7:30am–8pm daily (from 8am Sat, 9am Sun)

Probably the most popular outlet of this upmarket chain, this revamped café heaves with the rich and beautiful of Charlottenburg.

6 Café Hardenberg

MAP N3 ▪ Hardenbergstr. 10 ▪ (030) 312 26 44 ▪ 9am–1am daily ▪ no credit cards

A favourite of students and artists since the 1850s, this café has a great atmosphere and reasonable prices.

7 Balzac Coffee

MAP M3 ▪ Knesebeckstraße 1–2 ▪ 7am–8pm Mon–Fri, 8am–8pm Sat, 8am–7pm Sun ▪ no credit cards

A German gourmet coffee chain offering speciality drinks and snacks.

8 Der Kuchenladen

MAP N3 ▪ Kantstr. 138 ▪ (030) 31 01 84 24 ▪ 10am–6:30pm daily ▪ no credit cards

Enjoy lemon tart, crème brûlée cake and other delicious home-made delights at this tiny café.

9 Café Kleine Orangerie

MAP A3 ▪ Spandauer Damm 20 ▪ (030) 322 20 21 ▪ 10am–6pm Tue–Sun

A small, pleasant garden café at the Charlottenburg Palace.

10 Schwarzes Café

MAP N3 ▪ Kantstr. 148 ▪ (030) 313 80 38 ▪ open around the clock

This alternative rock café offers excellent all-day breakfasts and is often packed until dawn.

The bohemian Schwarzes Café

Restaurants

PRICE CATEGORIES
For a three-course meal for one with half
a bottle of wine (or equivalent meal),
taxes and charges included.

€ under €30   €€ €30–60   €€€ over €60

1 Francucci's
MAP B5 ▪ Kurfürstendamm 90
▪ (030) 323 33 18 ▪ noon–midnight
daily ▪ €€

This popular Tuscan restaurant
serves up excellent pizza,
home-made pasta and creative
meat and fish dishes.

2 Alt-Luxemburg
MAP B4 ▪ Windscheidstr. 31
▪ (030) 323 87 30 ▪ 5pm–midnight
Mon–Sat ▪ €€

Since 1982, chef Karl Wannemacher
has been dishing up exquisite French
and German classics here.

3 Eiffel
MAP B5 ▪ Kurfürstendamm
105 ▪ (030) 891 13 05 ▪ 9am–1am
daily ▪ €

A large but still charming French
restaurant with some traditional
Berlin and Mediterranean dishes
and outside tables.

4 Quadriga
MAP P4 ▪ Eislebener Str. 14
▪ (030) 21 40 50 ▪ 7–10:30pm Tue–
Sat ▪ €€€

With talented chef André Haufler at
the reins, this intimate restaurant
pairs creative French cuisine with
an excellent wine selection. The
elegant Art Deco salons overlook
a Japanese garden.

5 Kuchi
MAP N3 ▪ Kantstr. 30 ▪ (030)
31 50 78 16 ▪ noon–11pm daily ▪ no
credit cards ▪ €

Thanks mainly to its exquisite sushi
and mixed Asian hot dishes, this
minimalist restaurant has a loyal
clientele and ranks among the best
sushi bars in town.

Outside tables at Florian

6 Florian
MAP N3 ▪ Grolmanstr. 52
▪ (030) 313 91 84 ▪ 6pm–3am
daily ▪ €

Fine Franconian food – inventive,
robust and steadily high-quality –
is on offer at this famed restaurant.
Trendy and popular with film lovers,
particularly during the Berlinale.

7 Lubitsch
MAP N/P3 ▪ Bleibtreustr. 47
▪ (030) 882 37 56 ▪ 10am–midnight
Mon–Sat, 6pm–midnight Sun ▪ €

A small, elegant restaurant, serving
fresh, regional cuisine.

8 first floor
MAP N5 ▪ Budapester Str. 45
▪ (030) 25 02 10 20 ▪ noon–3pm,
6:30–11pm Tue–Sat ▪ €€

Award-winning gourmet restaurant
in the Hotel Palace (see p172) serving
German and French food.

9 Marjellchen
MAP P3 ▪ Mommsenstr. 9
▪ (030) 883 26 76 ▪ 5pm–midnight
daily ▪ €

This delightful restaurant serves
hearty dishes from East Prussia,
Pomerania and Silesia.

10 Ana e Bruno
MAP A3 ▪ Sophie-Charlotten-
Str. 101 ▪ (030) 325 71 10 ▪ 5pm–
midnight daily ▪ €€

Friendly and extremely elegant, Ana
e Bruno is probably the best Italian
restaurant in Berlin.

See map on pp118–19

🔟 Kreuzberg, Schöneberg and Neukölln

Checkpoint Charlie

Before the Wall fell, Kreuzberg was a hotbed of squatters, hippies and anarchists. Despite rapid gentrification it is still the city's most colourful area. Here, a diverse community of doctors, lawyers, artists, students and Turkish families harmoniously coexists in beautifully renovated petit-bourgeois flats. The adjacent Neukölln is Berlin's most trendy area for art galleries, grunge-hip bars and clubs, particularly along Weserstraße Schöneberg is not as daring as Kreuzberg, but still evokes a free-minded spirit. Here, Winterfeldtplatz is lined with inviting pubs, and Nollendorfplatz is the nexus of Berlin's lively gay scene.

KREUZBERG, SCHÖNEBERG AND NEUKÖLLN

- **1** Top 10 Sights
  see pp129–31
- **1** Restaurants
  see p135
- **1** The Best of the Rest
  see p132
- **1** Pubs, Bars and
  Nightclubs *see p134*
- **1** Shops and Markets
  see p133

① Deutsches Technikmuseum

MAP F5 ■ Trebbiner Str. 9
■ (030) 90 25 40 ■ 9am–
5:30pm Tue–Fri, 10am–6pm
Sat–Sun ■ Admission charge
(kids free after 3pm) ■ www.
sdtb.de

The history of technology
and crafts is the theme of
this museum, located in the
grounds of a former railway
goods yard. Visitors can
learn about developments
in aviation and admire 40
planes, including a Junkers
Ju 52 and a "raisin
bomber", the type of plane used for
the Berlin airlift. Old ships and
steam locomotives hark back to the
Industrial Revolution (see p64).

Exhibits at the Deutsches Technikmuseum

② Jüdisches Museum

MAP G5 ■ Lindenstr. 9–14
■ 10am–10pm Mon, 10am–8pm
Tue–Sun ■ Admission charge ■ www.
jmberlin.de

The Jewish Museum is architecturally unique, with the building
forming part of a philosophical
programme to illustrate the
repercussions of the Holocaust. Its
narrow galleries with slanting floors
and zig-zag turns evoke a sense of
dislocation, and are inter-
spersed by voids embodying
the vacuum left behind by
the destruction of Jewish
life. It documents nearly
1,000 years of
German-Jewish
cultural history; a
special exhibition
evokes everyday
Jewish life in
Berlin from the
end of the 19th
century (see p50).

Jüdisches Museum

③ Haus am Checkpoint Charlie

MAP G4 ■ Friedrichstr. 43–45
■ (030) 253 72 50 ■ 9am–10pm daily
■ Admission charge ■ www.
mauermuseum.de

This museum details the history of
the Wall and the means people used
to escape to West Berlin, from a hot-
air balloon to a car with a false floor.
Of the former border only a replica
control hut remains (see p51).

4 Topographie des Terrors
MAP F4 ▪ Niederkirchnerstr. 8
▪ **10am–6pm daily (to 8pm May–Sep)**
▪ **www.topographie.de/en**

Between 1933 and 1945, three Nazi institutions of persecution and terror were located in this area: the Secret State Police Office; the SS leadership; and, during World War II, the Reich Security main office. After World War II, all the buildings were bulldozed. A striking documentation centre, designed by Berlin architect Ursula Wilms, was inaugurated in 2010 on this site, providing information about the headquarters of the National Socialist SS and police state during the Third Reich and showing the extent of the Nazi reign of terror throughout Europe.

5 Anhalter Bahnhof
MAP F5 ▪ Askanischer Platz 6–7

Only pitiful fragments remain of the railway station that was once the largest in Europe. The giant structure was erected in 1880 by architect Franz Schwechten as a showcase station: official visitors to the Empire were meant to be impressed by the splendour and glory of the German capital as soon as they reached the railway station. In 1943 the station

The ruins of the Anhalter Bahnhof

TURKISH BERLIN

In the 1960s, thousands of Turkish *Gastarbeiter* ("guest workers") came to Berlin in response to a labour shortage. Today the community numbers around 176,000 and it is mainly their children who leave their mark on life in the city. There are few *Gastarbeiter* left; many Turkish Berliners own their own shops **(below)** and see themselves as true Berliners. The rate of naturalization is still low, and many German Berliners have no contact with everyday life in the Turkish community. At 40 per cent, the rate of unemployment among Turkish Berliners is depressingly high.

was badly damaged by bombs and in 1960 it was pulled down. The waste ground behind the façade was meant to become a park, but today the Tempodrom is based here, hosting concerts and cabaret shows.

6 Oranienstraße
MAP G4–H5 ▪ Between Lindenstr. and Skalitzer Str.

Oranienstraße is the heart of Kreuzberg. It is the wildest, most colourful and most unusual street of the district, where streetwear shops and pubs jostle for space with doner kebab takeaways and Turkish greengrocers. All aspects of life and politics in Kreuzberg are centred around this road.

7 Nollendorfplatz
MAP E5

Nollendorfplatz and neighbouring Winterfeldtplatz are right in the centre of Schöneberg. The former square has always been a focal point for Berlin's gay scene, and a plaque at the Nollendorfplatz U-Bahn station commemorates approximately 5,000 homosexuals killed in concentration camps by the Nazis. Today, gay life is concentrated more in the surrounding streets than the square itself. Before World War II, Nollendorfplatz was also a centre of entertainment. The Metropol-Theater, today a discotheque, then boasted Erwin Piscator as its director. And next door lived the writer Christopher Isherwood, whose novel formed the basis of *Cabaret*, the famous musical and film.

8 Viktoriapark
MAP F6 ■ Kreuzbergstr.

This rambling park *(see p61)* was set up as a recreational space for workers in Kreuzberg in 1888–94 to plans by Hermann Mächtig. It has an artificial waterfall, and the Neo-Gothic Schinkel memorial, 66 m (216 ft) high, commemorates Prussian victory in the Wars of Liberation against Napoleon.

Detail, Martin-Gropius-Bau

9 Martin-Gropius-Bau
MAP F4 ■ Niederkirchnerstr. 7 ■ (030) 25 48 60 ■ 10am–7pm Wed–Mon (check website) ■ Admission charge ■ www.berlinerfestspiele.de/gropiusbau

The richly ornamented former museum of arts and crafts hosts exhibitions on cultural history.

10 Riehmers Hofgarten
MAP F6 ■ Yorckstr. 83–86

Over 20 buildings make up this estate, built as officers' quarters in the Gründerzeit (after the founding of the German Empire in 1871). Restored in the 1970s, they include a pleasant hotel with restaurant.

A DAY IN KREUZBERG

▶ MORNING

Start from the ruins of **Anhalter Bahnhof**, which you can reach by S-Bahn. From here continue along Stresemannstraße in a northwesterly direction to the **Martin-Gropius-Bau**. While away a few hours in this impressive building, then take a break in the museum café. Afterwards, a visit to the neighbouring **Topographie des Terrors** exhibition will bring you face to face with the dark Nazi past of this area. Walk along Niederkirchnerstraße, past an original section of the Berlin Wall, to Wilhelmstraße. Continue to Zimmerstrasse and visit some of the many contemporary art galleries lining the street. Walk on to Friedrichstrasse to **Checkpoint Charlie** and the Wall Museum at the former border *(see p129)*.

AFTERNOON

You can have a tasty lunch at **Sale e Tabacchi** *(see p135)* in Rudi-Dutschke-Straße. Continue in an easterly direction to get to the heart of Kreuzberg. Make a detour south on Lindenstraße to the **Jüdisches Museum** *(see p129)* or carry on into **Oranienstraße**. Then take the U6 from U-Bahn station Hallesches Tor to Platz der Luftbrücke. **Viktoriapark** nearby is a good place for a rest, while shopaholics might prefer a stroll up Bergmannstrasse. At the end of the street, turn north into Baerwaldstraße and continue to Carl-Herz-Ufer, where you will be able to round off the day with a delicious evening meal at the **Altes Zollhaus** *(see p135)*.

See map on pp128–9

The Best of the Rest

1 Rathaus Schöneberg
MAP D6 ▪ John-F-Kennedy-Platz

It was from this town hall, on 26 June 1963, that the US President John F Kennedy made his famous speech, declaring "I am a Berliner" and expressing his commitment to the freedom of West Berlin.

2 Mehringplatz
MAP G5

Once Kreuzberg's prettiest square, Mehringplatz was destroyed in World War II and is today surrounded by modern residential buildings.

The old Tempelhof terminal

3 Tempelhofer Park
Tempelhof, built in 1939 by Ernst Sagebiel and at that point Germany's biggest airport, survives as the largest Fascist structure in Europe. The airport closed in 2008. The site is now home to a sports ground, park and offices. The old terminal building can be visited on a guided tour *(see p78)*.

4 Mariannenplatz
MAP H5

This square is dominated by the Gothic-style international cultural centre Künstlerhaus Bethanien. A former hospital, it is today used as studio space by experimental artists.

5 Oberbaumbrücke
Warschauer/Skalitzer Str.

Pedestrians and cyclists can cross to the other side of the Spree River from Kreuzberg to Friedrichshain on this red-brick bridge, one of Berlin's loveliest, which was built in 1894–6.

6 Altes Mosse-Palais
MAP G4 ▪ Kochstr.

One of Berlin's most influential publishing houses was based in this Jugendstil corner house in the former newspaper district.

7 Friedhöfe Hallesches Tor
MAP G6 ▪ Mehringdamm

Many celebrities lie buried in these four cemeteries, including the composer Felix Mendelssohn Bartholdy and the writer E T A Hoffmann, whose work inspired Offenbach to compose his *opéra fantastique The Tales of Hoffmann*.

8 Gasometer Schöneberg
MAP E6 ▪ Torgauer Str. 12–15

Once a massive gas holder, this Schöneberg landmark was decommissioned in the 1990s and turned into a viewing platform.

9 Kottbusser Tor
MAP H5

Social diversity in Kreuzberg is tucked away in between 1970s prefabricated buildings in the Turkish heart of the district.

10 Kammergericht
MAP E6 ▪ Potsdamer Str. 186

From 1947 to 1990, this magnificent supreme court, built in 1909–13, was used as Allied Control Council.

The façade of Kammergericht

Shops and Markets

Fruits at Winterfeldtmarkt

1 Winterfeldtmarkt
MAP E5 ▪ Winterfeldtplatz
▪ 8am–4pm Sat, 8am–1pm Wed

At Berlin's largest market you can buy fresh fruit and vegetables as well as other goods from around the world, such as clothes and New-Age items (see p77).

2 Türkenmarkt am Maybachufer
MAP H5 ▪ Maybachufer
▪ 11am–6:30pm Tue & Fri

The most vibrant market in Berlin. This is where Berliners and Turks alike buy unleavened bread and fresh goat's cheese (see p77).

3 Molotow
MAP G6 ▪ Gneisenaustr. 112
▪ (030) 693 08 18

Berlin designer Ute Hentschel's classy outfits are sold off-the-rack, and can be custom-made or altered for a perfect fit.

4 Oranienplatz and Oranienstraße
MAP H5 ▪ Oranienstr./corner Oranienplatz

Kreuzberg's main square and unofficial high street specialize in all things alternative.

5 Hot & Cold
MAP E5 ▪ Winterfeldtstr. 46
▪ (030) 23 63 44 30

Irresistible trinkets are sold at this charming Scandinvian design shop.

6 Depot 2
MAP H5 ▪ Oranienstr. 9 ▪ (030) 611 46 55

This small boutique sells the latest streetwear and hip-hop fashion of a local label.

7 High-Lite
MAP G6 ▪ Bergmannstr. 99
▪ (030) 691 27 44

Worried about standing out in the alternative crowd in Kreuzberg? This is the place to get your shades, body piercings and other counter-culture essentials.

8 Ararat
MAP G6 ▪ Bergmannstr. 99a ▪ (030) 693 50 80

One of Berlin's best-stocked and trendiest stationery, curiosity and gift shops, the colourful Ararat has many designer items for sale.

9 Marheineke-Markthalle
MAP G6 ▪ Marheinekeplatz
▪ 8am–8pm Mon–Fri, 8am–6pm Sat

This is one of the last remaining market-halls in Berlin. It boasts colourful fruit and vegetable stores and a wide range of organic produce, as well as numerous snack bars for hungry shoppers.

10 Grober Unfug Comics
MAP G6 ▪ Zossener Str. 33
▪ (030) 69 40 14 90

Comic books of all periods and in various languages, with an emphasis on Japanese manga. The store, whose name means "complete mischief" has all the latest comics, plus some bargains and rare editions.

Japanese manga

See map on pp128–9

Pubs, Bars and Nightclubs

The bar at Ankerklause

1 Ankerklause
MAP H5 ≡ Kottbusser Damm 104 ≡ (030) 693 56 49

An unrefined but hugely popular late-night place with a mixed crowd.

2 Yorckschlösschen
MAP F6 ≡ Yorckstr. 15 ≡ (030) 215 80 70

A pub-restaurant with a great old Berlin feel. Live jazz at the weekend.

3 Kuschlowski
MAP H6 ≡ Weserstr. 202 ≡ (0176) 24 38 97 01

This Russian vodka bar features bucket-shaped table lamps and bar stools designed by its owner, architect Daniel Neugebauer. Relaxed living-room vibe.

4 Van Loon
MAP G5 ≡ Carl-Herz-Ufer 5–7 ≡ (030) 692 62 93

Enjoy a snack surrounded by nautical artifacts on this old barge moored in Urbanhafen. In summer you can sit on the green banks.

5 Max & Moritz
MAP H5 ≡ Oranienstr. 162 ≡ (030) 69 51 59 11

Traditional Berlin tavern with touches of Jugendstil that fronts as a tango salon on Sundays. The bar opens at 5pm; lessons start at 8pm; the club starts at 9pm.

6 Rauschgold
MAP F6 ≡ Mehringdamm 62 ≡ (030) 78 95 26 68

Very popular, best late at night and very crowded at weekends. Karaoke, themed nights and a mixed crowd.

7 Golgatha
MAP F6 ≡ Dudenstr. 48–64 (Viktoriapark) ≡ (030) 785 24 53

This classic beer garden on the Kreuzberg attracts students and an older clientele, bopping to funk on the small and intimate dance floor.

8 SO36
A Kreuzberg classic, the SO36 is an über-alternative and very lively dance club. The crowd is a good mix of straight and gay (see p69).

9 Würgeengel
MAP H5 ≡ Dresdener Str. 122 ≡ (030) 615 55 60

The drinks at the "Angel of Death" are not, in fact, lethal, but the bar staff and most of the clientele are straight out of a Buñuel film.

10 Klunkerkranich
Karl-Marx-Str. 66 ≡ (030) 68 09 43 43

You might think a rooftop garden bar above a parking garage is less than glamorous, but it's hard to quibble with the fun-loving DJs, organic bistro stations and gorgeous views.

The rooftop bar at Klunkerkranich

Restaurants

PRICE CATEGORIES

For a three-course meal for one with half a bottle of wine (or equivalent meal), taxes and charges included.

€ under €30   €€ €30–60   €€€ over €60

1 Lavanderia Vecchia
MAP H6 ■ Flughafenstr. 46 ■ (030) 62 72 21 52 ■ noon–2:30pm & 7:30–11pm Tue–Fri, 7:30–11pm Sat ■ €€

Set in an old laundry, this creative Italian eatery excels in Roman tapas. Prepare to linger: a fixed four-course meal requires about 3 hours.

2 Entrecôte
MAP G4 ■ Schützenstr. 5 ■ (030) 20 16 54 96 ■ noon–midnight Mon–Fri, 6pm–midnight Sat, 6–11pm Sun ■ €€

Ever since Madonna enjoyed a meal here the usually low-key Entrecôte has become the talk of the town.

3 Altes Zollhaus
MAP G5 ■ Carl-Herz-Ufer 30 ■ (030) 692 33 00 ■ from 6pm Tue–Sat ■ €€

Former border control point on the banks of the Landwehrkanal serving international and German fare. Try the house speciality *Brandenburger Landente aus dem Rohr* (roast duck).

4 Viasko
MAP H5 ■ Erkelenzdamm 49 ■ (030) 88 49 97 85 ■ from 5pm (noon in summer) Mon–Fri, from 11am Sat–Sun ■ €

An imaginative vegan menu using fresh local produce is on offer here.

5 Restaurant Tim Raue
MAP G4 ■ Rudi-Dutschke-Str. 26 ■ (030) 25 93 79 30 ■ noon–1:30pm & 7pm–midnight Tue–Sat ■ €€€

Tasting menus explore combinations such as glazed partridge with Japanese chestnut. The Obamas ate here in 2013. Two Michelin stars.

Lavanderia Vecchia

6 Defne
MAP H5 ■ Planufer. 92c ■ (030) 81 79 71 11 ■ from 4pm daily ■ no credit cards ■ €

An intimate restaurant serving modern Turkish food.

7 Long March Canteen
MAP H5 ■ Wrangelstr. 20 ■ 0178 884 95 99 ■ 6pm–midnight daily ■ €€

A hip dim sum restaurant with communal tables and dim lighting, like a real Chinese street kitchen.

8 Henne
MAP H4 ■ Leu schnerdamm 25 ■ (030) 614 77 30 ■ from 6pm Tue–Sat, 5pm Sun ■ €

Only three dishes are served at this old-Berlin institution but all are cooked to perfection.

9 Lochner Weinwirtschaft
MAP D6 ■ Eisenacher Str. 86 ■ (030) 23 00 52 20 ■ 4pm–midnight Tue–Sun ■ €€

Wine and dinner bar with an outside terrace. Refined snacks also served.

10 Sale e Tabacchi
MAP G4 ■ Rudi-Dutschke-Str. 23 ■ (030) 252 11 55 ■ 10am–11:30pm daily ■ €€

Elegant Italian restaurant popular with the media crowd. In summer, reserve a table in the courtyard.

See map on pp128–9

Prenzlauer Berg

Having undergone dramatic changes in recent decades, this former East Berlin workers' district attracts locals and visitors like no other part of town. Even when Berlin was a divided city, the area was favoured by artists and an alternative crowd, and it exerts a similar pull today. Although structures on quiet side streets have not yet been restored and still give a sense of the old Berlin, Prenzlauer Berg is being steadily and noticeably transformed.

Gethsemane-kirche, detail

Many young professionals, decried as yuppies by locals, are restoring old buildings. Cafés and restaurants have taken over tenement blocks around Kollwitzplatz and Husemannstraße, giving the leafy streets an almost Parisian flair, while Kastanienallee, also known as "Casting Alley", is the catwalk of the hip young scene.

Schönhauser Allee, Prenzlauer Berg

1 Schönhauser Allee
MAP H1/2 ▪ Prenzlauer Berg

Schönhauser Allee, 3 km (2 miles) long and lined with shops and pubs, is the main artery of the district. Down the centre of the road runs the high-level viaduct of U-Bahn line U2. A few buildings have not yet been restored and give a good impression of the old Prenzlauer Berg, especially between Senefelderplatz and Danziger Straße.

2 Kollwitzplatz
MAP H2 ▪ Prenzlauer Berg

Once a quiet square, Kollwitzplatz is today the noisy heart of the district. All around the green square, locals congregate in the numerous cafés, pubs and restaurants. From the lavishly restored façades it is hard to tell that this was once one of the city's poorest areas. The district's 19th-century tenement blocks and impoverished past are today only recalled by the name of the square. The artist Käthe Kollwitz *(see p49)* once lived and worked at No. 25 (now destroyed), from where she highlighted the poverty of the local workers in her sculptures, drawings and sketches.

3 Prater
MAP H1 ▪ Kastanienallee 7–9 ▪ (030) 448 56 88 ▪ 6pm–midnight Mon–Sat, noon–midnight Sun

The Prater is one of the few remaining entertainment complexes that were once common in big German cities. It was built in 1837 just outside the original city gates, and was first jokingly called "Prater" after its world-famous counterpart in Vienna. A concert hall was added in 1857 and by the turn of the century it had become so popular that the nickname stuck. Today, you can enjoy beer and food at the restaurant of the same name *(see p141)*.

PRENZLAUER BERG

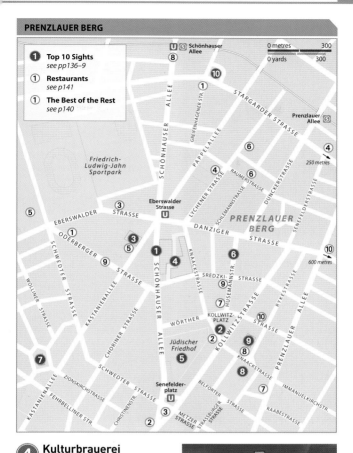

1 **Top 10 Sights**
see pp136–9

1 **Restaurants**
see p141

1 **The Best of the Rest**
see p140

Schönhauser Allee

Stargarder Strasse

Prenzlauer Allee

Friedrich-Ludwig-Jahn Sportpark

Greifenhagener Str

Pappelallee

Raumerstrasse

Dunckerstrasse

Seelfelderstrasse

Schönhauser Allee

Lychener Strasse

Schliemannstrasse

PRENZLAUER BERG

Eberswalder Strasse

Danziger Strasse

Eberswalder Strasse

Oderberger Strasse

Schwedter Strasse

Wolliner Strasse

Kastanienallee

Choriner Strasse

Schönhauser Allee

Knaackstrasse

Sredzki Strasse

Husemannstr.

Rykestrasse

Prenzlauer Allee

Wörther

Kollwitz-Platz

Kollwitzstrasse

Jüdischer Friedhof

Knaackstrasse

Immanuelkirchstr.

Senefelder-platz

Belforter Strasse

Raabestrasse

Zionskirchstrasse

Fehrbelliner Str

Kastanienallee

Schwedter Strasse

Christinenstr.

Metzer Strasse

Strassburger Strasse

0 metres 300
0 yards 300

250 metres

600 metres

---

4 **Kulturbrauerei**
MAP H1 ▪ Schönhauser Allee 36–39 (entrance: Knaackstr. 97) ▪ (030) 44 31 50 ▪ kulturbrauerei.de/en

This giant complex of buildings originally housed the Schultheiss brewery, one of the breweries that once made Prenzlauer Berg famous. The complex, parts of which are over 150 years old, was designed by Franz Schwechten. It was completely restored in 1997–9 and has become a lively and popular spot. Cafés, restaurants, a cinema, shops and even a theatre have sprung up in the red and yellow brick buildings and the numerous interior courtyards.

The Kulturbrauerei complex

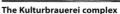

The peaceful Jewish Cemetery

5 Jewish Cemetery
MAP H2 ▪ Schönhauser Allee 23–25 ▪ www.jg-berlin.org/en.html

The small Jewish cemetery is among the city's most beautiful. The tombstones lie or stand amid dense scrub and high trees. The cemetery was set up in 1827, when the former Jewish cemetery in Große Hamburger Straße was closed. Two of the famous personalities who have found their final resting places here are the painter and printmaker Max Liebermann (1847–1935) and the composer Giacomo Meyerbeer (1791–1864).

6 Husemannstraße
MAP H1/2 ▪ Between Wörther and Danziger Str.

The East German regime undertook a perfect restoration of this idyllic street for Berlin's 750th anniversary celebrations. A stroll through the leafy roads lined with houses from the Gründerzeit (the years after the founding of the German Empire in 1871) is one of the loveliest ways to experience Prenzlauer Berg. Ancient-looking street lamps and signs, cobbled streets, antiquated shop signs and a few atmospheric pubs take the visitor back to the late 19th century.

7 Zionskirche
MAP G2 ▪ Zionskirchplatz ▪ (030) 449 21 91 ▪ 8–10pm Mon, 1–7pm Tue–Sat, noon–5pm Sun

Zionskirche, dating from 1866–73, and the square of the same name form a tranquil oasis in the middle of the lively district. The Protestant church has always been a political centre too. During the Third Reich, resistance groups against the Nazi regime congregated here and, during the East German period, the alternative "environment library" (an information and documentation centre) was established here. Church and other opposition groups who were active at Zionskirche played a decisive role in the political transformation of East Germany in 1989–90, which eventually led to the reunification of Germany.

8 Wasserturm
MAP H2 ▪ Knaackstr.

The unofficial symbol of the district is this giant 30-m (98-ft) high water tower, built in 1877 as a water reservoir, but shut down in 1914. The engine house in the tower was used as an unofficial prison by the SA from 1933 to 1945, a period recalled by a memorial

The Wasserturm

plaque. The water tower stands on Windmühlenberg (windmill hill), where some of the mills that had

---

PRENZLBERG OR PRENZLAUER BERG?

Many locals simply say Prenzlberg when talking about their quarter. But this name is used mainly by West Berliners and West Germans who have recently moved here – the real name is Prenzlauer Berg, just as it is written. The supposed nickname is just a new-fangled term for a neighbourhood that has become fashionable after the fall of the Berlin Wall.

made Prenzlauer Berg famous in the 19th century once stood. Today this round brick building has been converted into trendy apartments.

Interior of Synagoge Rykestraße

⑨ Synagoge Rykestraße
MAP H2 ▪ Rykestr. 53 ▪ (030) 88 02 83 16 ▪ guided tours 2–6pm Thu ▪ www.jg-berlin.org/en.html

Built in 1904, this synagogue is one of the few Jewish places of worship to have survived Kristallnacht on 9 November 1938, the violent attacks on Jewish property by the Nazis. The temple's historic interior was built from red bricks in the shape of a basilica. Today it is the largest synagogue in Berlin (see p59).

⑩ Gethsemanekirche
MAP H1 ▪ Stargarder Str. 77 ▪ (030) 445 77 45 ▪ May–Oct: 5–7pm Wed–Thu (otherwise by prior arrangement)

Outside this red-brick church, dating back to 1891–3, East German secret police beat up peaceful protesters. It was the starting point for the collapse of the East German regime.

Gethsemanekirche interior

▶ MORNING

Set off from the U-Bahn station in Senefelderplatz, one of the lively spots in Prenzlauer Berg. From here, explore the old tenement blocks and backyards. Now continue west along Fehrbelliner Straße to **Zionskirchplatz** with its eponymous church. There are numerous cafés on the square, such as **Kapelle**, where you could stop for a capuccino. Leave the square via Zionskirchstraße, then turn left into Kastanienallee. This is one of the most colourful streets in the quarter. At the end of the street you could pop into **Prater** (see p141). Then turn right into Oderberger Straße, one of the best preserved streets of the district. Continue east along Sredzkistraße until you reach **Husemannstraße**. Have a good look around the old Berlin streets, you may find something interesting to buy.

AFTERNOON

You could have lunch at one of the numerous restaurants in **Kollwitzplatz** (see p136): **Gugelhof** (see p141) and **Zander** are both recommended, the former for German and French cuisine, the latter for imaginative fish specialities. After lunch, walk along Knaackstraße to the **Synagoge Rykestraße**. From here it is a few paces back to the **Wasserturm**. Give your feet a rest at the small green space around the tower before continuing along Belforter Straße and Kollwitzstraße to Schönhauser Allee. You will find perfect tranquility there in the **Jewish Cemetery**.

See map on p137

The Best of the Rest

1 Greifenhagener Straße
MAP H1

Not the most beautiful, but one of the best-preserved red-brick residential streets of old Berlin.

2 Pfefferberg
MAP H2 ▪ Schönhauser Allee 176 ▪ (030) 44 38 30

This alternative cultural centre in a former brewery hosts concerts, performance art events and festivals.

3 Senefelderplatz
MAP H2

The wedge-shaped square is named after Alois Senefelder, a pioneer of modern printing techniques. At its centre is a "Café Achteck", housed in a historic octagonal public urinal.

4 Zeiss-Großplanetarium
Prenzlauer Allee 80 ▪ (030) 421 84 50 ▪ 9am–noon Tue–Thu, 6–9:30pm Fri, also pm Sat–Sun ▪ Closed for renovation until 2016

Lose yourself amidst uncountable stars, planets and galaxies under the vast silvery dome of the planetarium.

5 Mauerpark
MAP G1 ▪ Am Falkplatz

The vast park near the former border, comprising Max Schmeling Hall and Jahn Sports Park, was built for the Berlin Olympic bid in 2000. Today it hosts sports and music events, and a Sunday flea market.

Buildings at Helmholtzplatz

6 Helmholtzplatz
MAP H1

Apart from the trendy cafés and bars, time seems to have stopped here in 1925, with buildings reminiscent of a social housing programme.

7 Prenzlauer Berg Museum
MAP H2 ▪ Prenzlauer Allee 227–228 ▪ (030) 902 953 917 ▪ 9am–7pm Mon–Fri

This museum charts the history of the district and its poor working-class inhabitants in the 19th century.

8 Konnopke
MAP H1 ▪ At the southern exit of U-Bahn Schönhauser Allee ▪ (030) 442 77 65 ▪ 10am–8pm Mon–Fri, noon–8pm Sat

This legendary *Currywurstimbiss* was opened in 1930 under the U-Bahn steel viaduct. The spicy sausages are among the best in the city.

9 Oderberger Straße
MAP G/H1

This leafy street is lined with cafés, boutiques and a few historic buildings. The old swimming baths of Prenzlauer Berg at No. 84 were renovated in 2015.

10 Thälmannpark
MAP H1 ▪ Prenzlauer Allee

One of few parks in the northeast of the city, dominated by Socialist prefabricated buildings. It has a monument to Ernst Thälmann, a communist murdered by the Nazis.

Toy stall, Mauerpark flea market

Restaurants

1 Oderquelle
MAP G1 ■ Oderberger Str. 27
■ (030) 44 00 80 80 ■ 6pm–1am daily
■ €

Basic Berlin and German dishes are served up in an alternative, relaxed setting in this quaint little *Kiez* (neighbourhood) place.

2 Gugelhof
MAP H2 ■ Knaackstr. 37
■ (030) 442 92 29 ■ 4pm–1am Mon–Fri, 10am–1am Sat–Sun ■ €€

Bill Clinton was once a guest at this restaurant, which attracts clients from all over Berlin. The menu features an original combination of German and French cuisine.

Outdoor tables at Gugelhof

3 Cotto e Crudo
MAP G/H1 ■ Eberswalder Str. 33 ■ (030) 44 03 71 11 ■ noon–midnight daily ■ €

Homely little restaurant, Cotto e Crudo offers authentic Sicilian cuisine. It is located close to the southern end of Mauerpark.

4 Weinstein
MAP H1 ■ Lychener Str. 33
■ (030) 441 18 42 ■ 5pm–2am daily (from 6pm Sun) ■ €€

A friendly, rustic wine bar with a great selection of Austrian and German wines and solid bistro fare.

PRICE CATEGORIES

For a three-course meal for one with half a bottle of wine (for equivalent meal), taxes and charges included.

€ under €30   €€ €30–60   €€€ over €60

5 Prater
MAP H1 ■ Kastanienallee 7–9
■ (030) 448 56 88 ■ 6pm–midnight Mon–Sat, noon–midnight Sun ■ no credit cards ■ €

Surprises at the Prater include a beer garden, a rustic restaurant in the courtyard and free live concerts.

6 Sasaya
MAP H1 ■ Lychener Str. 50
■ (030) 44 71 77 21 ■ noon–3pm, 6–11:30pm Thu–Mon ■ no credit cards ■ €

Head to Sasaya for some of Berlin's best sushi. Reservations needed.

7 Restauration 1900
MAP H2 ■ Husemannstr. 1
■ (030) 442 24 94 ■ from 10am daily
■ €€

This venerable restaurant still pulls in the crowds with its deliciously light German cuisine.

8 Pasternak
MAP H2 ■ Knaackstr. 22 ■ (030) 441 33 99 ■ 9am–1am daily ■ €

Go Russian at this Moscow-style venue, with borscht, Russian music and vodka.

9 Café November
MAP H1 ■ Husemannstr. 15
■ (030) 442 84 25 ■ 10am–1am Mon–Fri, 9am–2am Sat–Sun ■ €

A Prenzlauer Berg institution with a small but tempting menu.

10 Mao Thai
MAP H2 ■ Wörther Straße 30
■ (030) 441 92 61 ■ noon–11:30pm daily ■ €

One of the best and friendliest Thai restaurants in town, this serves traditional and artistically presented food.

See map on p137

⟦TOP 10⟧ Berlin's Southeast

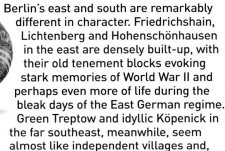

Sculpture detail, Treptower Park

Berlin's east and south are remarkably different in character. Friedrichshain, Lichtenberg and Hohenschönhausen in the east are densely built-up, with their old tenement blocks evoking stark memories of World War II and perhaps even more of life during the bleak days of the East German regime. Green Treptow and idyllic Köpenick in the far southeast, meanwhile, seem almost like independent villages and, together with Großer Müggelsee, are popular day trip destinations for visitors and Berliners alike.

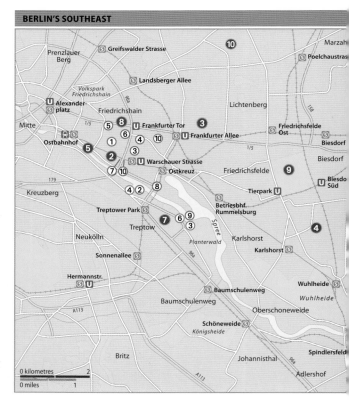

BERLIN'S SOUTHEAST

Previous pages The Berliner Dom with the shimmering Sony Center in the background

A view of the small town of Köpenick from the Spree River

① Köpenicker Altstadt and Köpenicker Schloss

Schloss: Schlossinsel ▪ **11am–6pm Tue–Sun (to 5pm in winter)** ▪ **Adm charge** ▪ **www.smb.museum**

The island community of Köpenick has a venerable history: as early as the 9th century, people had settled on Schlossinsel. The village stayed independent until 1920. Its coat of arms still features two fish, and the Altstadt (old town) on the Dahme River has 18th–19th-century fishermen's huts. On 16 October 1906, Wilhelm Voigt, dressed as a captain, led soldiers into the Rathaus (town hall) on Alt-Köpenick, arrested the mayor and "confiscated" the municipal coffers. The "Hauptmann von Köpenick" (Captain of Köpenick) is commemorated by a statue in front of the Rathaus. The 1904 structure is a good example of Gothic brick architecture from Brandenburg. The charming Baroque Köpenick palace, on Schlossinsel in the south of the district, was built in 1677–81 for the future King Frederick I by Dutch architect Rutger van Langervelt. It now houses collections from the Kunstgewerbemuseum *(see p51)*.

② Mercedes-Benz Arena

Mühlenstr. 12–30/O2-Platz 1 ▪ **Ticket hotline (030) 20 60 70 88 99** ▪ **www.mercedes-benz-berlin.de**

The city's largest entertainment arena, seating 17,000 people, hosts pop concerts and shows of all kinds, as well as being home to the Alba Berlin basketball team and the Eisbären Berlin ice-hockey club.

Map Legend

① **Top 10 Sights**
see pp145–7

① **Restaurants**
see p149

① **Bars and Clubs**
see p148

Kaulsdorf

⑤ Kaulsdorf

Mahlsdorf

Kaulsdorf Süd

Waldesruh

Mittelheide

⑤ Köpenick

Friedrichshagen

Köpenick

① ⑨

② ①

⑦

Friedrichshagen ⑤

Spree

⑧

Kämmereiheide

⑥ Großer Müggelsee

The Mercedes-Benz Arena

3 Stasi-Museum Berlin

Ruschestr. 103, Haus 1
■ 10am–6pm Mon–Fri,
noon–6pm Sat–Sun
■ Adm ■ www.
stasimuseum.de

Button spy camera, Stasi-museum

The former headquarters
of the feared Stasi, East
Germany's secret police,
is now a memorial commemorating
the victims of the East German
regime and of Erich Mielke, the min-
ister in charge of the secret police.
Visitors can see his offices, the can-
teen and spying equipment used by
the Socialist big-brother regime.

4 Deutsch-Russisches Museum

Zwieseler Str. 4 ■ 10am–6pm Tue–Sun
■ www.museum-karlshorst.de

World War II ended here on 8 May
1945, when Germany signed its
unconditional surrender. Documents,
uniforms and photographs, displayed
in the former officers' casino, relate
the story of the war.

5 East Side Gallery

A 1.3-km (0.8-mile) section
of the Berlin Wall was left standing
next to the Spree River. In 1990, 118
artists from around the world painted
colourful images onto the grey concrete, making it a unique work of art.
Particularly famous is a mural by
Russian Dmitri Vrubel showing Erich
Honecker and Leonid Brezhnev kissing. Most murals were restored by
the original artists in 2009 (see p78).

6 Großer Müggelsee

Treptow-Köpenick district

Nicknamed Berlin's
"Large Bathtub", the
Großer Müggelsee is
the city's biggest lake,
covering 766 ha (1,892
acres). Müggelsee is
not as popular as Großer
Wannsee, mainly because it is so far
from the centre of town. It is known
for the beer gardens on its south
side, which can be reached on foot or
by boat from Friedrichshagen. You
can swim in the lake, and around it
are great walking and cycling paths.

7 Treptower Park

Alt-Treptow

Established in the 19th century for
the city's working classes, Treptower
Park is today best known for its
Sowjetisches Ehrenmal (Soviet
Memorial). In April 1945, 7,000 Red
Army soldiers who died during the
liberation of Berlin were buried here.
Beyond the mass graves is a 12-m
(39-ft) bronze statue of a Russian
soldier holding a child and a sword
with which he has destroyed the Nazi
hakenkreuz symbol (see p61).

8 Friedrichshain

MAP H2

This densely built-up area grew
rapidly during the industrialization of
the late 19th century. Its industries
made it an Allied target during the
war and it was one of Berlin's most
damaged districts. After the fall of

Colourful murals at the city's East Side Gallery

the Wall, Friedrichshain attracted a vibrant young population, and it is now one of the city's most popular and bohemian areas, home to trendy design and media companies, bars, clubs, and cafés, mostly set around Boxhagener Platz and Simon-Dach-Straße. Its Volkspark is an oasis of tranquillity, with Ludwig Hoffman's charming Märchenbrunnen fountain, decorated with fairy-tale characters, and the wooded Großer and Kleiner Bunkerberg hillocks *(see p61)*.

Märchenbrunnen, Volkspark

⑨ Tierpark Berlin

Am Tierpark 125 ▪ (030) 51 53 10 ▪ Opening times vary, check online ▪ Adm ▪ www.tierpark-berlin. de/tierpark

Located in the Friedrichsfelde Palace park, Europe's largest zoological garden hosts several rare species. The Siberian tigers in their rocky outdoor enclosures are worth a visit. The park is known for its successful elephant breeding programme. The 1695 palace sits in the middle of this 160-ha (400-acre) estate *(see p61)*.

⑩ Gedenkstätte Hohenschönhausen

Genslerstr. 66 ▪ English guided tours 11am & 2:30pm Apr–Oct, 2:30pm Nov–Mar ▪ Adm ▪ en.stiftung-hsh.de

This former secret police prison for political prisoners was in use until 1990. Before 1951, it served as a reception centre for the Red Army. You can visit the watchtowers and cells – particularly horrifying are the windowless "submarine cells" for solitary confinement and torture.

A DAY IN BERLIN'S SOUTHEAST

Alexanderplatz station
Stasi-Museum Berlin
U-BAHN
Magdalenenstr. station
Tierpark station
Tierpark Berlin
BUS
Deutsch-Russisches Museum
Karlshorst tram stop
TRAM
Friedrichs-hagen
TRAM
Köpenick Old Town, Köpenicker Schloss
BOAT
Grosser Müggelsee
Müggelsee-Terrassen

▶ MORNING

Begin your tour of Berlin's Southeast at Alexanderplatz. Sights on this tour are not always near each other, so using public transport is recommended.

Take the U-Bahn line U5 to Magdalenenstraße station, from where it is a short walk to the **Stasi-Museum Berlin**. Return to the station and continue on U5 to **Tierpark Berlin**, where you can spend some time exploring both the zoological garden and the beautifully restored **Schloss Friedrichsfelde**, built in early Neo-Classical style. Then catch bus No. 296 from the Tierpark U-Bahn station to the **Deutsch-Russisches Museum**.

AFTERNOON

From the museum, either walk (15 minutes) or take bus No. 296 southwest down Rheinsteinstraße to the S Karlshorst tram stop. No. 27 goes direct to **Rathaus Köpenick**. Stop for a typically German meal in the **Ratskeller** *(see p149)*, the town hall's cellar restaurant. Afterwards explore **Köpenick Old Town** *(see p145)*. The old fishing village is especially worth a visit. There are many cafés near **Köpenicker Schloss** *(see p145)* where you could stop for coffee and cake. Continue your journey by tram No. 60 to Friedrichshagen, the access point for the **Großer Müggelsee**. From here take one of the tourist boats across the lake to **Müggelsee-Terrassen**, where you can round off the day with an evening meal at a choice of restaurants.

See map on pp144–5 ⬅

Bars and Clubs

1 Berghain
Located in a former power station, this club has a strict door policy – be prepared to queue. A good sound system and cool crowds make the wait worthwhile *(see p75)*.

2 Arena
Eichenstr. 4 ▪ (030) 533 20 30 ▪ **Check opening days in advance**
This sprawling post-industrial riverside complex of concert halls, a club ship *(Hoppetosse)* and a moored swimming pool *(Badeschiff)* is unusual even by Berlin standards.

3 Cassiopeia
Revaler Str. 99 ▪ (030) 47 38 59 49 ▪ From 7pm Wed–Sat
Join hippies, punks and freestylers in this underground urban enclave for ungentrified clubbing and live gigs.

4 Astro Bar
Simon-Dach-Str. 40 ▪ (030) 29 66 16 15 ▪ from 7pm daily
This retro sci-fi-styled bar has moderately priced cocktails, pin-ball machines and a trashy charm.

5 CSA
Karl-Marx-Allee 96 ▪ (030) 29 04 47 41 ▪ From 7pm daily ▪ No credit cards
Named after the Czech Airlines office that was based here, CSA is a stylish cocktail bar serving perfect drinks to pleasant lounge music.

6 Red Rooster Bar
Grünberger Str. 23 ▪ (030) 29 00 33 10 ▪ From 4pm daily
Attached to a hostel, this is a good low-budget option in Friedrichshain's generally expensive bar scene.

7 Monster Ronson's Ichiban Karaoke Bar
Warschauer Str. 34 ▪ (030) 89 75 13 27 ▪ From 7pm daily
At this lively bar, karaoke fans either practise their art in soundproof booths that can fit up to 16 people, or go up to sing on a stage. Try the brunch on Sundays.

8 Salon zur Wilden Renate
Alt Stralau 70 ▪ (030) 25 04 14 26 ▪ 6pm–2am Wed–Thu, 6pm–8am Fri, 6pm–6am Sat–Sun ▪ No credit cards ▪ No disabled access
Styled like a living room, this club is spread across several floors. It plays house and techno house music and often has a queue at the door.

9 Insel
Alt-Treptow 6 ▪ (030) 53 60 80 20 ▪ Club 7pm–1am Wed, 8pm–late Fri–Sat
This miniature castle on a Spree island houses a beer garden by day and a club by night. Live concerts in summer; poetry slams and ping pong in winter.

10 Matrix
Warschauer Platz 18 ▪ (030) 29 36 99 90 ▪ 10pm–7am daily
Located in vaults under the Warschauer Straße train station, Matrix is one of the largest clubs in the city. Popular with a young crowd, it attracts Berlin's best DJs.

Matrix, set under railway arches

Restaurants

PRICE CATEGORIES

For a three-course meal for one with half
a bottle of wine (or equivalent meal),
taxes and charges included.

€ under €30 €€ €30–60 €€€ over €60

1 freiheit fünfzehn
Freiheit 15 ■ (030) 65 88 78 25
■ From 4pm Mon–Sat, 11am–
midnight Sun ■ €

German and French cuisine served
aboard a schooner moored on the
Müggelspree. If you prefer dry land,
you can dine in the beer garden.

Vast vaults of Ratskeller Köpenick

2 Ratskeller Köpenick
Alt-Köpenick 21 ■ (030) 655 51
78 ■ 11am–11pm daily ■ €

Traditional Berlin fare is served in
the vaulted cellars where Wilhelm
Voigt once famously conned gullible
local civil servants (see p145).

3 Klipper Schiffsrestaurant
Bulgarische Str. ■ (030) 53 21 64 90
■ 10am–1am daily ■ no credit cards
■ €

This two-masted 1890 boat has been
turned into a cosy restaurant; the
menu features fish and game dishes.

4 White Trash Fast Food
Am Flutgraben 2 ■ (030) 50 34
86 68 ■ Noon–late daily ■ €

This quirky all-in-one venue has a
"zen" beer garden, cinema, tattoo
parlour and an organic restaurant-
club hosting raucous indie bands.

5 Die Spindel
Bölschestr. 51 ■ (030) 645 29 37
■ Noon–2:30pm and from 6pm Tue–
Sun ■ €€

This rustic restaurant serves
gourmet cuisine and excellent wines.

6 Eierschale Haus Zenner
Alt-Treptow 14–17 ■ (030) 533
73 70 ■ 10am–10pm Mon–Thu & Sun,
10am–4am Fri–Sat ■ no credit cards
■ €

A classic day trip destination: once,
families used to "bring and brew
their own coffee". Today it is a popular outdoor café and beer garden.

7 Krokodil
Gartenstr. 46–48 ■ (030) 65 88
00 94 ■ 5pm–midnight Mon–Sat,
11am–11pm Sun (brunch 11am–3pm)
■ €

Situated in Köpenick's Old Town,
near the river baths in Gartenstraße,
this is one of the nicest garden
venues, especially in summer.

8 Bräustübl
Müggelseedamm 164 ■ (030)
37 44 67 69 ■ 11am–midnight daily
■ €

This typical beer garden, belonging
to the neighbouring Berliner Bürger-
Brau brewery, serves game dishes.

9 Lehmofen
Freiheit 12 ■ (030) 655 70 44
■ noon–midnight daily (from 10am
Sun) ■ €

Meat and vegetarian dishes, freshly
cooked in a clay oven, are the top
attractions in this Anatolian restaurant with a summer terrace.

10 Leander
Jungstr. 29 ■ (030) 29 00 48 03
■ Apr–Oct: from 10am daily; Nov–
Mar: from 3pm Mon–Fri & from 10am
Sat–Sun ■ €

This romantic bistro with an
old-time feel offers creative and
cosmopolitan food – and it is a
bargain to boot.

See map on pp144–5

Grunewald and Dahlem

Berlin's green southwest, which includes the districts of Grunewald and Dahlem, is dotted with lakes, rivers, residential villas, private estates and small castles. Grunewald and Dahlem have a charming suburban character that has always drawn affluent and famous Berliners here. Visitors can enjoy extensive walks in the Grunewald forest, take a ferry ride across picturesque Wannsee to the romantic ruins at Pfaueninsel or relax at Europe's largest inland beach. Dahlem's museum complex has outstanding ethnographic and art collections, while the Haus der Wannsee Konferenz and Alliiertenmuseum recall a more painful period in Berlin's history.

Benin bronze, Dahlem Museums

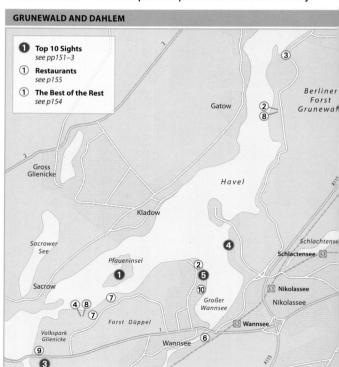

GRUNEWALD AND DAHLEM

1 Top 10 Sights
see pp151–3

1 Restaurants
see p155

1 The Best of the Rest
see p154

Friedrich Wilhelm II's charming ruined castle folly on Pfaueninsel

1 Pfaueninsel
Pfaueninselchaussee ▪ (030) 80 58 68 30 ▪ 10am–sunset daily ▪ Admission charge (castle) ▪ www.spsg.de

Visitors to Pfaueninsel are immediately enchanted by the romantic palace ruins and the eponymous peacocks that run around here. The Wannsee island, which can only be reached by ferry, is one of the most charming spots for a walk in Berlin *(see p60)*.

2 Dahlem Museums
Lansstr. 8 (Museum of European Cultures: Arnimallee 25) ▪ 10am–6pm Tue–Fri, 11am–6pm Sat–Sun ▪ Admission charge ▪ www.smb.museum

This complex of three museums is dedicated to foreign cultures and peoples. The Ethnological Museum has full-scale wooden huts and boats from the South Pacific islands and ceramic and stone sculptures from the Mayas, Aztecs and Incas. Highlights of the Museum of Asian Art include Japanese painting, Chinese porcelain, Buddhist cave paintings and early Indian sculptures. The Museum of European Cultures has objects from all over the continent.

3 Schloss Glienicke
Königstr. 36 ▪ (0331) 969 42 00 ▪ Apr–Oct: 10am–6pm Tue–Sun; Nov–Mar: 10am–5pm Sat–Sun ▪ Admission charge ▪ www.spsg.de

One of Berlin's most beautiful Hohenzollern palaces, this romantic castle was built by Schinkel in 1824–60 as a summer residence for Prince Carl of Prussia. The landscaped garden, designed by Lenné, includes pavilions called "Große" and "Kleine Neugierde" (large and small curiosity), a teahouse and the Orangerie.

White-sand artificial beaches at the beautiful Wannsee lake

④ Strandbad Wannsee
Wannseebadeweg 25
■ Call for opening times: (030) 803 54 50 ■ Admission charge

Europe's largest inland beach is a picturesque spot on the edge of the city, attracting up to 40,000 daily visitors. The renovated swimming baths were built in 1929–30 as a recreation area for workers *(see p61)*.

⑤ Gedenkstätte Haus der Wannsee-Konferenz
Am Großen Wannsee 56–58 ■ 10am– 6pm daily ■ www.ghwk.de

It is hard to believe that something as abhorrent as the Holocaust could have been planned at this elegant villa. Built by Paul Baumgarten in

1914–15 in Neo-Baroque style for businessman Ernst Marlier, it hosted the Nazi elite, among them the infamous Adolf Eichmann, on 20 January 1942. They met to discuss the details of the mass extermination of Jews. An exhibition documents the conference and its consequences, as well as the history of the villa.

⑥ Alliiertenmuseum
Clayallee 135 ■ (030) 818 19 90
■ 10am–6pm Sun–Tue ■ www. alliiertenmuseum.de/en

This museum recalls the 50 or so years of partnership between West Berliners and the Western Allies. Based in a former US barracks, the museum uses uniforms, documents, weapons and military equipment to tell the story of Berlin's post-war history, though not only from the military point of view.

⑦ Grunewald Villas
Am Großen Wannsee

Some of Berlin's most attractive 19th-century villas are found in the streets around the Grunewald S-Bahn station. Especially worth seeing are Nos. 15 and 11 in Winklerstraße, the latter of which was built by Hermann Muthesius in the style of an English country house. Villa Maren at No. 12 is a beautiful example of the Neo-Renaissance style. The villas on Furtwänglerstraße and Toni-Lessler-Straße are also worth a detour.

PRUSSIA AND ANTIQUITY

From 1821, Lenné and Schinkel tried to turn the Potsdam countryside into an "island paradise". Their idea was based on Classical ideas of the harmonious ensemble of architecture and landscape, in line with the idealized views of antiquity prevalent in the Neo-Classical period. The architectural style of Prussian palaces such as Sanssouci (left) thus harks back to Greek and Roman models and the Italian Renaissance.

8 Jagdschloss Grunewald

Hüttenweg 100, Grunewaldsee
▪ (030) 813 35 97 ▪ Apr–Oct: 10am–
6pm Tue–Sun; Nov–Mar: tours only,
11am, 1 & 3pm Sat–Sun ▪ Admission
charge ▪ www.spsg.de

This small white 1542 palace is the
oldest in the city area. It was once a
hunting lodge for the Electors. Built
in the Renaissance and Baroque
styles, it holds paintings by Cranach
the Elder and 16th–19th-century
portraits of Hohenzollern rulers.

9 Museumsdorf Düppel

Clauerstr. 11 ▪ (030) 802 66 71
▪ Apr–Oct: 3–7pm Thu, 10am–5pm
Sun ▪ Admission charge
▪ www.stadtmuseum.de

This lively open-air museum is a
reminder that Berlin was once a
series of villages dating back to the
13th century. Costumed actors enact
the daily life of the Middle Ages, and
there are bread-baking, pottery and
basket-weaving demonstrations. The
gardens are very interesting.

Villas of Mexikoplatz

10 Mexikoplatz

Idyllic Mexikoplatz in the
southern district of Zehlendorf is
one of the most atmospheric and
architecturally fascinating squares
in Berlin. It is flanked by elegant
semicircular Jugendstil apartment
blocks, and in front of these stands
Berlin's last remaining Art-Deco-
style S-Bahn station. In summer,
the buildings' balconies are richly
decked with greenery and flowers.
Some of Berlin's most magnificent
mansion houses line Argentinische
and Lindenthaler Allee, the streets
leading into the magnificent square.

A DAY IN THE SOUTHWEST

▶ MORNING

Start your morning walk through
Berlin's southwestern districts
by taking the S-Bahn (line S1)
to **Mexikoplatz**. Here you can
admire the beautiful villas and
the lovely green square before
dropping in at **Café Krone** (No. 2
Argentinische Allee) for a late
breakfast. Then take bus No. 118
southwards to the open-air
museum **Museumsdorf Düppel**.
From there, take bus No. 115
north to the **Alliiertenmuseum**.
Afterwards, a 20-minute walk
through the park opposite leads
right up to the beer garden **Luise**
(see p155) near the Free University,
where you may like to have lunch.

AFTERNOON

Resume your explorations with
a stop at the **Dahlem Museums**
(see p151), a 2-minute walk south
of the café, or discover exotic
flora in the giant greenhouses of
the **Botanischer Garten** (pp60–61),
a 20-minute walk east. The
seasonal displays are spectacular
at any time of year. Then find your
way to the Botanischer Garten
S-Bahn station to take the train to
the Wannsee station, gateway to
the sights of southwestern Berlin.
When the weather is right, head
to the beaches of **Strandbad
Wannsee**. Alternatively, pay a
visit to the **Gedenkstätte Haus
der Wannsee-Konferenz** and
then admire the park and **Schloss
Glienicke** (see p151). After your
day out, allow yourself to be
tempted by coffee and cake or
supper at **Restaurant Remise im
Schloss Glienicke** (see p155). Your
best option for the return journey
is the S-Bahn from Wannsee.

See map on pp150–1

The Best of the Rest

1 Open Air Museum Domäne Dahlem

Königin-Luise-Str. 49 ▪ 10am–6pm Mon & Wed–Sun ▪ Adm ▪ www.domaene-dahlem.de

Learn about modern organic farming techniques at this historic working farm.

2 Grunewaldturm

Havelchaussee

This Neo-Gothic brick tower was built in 1897 as a memorial to Kaiser Wilhelm I.

Grunewaldturm

3 Onkel-Tom-Siedlung

Argentinische Allee

The "Uncle Tom's Hut" settlement, developed in 1926–32 according to designs by Bruno Taut and others, was intended to create a modern housing estate for workers, unlike the narrow and dark old tenement blocks they lived in.

4 Free University

Habelschwerdter Allee 45 ▪ Library: 9am–10pm Mon–Fri (to 5pm Sat–Sun)

The campus of Berlin's largest university, founded in 1948 as a rival to the East-Berlin Humboldt University, covers large parts of Dahlem. It is worth looking at the 1950s Henry-Ford-Bau and the Philological Library, designed by Lord Norman Foster.

5 Teufelsberg

Both the hill and the dark green Teufelssee lake are popular destinations for flying kites and biking. Swimming and sunbathing at the lake is mainly nude.

6 Heinrich von Kleist's Tomb

Bismarckstr. 3, Am Kleinen Wannsee

German playwright Kleist and his companion Henriette Vogel committed suicide by shooting themselves in 1811; they are buried here together (near the S-Bahn overpass).

7 St-Peter-und-Paul-Kirche

Nikolskoer Weg 17 ▪ (030) 805 21 00 ▪ 11am–4pm daily

This charming stone church, built in 1834–7 by Stüler, resembles Russian-Orthodox churches and is used for marriage ceremonies.

8 Blockhaus Nikolskoe

Nikolskoer Weg 15 ▪ (030) 805 29 14 ▪ 10:30am–6pm daily (to 10pm summer)

This wooden, Russian-style *dacha*, built in 1819, was a gift from King Friedrich Wilhelm III to his daughter Charlotte and his son-in-law, the future Tsar Nicholas I. The house is now a restaurant.

9 St-Annen-Kirche

Königin-Luise-Str./Pacelliallee

This 14th-century Gothic church has attractive murals depicting scenes from the life of St Anna, as well as late Gothic figures of saints and a Baroque pulpit.

10 Liebermann-Villa

Colomierstr. 3 ▪ Summer: 10am–6pm Wed–Mon (to 7pm Thu & Sun); winter: 11am–5pm Wed–Mon

The home of Berlin painter Max Liebermann, on the Wannsee shore, is now a museum of his art.

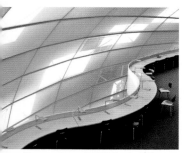

Norman Foster's Philological Library

Restaurants

PRICE CATEGORIES
For a three-course meal for one with half a bottle of wine (or equivalent meal), taxes and charges included.

€ under €30 €€ €30–60 €€€ over €60

The splendid Forsthaus Paulsborn

1 Forsthaus Paulsborn
Hüttenweg 90 ▪ (030) 818 19 10 ▪ Summer: 11am–11pm Tue–Sun; winter: noon–7pm Tue–Sun (to 9pm Fri & Sat) ▪ €€€
This pastoral restaurant next to Jagdschloss Grunewald is based in an old hunting lodge *(see p176)*.

2 Haus Sanssouci
Am Großen Wannsee 60 ▪ (030) 805 30 34 ▪ 11:30am–11pm Tue–Sun ▪ €€–€€€
Offering great Wannsee views, this idyllic cottage-style restaurant offers up mostly German food, but it has lobster nights and other specials too.

3 Wirtshaus Schildhorn
Havelchaussee/Straße am Schildhorn 4A ▪ (030) 30 88 35 00 ▪ Summer: noon–midnight daily; winter: noon–10pm Sat–Sun ▪ €€
In summer enjoy your *bratwurst* outside, in this picturesque spot on the Havel riverside.

4 Blockhaus Nikolskoe
Nikolskoer Weg 15 ▪ (030) 805 29 14 ▪ from 10:30am daily ▪ no credit cards ▪ €€
Traditional German fare in a historic log cabin, built as a Russian *dacha*.

5 Alter Krug Dahlem
Königin-Luise-Str. 52 ▪ 10am–midnight daily ▪ (030) 832 70 00 ▪ no credit cards ▪ €€
Relax in this large beer garden that boasts porch swings and a barbecue.

6 Luise
Königin-Luise-Str. 40 ▪ (030) 84 18 88 0 ▪ 10am–1am daily ▪ €€
One of Berlin's nicest beer gardens, on the Free University campus, Luise's is always crowded and always has a good atmosphere. Try the delicious salads and sandwiches.

7 Wirtshaus zur Pfaueninsel
Pfaueninselchaussee 100 ▪ (030) 805 22 25 ▪ Summer: 10am–8pm daily; winter: 10am–6pm Wed–Mon ▪ €€
A small venue serving rustic German food in the open air. An ideal place for a break before a Pfaueninsel visit.

8 Grunewaldturm-Restaurant
Havelchaussee 61 ▪ (030) 41 72 00 01 ▪ 10am–7pm daily ▪ €€
This restaurant is a great place to relax after a long hike and enjoy the views of Wannsee.

9 Restaurant Remise im Schloss Glienicke
Königstr. 36 ▪ (030) 805 40 00 ▪ Mar–Jan: 11am–late daily ▪ €€€
Sophisticated surroundings and cuisine. Fish dishes and salads in summer, game and roasts in winter.

10 Chalet Suisse
Clayallee 99 ▪ (030) 832 63 62 ▪ noon–midnight daily ▪ €€€
A cosy atmosphere and Swiss hospitality are the order of the day. Local and exquisite Swiss cooking features strongly on the menu.

See map on pp150–1

🔟 Potsdam and Sanssouci

Marmorpalais

Potsdam is an important part of European cultural history – a splendid centre of the Enlightenment, which reached its climax in the 18th century in the architectural and artistic design of Frederick the Great's palace of Sanssouci. The palace complex, with its beautiful, extensive park, is both magnificent and playful. It has been designated a World Heritage Centre of Culture by UNESCO and enchants millions of visitors every year. The town of Potsdam, numbering some 300,000 inhabitants, is the capital of the federal province of Brandenburg. This former garrison town has much to delight visitors, including small palaces and old churches, idyllic parks and historic immigrant settlements.

POTSDAM AND SANSSOUCI

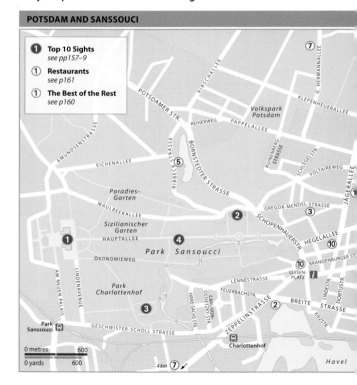

1 Top 10 Sights
see pp157–9

1 Restaurants
see p161

1 The Best of the Rest
see p160

① Neues Palais

Am Neuen Palais ▪ (0331) 969 42 00 ▪ 10am–6pm Wed–Mon (Nov–Mar: to 5pm) ▪ The visitor centre is at the south gate; audio guide available ▪ Admission charge ▪ www.spsg.de

One of Germany's most beautiful palaces, the Baroque Neues Palais was built in 1763–9 for Frederick the Great by Johann Gottfried Büring, Jean Laurent Le Geay and Carl von Gontard. The vast structure has 200 rooms, including the Marmorsaal (marble hall), a lavishly furnished ballroom, and the Schlosstheater, where plays are once more performed today. Frederick's private chambers are equally splendid, especially his Rococo study, the upper gallery with valuable parquet flooring and the Oberes Vestibül, a room clad entirely in marble.

The beautiful Baroque Neues Palais

② Schloss Sanssouci

Maulbeerallee ▪ (0331) 969 42 00 ▪ Apr–Oct: 10am–6pm Tue–Sun; Nov–Mar: 10am–5pm Tue–Sun; guided tour obligatory ▪ Admission charge ▪ www.spsg.de

Frederick the Great wished to live "sans souci" ("without worries") in a palace outside the city. In 1745, he commissioned his favourite architect Georg Wenzeslaus von Knobelsdorff to construct this magnificent Rococo palace according to his own designs. The structure rises proudly above the former terraced vineyards, leading up to the domed building and its marble hall at the centre of the complex. In both its design and shape, the hall pays homage to Rome's Pantheon. To its left and right are attractive rooms designed by von Knobelsdorff and Johann August Nahl; these include the famous concert room and the king's library. In this wing, the monarch liked to play the flute or to philosophize with Voltaire. Works by the king's favourite painter, Antoine Watteau, adorn the palace walls.

③ Schloss Charlottenhof

Geschwister-Scholl-Str. 34a ▪ (0331) 969 42 28 ▪ May–Oct: 10am–6pm Tue–Sun ▪ www.spsg.de

A small Neo-Classical palace in Park Sanssouci, built in 1829 by Schinkel for the heir to the throne, Friedrich Wilhelm IV. Particularly worth seeing is the tent-like Humboldtsaal.

④ Schlosspark Sanssouci

Chinesisches Haus: Am Grünen Gitter ▪ (0331) 969 42 25 ▪ May–Oct: 10am–6pm Tue–Sun ▪ Römische Bäder: Lennéstr. ▪ (0331) 969 42 25 ▪ May–Oct: 10am–6pm Tue–Sun ▪ Orangerie: An der Orangerie 3–5 ▪ (0331) 969 42 22 ▪ Apr: 10am– 6pm Sat–Sun; May–Oct: 10am–6pm Tue–Sun ▪ www.spsg.de

It is easy to spend a day in the park, which covers 287 ha (709 acres). Among the many charming buildings hidden in the landscaped garden is the Rococo-style Chinesisches Haus, built in 1754–6 by Johann Gottfried Büring. It originally served as a teahouse and dining room, and now houses an exhibition of East Asian porcelain. The Römische Bäder (Roman Baths) are lakeside pavilions modelled on an Italian Renaissance villa. They were built as bath- and guesthouses between 1829 and 1840 by Schinkel. The Orangerie, built in 1851–60 by Stüler, was also originally intended for the king's guests. Today it houses a small gallery of paintings.

⑤ Schloss Cecilienhof

Im Neuen Garten ▪ (0331) 969 42 00 ▪ Apr–Oct: 10am–6pm Tue–Sun; Nov–Mar: 10am–5pm Tue–Sun ▪ www.spsg.de

The 1945 Potsdam Conference was held in this little palace, built in 1914–17 in the style of an English country house. It is a UNESCO World Heritage Site and is now used as a hotel. It also houses a small exhibition documenting the Conference and the palace's furnishings.

⑥ Marmorpalais

Heiliger See (Neuer Garten) ▪ (0331) 969 45 50 ▪ May–Oct: 10am– 6pm Tue–Sun; Nov–Apr: 10am–4pm Sat–Sun ▪ www.spsg.de

This small, early Neo-Classical palace by the Heiliger See was built in 1791–7 by Carl Gotthard Langhans and others. It features an elegant concert hall as well as contemporary furniture and porcelain.

House in the Holländisches Viertel

⑦ Holländisches Viertel

Friedrich-Ebert-, Kurfürsten-, Hebbel-, Gutenbergstr.

A pleasant way to explore Potsdam is a walk through the historic Old Town, with its art galleries, cafés and restaurants. Built between 1733 and 1742, the area originally served as a settlement for Dutch workers after

THE POTSDAM CONFERENCE

In July and August 1945, the heads of the governments of the United States (Harry Truman), the USSR (Joseph Stalin) and Great Britain (Winston Churchill) met in Schloss Cecilienhof in order to seal the future of Germany through a treaty. Vitally important points such as the level of reparations to be paid by Germany, the demilitarization of the country, its new borders, and the punishment of war criminals, and the resettlement of Germans from Poland were decided here.

whom it is now named. The small red-brick buildings are decorated with attractive stucco ornaments.

8 Marstall (Filmmuseum)
Breite Str. 1a ■ (0331) 27 18 10 ■ 10am–6pm Tue–Sun ■ www. filmmuseum-potsdam.de

This small museum in the Baroque former stable buildings of the king's town residence uses old cameras, props and projectors to document the history of German film.

9 Filmpark Babelsberg
The Filmpark offers visitors a tour of the legendary UFA-Studios, which were among the world's most prestigious when they operated here in Babelsberg from 1917 to 1945. Exciting U-boat trips and thrilling stunt performances and special effects are shown (see p65).

10 Nikolaikirche
Am Alten Markt ■ (0331) 270 86 02 ■ 9am–6pm Mon–Sat, 11:30am–5pm Sun

Potsdam's most attractive church was designed by Schinkel in 1830 in an early Neo-Classical style. Its giant dome is particularly striking, and you can ascend it for a breathtaking view over the Stadtschloss, the city palace that is now home to the parliament of Brandenburg.

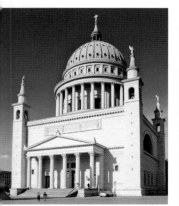

The Neo-Classical Nikolaikirche

A DAY IN POTSDAM

▶ MORNING

Begin your exploration in the **Schlosspark Sanssouci** as early as possible in order to get ahead of the daily influx of visitors. Start with **Schloss Sanssouci** (see p157) and **Neues Palais** (see p157) then visit the Chinesisches Haus, Römische Bäder and Orangerie. From the orangery's viewing terrace you will have magnificent views over the entire palace complex. If you are up for it, you could also climb up to **Schloss Belvedere** on top of the hill. From Schlosspark walk along Voltaireweg to Neuer Garten in the northeast of Potsdam, where you can recover over a tasty lunch at **Schloss Cecilienhof** (see p161).

AFTERNOON

Start the afternoon looking around **Schloss Cecilienhof** and stroll through Neuer Garten. Stop for a break at Heiliger See, then head to the centre of Potsdam, starting with the **Holländisches Viertel** (Dutch quarter) where you could pop into one of the numerous cafés. Stroll past the **St Peter-und-Paul Kirche** (see p160), the **Französische Kirche** (see p160), the **Nikolaikirche** and the **Altes Rathaus** (see p160) to the **Marstall** film museum. If you have the time, extend your tour by driving to nearby Babelsberg. You could either visit the **Filmpark**, admire **Schloss Babelsberg** (see p160) or walk up **Telegrafenberg** (see p160). To round off your day, a delicious evening meal awaits you at **Pino** (see p161) in Potsdam.

See map on pp156–7

The Best of the Rest

① Alexandrowka
Russische Kolonie/ Puschkinallee

The Russian colony feels like a village in Tsarist Russia. Decorated log cabins with picturesque gardens were built here in 1826 for a Russian military choir. Don't miss the museum and the Alexander Newski church.

② Dampfmaschinen- haus Sanssouci
Breite Str. 28 ▪ (0331) 969 42 25 ▪ May–Oct: 10am–6pm daily ▪ www.spsg.de

This building, resembling a mosque with minarets, is the water pumping station for Sanssouci. The 1842 pump can be seen inside.

③ Telegrafenberg
Albert-Einstein-Str. ▪ Einsteinturm tours Oct–Mar: (0331) 29 17 41 ▪ Admission charge

The elegant Einstein tower on top of Telegraph Hill was designed by Erich Mendelssohn in 1920 to see the sun.

④ Schloss Babelsberg
Park Babelsberg ▪ Closed for renovation until 2015 ▪ www.spsg.de

Built by Schinkel in 1833–5, this Neo-Gothic palace sits in an idyllic park on the banks of the Havel River.

The Neo-Gothic Schloss Babelsberg

⑤ Potsdamer Stadtschloss
Neuer Markt

The Hohenzollern palace that was once the residence of Frederick the Great was badly bombed in World War II and had to be demolished in 1960. It has since been rebuilt as a cultural centre and the seat of the Potsdam legislative assembly.

⑥ Altes Rathaus
Am Alten Markt

The old town hall, built in 1753, is decorated with sculptures and Potsdam's coat of arms – two gilded Atlas figures, each carrying a globe on its back.

Altes Rathaus

⑦ Biosphäre
Georg-Hermann-Allee 99 ▪ (0331) 55 07 40 ▪ 9am–6pm Mon– Fri, 10am–6pm Sat–Sun ▪ Adm ▪ www.biosphaere-potsdam.de

This indoor tropical botanical garden provides visitors with an authentic rainforest experience, complete with waterfalls, iguanas and butterflies.

⑧ Französische Kirche
Am Bassinplatz ▪ (0331) 29 12 19 ▪ late Mar–mid-Oct: 1:30–5pm Tue–Sun

In 1752, Johann Boumann built this elliptical Huguenot church with its columned portico; Schinkel designed the beautiful interior in the 1830s.

⑨ St-Peter-und-Paul- Kirche
Am Bassinplatz ▪ (0331) 230 79 90 ▪ 10am–6pm daily (winter: to 5pm)

The Catholic church of saints Peter and Paul, modelled on Haghia Sophia in Istanbul, was built in 1867– 70 by Stüler.

⑩ Brandenburger Tor
Luisenplatz

The most attractive of five former town gates was built by Gontard and Unger in 1770 to celebrate Prussian victory in the Seven Years' War.

Restaurants

PRICE CATEGORIES
For a three-course meal for one with half
a bottle of wine (or equivalent meal),
taxes and charges included.
....
€ under €30   €€ €30–60   €€€ over €60

1 Speckers Landhaus
Jägerallee 13 ▪ (0331) 280 43
11 ▪ noon–2pm, 6–11pm Tue–Sat ▪
€€

The combination of a Prussian
interior, friendly service and light
cuisine make Speckers Landhaus
one of Potsdam's best restaurants.

2 Schloss Cecilienhof
Neuer Garten ▪ (0331) 370 52
33 ▪ noon–11pm daily ▪ €€
The palace is now a luxury hotel. Its
restaurant serves solid German food.

3 Pino
Weinbergstr. 7 ▪ (0331) 270 30
30 ▪ 6pm–midnight Mon–Sat ▪ €€
Close to Park Sanssouci, Pino serves
a daily changing menu of exquisite
Sicilian fare. The wine list reads like
a Who's Who of Italian vintages.

4 Restaurant Juliette
Jägerstr. 39 ▪ (0331) 270 17 91
▪ noon–3:30pm, 6pm–midnight
Wed–Mon ▪ Closed Jul ▪ €€
A former manor house is the setting
for this French restaurant, one of the
most charming in Potsdam. It serves
top-quality French classics.

5 Brauhaus
Ribbeckstr. 6–7 ▪ (0331) 550 65
48 ▪ 11am–10pm daily ▪ €
This rustic restaurant, set in the
brewery of a historic country manor,
Krongut Bornstedt, serves hearty
meals with local fish, game,
sausages and home-brewed beers.

6 Maison Charlotte
Mittelstr. 20 ▪ (0331) 280 54 50
▪ noon–11pm daily ▪ €€
An olde-worlde wine bar in a red-
brick Dutch house with outdoor

seating in a pleasant courtyard,
Maison Charlotte serves French
country fare and fine wines.

7 Friedrich Wilhelm
Im Wildpark 1 ▪ (0331) 550 50
▪ 6pm–late Tue–Sat ▪ €€€
This Michelin-starred restaurant in
Hotel Bayrisches Haus (see p176)
is probably Potsdam's best. Light
German dishes are exquisitely pre-
pared and presented by Alexander
Dressel. In summer, eat on a terrace
overlooking a wildflower meadow.

8 Waage
Am Neuen Markt 12 ▪ noon–
midnight Tue–Sun ▪ €€
Attractive historic restaurant in
central Potsdam. Regional meat and
fish dishes in unusual variations are
particularly worth trying.

Café Heider's vintage car shuttle

9 Café Heider
Friedrich-Ebert-Str. 29 ▪ (0331)
270 55 96 ▪ 8am–1am Mon–Fri,
9am–1am Sat, 10am–1am Sun ▪ €
This lovely café in the middle of
Potsdam's Old Town offers a
fantastic breakfast, which you can
enjoy outside on the terrace in
summer. A vintage Ford can be hired.

10 La Madeleine
Lindenstr. 9 ▪ (0331) 270 54 00
▪ noon–midnight daily ▪ no credit
cards ▪ €
A little bistro serving all sorts of
crêpes, such as sweet with jam or
savoury with ham – the ideal spot
for a quick snack.

See map on pp156–7

Streetsmart

Interior of Berlin Hauptbahnhof

Getting To and Around Berlin

Arriving by Air

Berlin is served by two international airports, Tegel and Schönefeld. A new regional hub, Berlin-Brandenburg Airport (BER, or Willy-Brandt-Flughafen), is planned to open in late 2017 to replace them.

Tegel Airport (TXL), located about 8 km (5 miles) northeast of the city centre, has excellent public transport links into town. Buses 109 and 128, and the express buses X9 and TXL (both of which stop right outside the terminal) connect to convenient S- and U-Bahn stops, and to the Berlin Hauptbahnhof (Berlin Central) and Zoologischer Garten stations, taking about 20 minutes.

Schönefeld Airport (SXF) is about 18 km (11 miles) southeast of the centre. The fastest way to get there and away is the S-Bahn commuter train or Deutsche Bahn's RB14 and RE7 Airport Express trains, which whisk you to Berlin Hauptbahnhof in around 30 minutes. City buses link the airport to the U-Bahn network.

Arriving by Rail

The city's gleaming new main station, **Berlin Hauptbahnhof**, is centrally located and close to the government district. All long-distance trains arrive and depart from here. Other key stations include Gesundbrunnen on the northern side of town, Zoologischer Garten in the west, Ostbahnhof in the east and Südkreuz in the south. The stations connect seamlessly to the S- and U-Bahn and city bus networks.

The national railway, **Deutsche Bahn (DB)**, often gives steep online discounts on regular fares. Buy train tickets in advance, as onboard fares are more expensive. DB's high-speed ICE trains link Berlin to Hamburg (2.5 hrs), Munich (6.5 hrs) and Frankfurt (4.25 hrs). Private rail **Harz-Elbe Express (HEX)** has cheap fares for journeys to Magdeburg and Harz Mountains ski resorts.

Arriving by Road

The central coach station, **Zentraler Omnibus-bahnhof (ZOB)**, is located near Charlottenburg's Funkturm (see p122) and offers good-value links from all major German and European cities. The ZOB website lists daily departures and arrivals as well as coach lines, which include **Eurolines**, **FlixBus** and **Berlinienbus**. Seats fill up fast during the summer and holiday seasons, so book early.

When driving to Berlin, you will arrive via the Berliner Stadtring, the orbital motorway around the city. From the south you come in on the A115 – the famous Avus Autobahn. From the north you arrive on the A111 via Stolpe in the direction of Autobahndreieck Funkturm. The speed limit on the Stadtring is generally 100 kmh (62.5 mph), and on urban motorways 80–100 kmh (50–62.5 mph). Drivers should be aware there are frequent radar checks.

Travelling by Underground

The transport network is run by the **Berliner Verkehrsgesellschaft (BVG)** and Deutsche Bahn. BVG tickets are transferable between all modes of public transport in Berlin.

The Berlin U-Bahn, or underground railway, has one of Europe's largest networks and provides a fast, convenient means of getting around the city. There are 10 U-Bahn lines, each identifiable by number and colour. The U-Bahn runs from 5am to 1am; at weekends most lines run throughout the night. The station indicated on the platform is the train's final destination.

The Stadtbahn or S-Bahn (city commuter railway) has 15 lines connecting the centre with the suburbs. They run every 5 to 20 minutes. Many lines share tracks so you need to pay attention to indicator boards.

By Bus and Tram

Buses and trams are also operated by BVG. Berlin has a dense bus network. All lines have three-digit numbers except for express services, which are preceded by "X". Buses and trams marked "M" go to areas that have no direct S- or U-Bahn links. Board via the front door (unless you have a buggy, in which case the back door will be opened) and present your ticket or fare money to the driver. Trams operate only in the eastern part of the city.

Tickets

Berlin is divided into three fare zones: A, B and C. Most destinations are covered by an AB ticket, available from BVG ticket machines. For most visitors, the best value is an AB day ticket at €6.90, valid until 3am the following day. A single AB journey costs €2.70 and is valid for two hours in one direction. A *Kurzstrecke* (short distance ticket) is valid for up to three S- or U-Bahn stations or six bus stops, and costs €1.60. Children under 14 years pay a reduced rate; those under six travel free.

Tickets for buses and S- and U-Bahn trains are available at stations and from bus drivers. Trams and some buses have onboard ticket machines. At the station, you must validate your ticket in the red machine before boarding; on the bus, find the yellow validation machine after you board.

By Taxi

There are taxi stands all over Berlin, and you can also hail a taxi in the street. Taxis from companies such as **Würfelfunk**, **City Funk**, **Taxi Berlin** and **Talixo** can also be booked on the phone or online. The starting price is €3.40, and a further €1.30–1.79 is charged per kilometre (0.6 mile). If you hail a taxi, you can travel up to 2 km (1 mile) for €4

but you must ask at the start for the *Kurzstrecke* (short distance tariff).

The **Velotaxi** (bicycle rickshaws) is an unusual way to explore the city. These can be found in the city centre at several popular visitor locations from April to October.

By Car

All of Berlin inside the S-Bahn ring is a green zone, which means that only vehicles bearing a special environmental badge are allowed in. Order these in advance through **Green Zones**, which processes 24-hour rush orders for an extra fee. Drivers without this badge face a €40 fine.

To hire a car you'll need a valid full driving licence, passport and credit card; some agencies will only accept customers over 21 years. There are rental agencies at the airports and across central Berlin. Search websites such as **billiger-mietwagen.de** help find the best deals.

By Bicycle

Berlin is bicycle-friendly, with an extensive network of cycle lanes, although most run directly along the street. The red-and-silver bikes of DB's **Call a Bike** scheme are found across the city. You have to pre-register and provide credit card details. The website is only in German, but the phone hotline usually has someone who can speak English. There are bike hire places all over town, and hotels and hostels often rent cycles to their guests for €5–10 per day.

Practical Information

Passports and Visas

Visitors from outside the European Economic Area (EEA), European Union (EU) and Switzerland need a valid passport to enter Germany. EEA, EU and Swiss nationals can use their national identity cards instead. Citizens of Canada, the US, Australia and New Zealand can visit Germany for up to 90 days without a visa as long as their passport is valid for 6 months beyond the date of entry. For longer stays, a visa is necessary and needs to be obtained in advance from the German embassy. Most other non-EU nationals need a visa, and should consult the German **Federal Foreign Office** website or their German embassy for details. Schengen visas are valid for Germany.

Customs and Immigration

For EU citizens there are no limits on most goods carried in or out of Germany as long as they are for personal use only. Exceptions include firearms and weapons, some types of food and plants and endangered species. Non-EU citizens may import 200 cigarettes and a litre of spirits per adult, and can claim back VAT on EU purchases over €25 – do this at the airport when leaving the EU.

Travel Insurance

All travellers are advised to buy insurance against accidents, illness, theft or loss and travel delays or cancellations. Germany has a reciprocal health agreement with other EU countries, and EU citizens receive emergency treatment under the public healthcare system if they have with them a valid European Health Insurance Card (EHIC). Prescriptions have to be paid for upfront. Non-EU visitors should check if their country has reciprocal arrangements with Germany.

Emergency Services

The police and fire brigade can be reached on dedicated hotlines, as can emergency dentists. There are also hotlines for narcotics- and poison-related emergencies.

Health

Germany has one of the best health services in the world, and Berlin is no exception. Ambulances arrive swiftly when called. Those able to reach a hospital themselves should use the entrance marked *Notaufnahme* (Accident and Emergency). Less serious cases can be dealt with in one of the many private walk-in clinics.

Charité Krankenhaus, Berlin's main central hospital, has a 24-hour emergency room. The US and UK embassies can provide a list of English-speaking physicians.

No vaccinations are required to enter the country, but flu jabs and routine vaccines should be kept up to date.

Apotheken (chemists or pharmacies) are signalled by a red "A" sign. Staff can offer advice for medical treatment. After 8pm, the address of the nearest all-night pharmacy is posted on the door of each outlet; alternatively, you can call the **Ärztlicher Bereitschaftsdienst der KV Berlin** to help locate the nearest doctors and open pharmacies. Those covered by private health insurance can also contact **Doctors on Call**.

Visitors who suspect they may have caught a sexually transmitted disease (STD) can have a "quick test" done at **Berliner AIDS-Hilfe**. Results are delivered in half an hour. Emergency contraception is available on prescription.

Personal Security

Care should be taken in crowded trains, stations and tourist areas where pickpockets tend to operate. At night, the following are best avoided: U-Bahn line U9 north of the Zoo; the areas of Lichtenberg, Marzahn and Wedding; behind the Kaiser-Wilhelm-Gedächtnis-Kirche; and Görlitzer Park in Kreuzberg. Black or openly homosexual visitors are advised not to take the S-Bahn at night east of Alexanderplatz, or into the surrounding region of Brandenburg.

Lost Property

The **Zentrales Fundbüro** (central lost property office) keeps anything that has been lost and found anywhere in Berlin. If you have left an item on public transport, enquire at the **Fundbüro der BVG**. Items lost on the S-Bahn or the national railways are sent to the **Fundbüro der Deutschen Bahn**.

Women Travellers

Berlin is quite safe for women on their own, but avoid parks and dark, quiet streets at night. On trains or buses late at night, take a seat near the driver's compartment.

Disabled Travellers

Visitors with mobility issues will find Berlin is reasonably well-equipped

for their needs. Nearly all streets and pavements are sloped at junctions for wheelchair users. Most public buildings, shopping malls and cinemas are fitted with lifts, ramps and extra-wide doors. The **German Red Cross** (DRK) rents out wheelchairs at a nominal daily cost.

S- and U-Bahn trains are wheelchair accessible, but not all stations are equipped with lifts. In the U-Bahn, wait at the head of the platform, and the driver will put up a ramp. In the S-Bahn, speak to the station manager to have a ramp set up. BVG network maps show all accessible stations.

All buses displaying a wheelchair symbol are

equipped for disabled access; most buses in the centre have one door with a ramp that can be lowered down.

Look out for silver *City Toiletten* public conveniences in central Berlin. Over 160 of them are fully accessible.

Disabled visitors who wish to drive around Berlin and Brandenburg, or share a car with driver with other disabled visitors, can contact specialist travel agents **BBV Tours** or **Micky Tours**.

Berlin's charitable association for the blind and sight-impaired, the **Allgemeiner Blinden- und Sehbehindertenverein**, offers practical advice on suitable facilities.

Currency and Banking

Germany is one of the 19 European countries using the euro (€), which is divided into 100 cents. Paper notes are in denominations of €5, €10, €20, €50, €100, €200 and €500. Coins are €2, €1, 50c, 20c, 10c, 5c, 2c, 1c.

All large German banks have city centre branches. Cash machines or ATMs (*Geldautomaten*) are dotted throughout the city. A fee list should be posted next to the screen; if you withdraw cash from a bank not affiliated with your home institution, expect to pay a handling fee. Stiff fees are charged by "independent" ATMs for withdrawals. Inquire about credit card ATM cash withdrawal fees (which can be high) before departure. German banks charge up to 2% per credit card withdrawal.

Mastercard and **VISA** credit and debit cards are taken by many cafés, restaurants and shops but not all, so it is a wise to carry some cash. **Diners Club** and **American Express** are less common.

Should your card be lost/stolen, it is essential you inform your bank immediately. Germany has a free 24-hour national **Lost Card Hotline** which will direct you to your bank.

Pre-paid currency cards (cash passports) are a more secure way of carrying money. They can be preloaded with euros, fixing exchange rates before you leave, and used like a debit card.

You'll be able to buy euros at *Wechselstuben* (banks and bureaux de change); many are based around train stations. Hotels will also change money but may charge higher fees.

Travellers' cheques can be exchanged at all larger banks or at branches of the issuers. Most banks charge a fee.

Internet and Telephone

While connection speeds can lag behind those in some other European countries, Germans are more wired than ever. Berlin has over 400 wireless Internet hotspots – many free – in bars, cafés, department stores, hotels and public places such as the Sony Center. Deutsche Bahn gives you up to 30 minutes of free surf time per day at over 100 stations across the country. Kabel Deutschland, an internet services company, does the same thing at 75 outdoor Wi-Fi hotspots across town.

To use your mobile device in Germany, it will need to be equipped for GSM network frequencies 900 and 1800 MHz. It is advisable to sign up for an international usage plan to keep costs down. Europe-based companies such as Ortel also offer prepaid plans at competitive rates. Upon arrival consider buying a local SIM card or cheap mobile phone with a German number so you can take advantage of local rates. If needed, ask your home carrier for the unlock code to use a different SIM card/service.

There are public phones (both enclosed booths and open handsets) in the town centre, though they are slowly vanishing. Most are card-operated, but a few will take coins. Phone cards can be bought from post offices, department stores and kiosks.

Postal Services

German mail is efficient, reliable and fast. Offices of Deutsche Post, the national mail service, usually open 8am–6pm (till noon on Saturday), with some variation for smaller outlets. Offices in train stations and airports open on Sunday as well. Buy stamps from the post office counter or vending machines (often outside the entrance). A standard letter weighing up to 20g or a postcard to anywhere outside Germany costs €0.75. For non-standard postcards and letters bigger than 235 x 125mm (9.25 x 4.9 in) the recipient incurs a charge.

Public postboxes in Berlin generally have two slots: *Postleitzahlen* (postal codes) 10000–169999 for addresses in Brandenburg and Berlin, and *Andere Postleitzahlen* (other postal codes) for destinations elsewhere in Germany and abroad.

Television and Radio

Public television is built on two national networks, ARD and ZDF. Private channels such as RTL and SAT 1 have stolen a big chunk of their audience. The most authoritative news broadcasts are ARD's *Tagesschau* at 8pm and the 10:30pm ZDF evening news *Heute*. Thanks to satellite and cable you can tune into global English channels including CNN and BBC World. The most popular radio station is RBB's **Radio Eins** (livestream and 95.8 MHz), with pop, news, and chat shows.

Newspapers and Magazines

Serious newspapers include the *Tagesspiegel*, *Berliner Morgenpost* and *Berliner Zeitung*, the only major East Berlin paper to survive reunification. The tabloid *BZ*, with the greatest circulation, is similar to the US *National Enquirer* or Britain's *Sun*. Another saucy broadsheet is the *Berliner Kurier*. The heavyweight nationals include the *Frankfurter Allgemeine Zeitung* and *Süddeutsche Zeitung*. The country's best-established weekly magazine is *Der Spiegel*, which has an English online edition.

Free event guides such as *030* are available in restaurants and cafés. For entertainment listings, try the twice-monthly magazines *Tip*, *Zitty* or *Prinz*; their online listings are updated more frequently. The *ExBerliner* magazine carries useful articles on Berlin life and culture, as does *The Local* online, both in English.

Opening Hours

By law, Berlin retailers may conduct business 24 hours a day from Monday to Saturday. Few do so, however. On weekdays, small retailers generally open at 9am or 10am and shut by 7pm, while department stores close at 10pm. Large supermarkets open 8am–10pm. Most shutters go down at 4pm on Saturdays. Shops in large train stations and service stations and convenience stores (*Spätkauf*) stay open until at least midnight, and are also open on Sundays.

Banks in the city centre work 9am–4pm Monday–Wednesday, till 6pm on Thursday, and till 2pm on Friday. Small branches may take a hour's lunch break around 12:30pm. Larger post offices work 8am–6pm Monday–Friday, and till at least noon on Saturday. Pharmacies open 9am–7pm Monday–Friday, and until 4pm on Saturday. Public museums generally open 10am–6pm; many close on Monday, but stay open late on Thursday.

Time Difference

Germany is on Central European Time (CET), an hour ahead of Greenwich Mean Time, 6 hours ahead of US Eastern Standard Time and 11 hours behind Australian Eastern Standard Time. The clock moves forward 1 hour during daylight saving time from the last Sunday in March until the last Sunday in October.

Electrical Appliances

The electric current is 220 volts. Many electrical appliances such as hair dryers have 110/220V transformers built in, so converters may be less of a concern, especially if you're coming from North America. Bring an adaptor with two round pins. Some hotel bathrooms provide a lower current as a safety measure.

Driving Licences

Germany recognizes UK, Australian, Canadian and US licences *(see p165)*.

Weather

The weather in Berlin is better than its reputation. The continental climate guarantees mild and dry weather from May to September. In spring and autumn it can be cold and wet, and from November to February it is often cloudy, with a biting cold, easterly wind whistling through the city.

DIRECTORY

CURRENCY AND BANKING

American Express
☎ (069) 979 70

Diners Club
☎ (041) 587 508 008

Lost Card Hotline
☎ 116 116

Mastercard
☎ (0800) 819 10 40

VISA
☎ (0800) 811 84 40

TELEVISION AND RADIO

Radio Eins
🖳 radioeins.de/livestream/

NEWSPAPERS AND MAGAZINES

Der Spiegel
🖳 spiegel.de/international/

ExBerliner
🖳 exberliner.com

Prinz
🖳 prinz.de

Tip
🖳 tip-berlin.de

The Local
🖳 thelocal.de

Zitty
🖳 zitty.de

Visitor Information

The municipal **Berlin Tourist Info** service has seven offices in the city. Here you can book tickets for events and sightseeing tours, buy the Museum Pass and WelcomeCard, and make reservations at hotels and hostels (for a €3 fee). The city-run websites **Berlin.de** and **VisitBerlin.de**, both available in English, provide useful information.

There is a wide variety of Berlin apps. Good ones in English include BVG Fahrinfo Plus (real-time public transport connections) and 360° Berlin (guided walks with panoramas), both on Android as well as iPhone, and WhatWasHere_Berlin (interactive historical city guide) for iPhone.

Some of the best English-language blogs exploring fashion, people, places, art and food are **Finding Berlin**, **I Heart Berlin** and **Stil in Berlin**.

Excursions and City Tours

The watery landscape of the **Spreewald**, southeast of Berlin, is a unique, UNESCO-protected area of natural beauty. You can explore by traditional punt the old settlements of the Slavic Sorb peoples in the tree-lined waterways of Lübben and Lübbenau.

Sachsenhausen, the site of Germany's first Nazi concentration camp, where 100,000 people were murdered between 1936–45, is a poignant, haunting experience.

Schloss Rheinsberg in the Mecklenburg lakes district makes a splendid day trip. The summer residence of the young Frederick the Great can be visited by guided tour.

Near Potsdam lies the hamlet of Sacrow with its dreamy Saviour's Church, on the lake of the same name. Not far away, picturesque Caputh boasts the charming Baroque **Schloss Caputh** and Einstein's summer home, the **Einsteinhaus** (open only by guided tour at weekends in summer).

Hop-on-hop-off tours on double-decker buses, some of which are open-top in summer, are run by **City Circle**, **BEX**, **Berolina**, **Top Tour** and **Berlin City Tour**. The buses stop at all the main sights, and you can board at any one.

The cheapest, fastest way to see the city is to take a ride on buses No. 100 or 200. These double-deckers go from Bahnhof Zoo and Alexanderplatz right into Prenzlauer Berg, passing all the key sights en route for the price of a single fare.

Berlin Walks runs daily themed English-language walks, leaving from the taxi rank outside the zoo and Hackescher Markt. **Berliner Unterwelten** leads walks through the city's spooky underbelly into bunkers and tunnels.

Fat Tire Bike Tours operates Segway and bike tours through Berlin.

Berlin's waterways – the Landwehrkanal, Havel and Spree Rivers, and the Wannsee and Müggelsee lakes – can all be toured by boat. **Reederei Riedel** and **Stern- und Kreis-Schifffahrt** take in historic sights between the centre and Charlottenburg over 2 to 3 hours.

Shopping

Kurfürstendamm (see p30–31), Tauentzienstraße and Friedrichstraße are Berlin's main three shopping streets. Galeries Lafayette, Department Store Quartier 206 and Ku'damm are at the upper end of the scale, but you'll also find inexpensive shops around Tauentzienstraße and Alexanderplatz.

A good mix of shops can be found in the huge malls at Potsdamer Platz and Leipziger Platz, the Alexa shopping centre at Alexanderplatz, Schlossstraße in the south and the Gesundbrunnencenter in the north.

The best fashion and designer stores, selling coveted labels such as Gucci, Versace, Jil Sander, DKNY or Prada, are on Friedrichstraße and the west side of Ku'damm. Kaufhaus des Westens (KaDeWe) sells a good range of fashions for men and women (see p76).

The best selection of CDs is at Kulturkaufhaus Dussmann (see p91). For gifts and souvenirs try KaDeWe and the souvenir shops on Unter den Linden near Pariser Platz, Potsdamer Platz and at Checkpoint Charlie.

Most antiques shops are clustered south of Nollendorfplatz (see p130) and in the smaller streets off Ku'damm. However, the antiques and flea market on the Straße des 17. Juni (see p76) and the antiques located in the S-Bahn arches between Friedrichstraße and the Museumsinsel often turn out to be much better value.

Dining

Berlin cuisine doesn't have a stellar reputation, but there is a huge range of well-priced restaurants and growing numbers of young, adventurous chefs. Old-style meaty, artery-clogging meals are giving way to inventive, lighter fare with global influences.

Popular dining strips include Kurfürstendamm, Kastanienallee (see p139); Oranienburger Straße in Mitte (see p95); Wühlisch Straße in Friedrichshain; Oranienstraße (see p130) and Schlesische Strasse, both in Kreuzberg; and Akazienstraße in Schöneberg. Berlin has more Michelin-starred restaurants than Munich or Hamburg, and this guide lists several two-star places: Fischers Fritz and Facil (see p71), Lorenz Adlon Esszimmer (see p117), Reinstoff (see p70) and Restaurant Tim Raue (see p135).

Where to Stay

Whatever your budget, finding a good, affordable place to stay generally isn't a problem. Surging tourism has produced a glut of beds in enticing surrounds, especially in eastern Berlin, where most of the main sights are located. There is a range of options from sleek luxury and boutique hotels to budget B&Bs and quirky stays in indoor camping trailers and former East German prison cells. Youth hostels are smartly equipped and attract guests of all ages. Kreuzberg has several Pensionen (guesthouses) and small hotels. Most of the business hotels are in west Berlin, particularly around the trade-fair grounds. Places outside the city centre can offer good value in green areas, and are often close to S- and U-Bahn lines. Sites such as **Berlin30.com**, **Airbnb**, **Trivago**, **HRS** and **Booking.com** are good places to look.

Rates are reasonable by European standards. It is not hard to find premium/middle/cheap double rooms in great locations for around €110/75/50. The average hotel room price is around €90. The former East German districts have cheaper options, with good deals to be found in parts of Prenzlauer Berg and in Mitte and Friedrichshain.

DIRECTORY

VISITOR INFORMATION

Berlin Tourist Info
🔳 visitberlin.de/en/plan/on-site/tourist-information

Berlin.de
🔳 berlin.de

Finding Berlin
🔳 findingberlin.com

I Heart Berlin
🔳 iheartberlin.de

Stil in Berlin
🔳 stilinberlin.de

VisitBerlin
🔳 visitberlin.de

EXCURSIONS AND CITY TOURS

Berlin City Tour
🔳 berlin-city-tour.de

Berliner Unterwelten
🔳 berliner-unterwelten.de

Berlin Walks
🔳 berlinwalks.com

Berolina Berlin
🔳 berolina-berlin.com

BEX
🔳 en.bex.de

City Circle
🔳 city-circle.de

Einsteinhaus
Am Waldrand 15-17
📞 (0331) 27 17 80
🔳 einsteinsommerhaus.de

Fat Tire Bike Tours
🔳 fattirebiketoursberlin.com

Gedenkstätte und Museum Sachsenhausen
MAP H3 ▪ Str. der Nationen 22
📞 (03301) 20 02 00
🔳 stiftung-bg.de/gums

Reederei Riedel
🔳 reederei-riedel.de

Schloss Caputh
Str. der Einheit 2
📞 (033209) 703 45
🔳 spsg.de

Schloss Rheinsberg
Mühlenstr. 1
📞 (033931) 72 6
🔳 spsg.de

Spreewald Tourism
Lindenstr. 1, Raddusch
📞 (035433) 722 99
🔳 spreewald.de

Stern- und Kreis-Schifffahrt
🔳 sternundkreis.de

Top Tour
🔳 top-tour-sightseeing.de

WHERE TO STAY

Airbnb
🔳 airbnb.com

Berlin30.com
🔳 berlin30.com

Booking.com
🔳 booking.com

HRS
🔳 hrs.de

Trivago
🔳 trivago.com

Places to Stay

PRICE CATEGORIES

For a standard double room per night (with breakfast if included), taxes and extra charges.

€ under €100   €€ €100–€200   €€€ over €200

Luxury Hotels

Grand Hotel Esplanade

MAP N6 ▪ Lützowufer 15 ▪ (030) 25 47 80 ▪ www.esplanade.de ▪ €€

Glitzy and modern, with furnishings somewhere between Bauhaus style and functional sobriety. Service at this Sheraton group hotel is excellent and its first-class facilities include a state-of-the-art spa and fitness centre, with a pool, massage area, gym, solarium and three saunas. Harry's New York Bar, sister to the historic Harry's in Paris, is one of central Berlin's most popular venues, serving up cocktails with unexpected ingredients such as rosemary, pepper and paprika.

Hotel Intercontinental Berlin

MAP N6 ▪ Budapester Str. 2 ▪ (030) 260 20 ▪ www.berlin.intercontinental.com ▪ €€

A luxury hotel in the Tiergarten, nicely situated with great views over the central park, this establishment is popular with business travellers.The building itself is not particularly attractive, but the rooms are furnished in a timelessly elegant style. Its two restaurants offer first-class food – the elegant, fine-dining Hugos (see p70) has a

Michelin star – and the Marlene Bar, the Cigar and Rum Lounge, and the pool and fitness area are also excellent.

Hotel Palace

MAP N5 ▪ Budapester Str. 45 ▪ (030) 250 20 ▪ www.palace.de ▪ €€

This expensively restored hotel on the second floor of the Europa-Center is a real find – all the rooms are exquisitely designed and two suites – Panda and Zackenbarsch – were styled by the director himself. It boasts a spa and fitness centre, and the Michelin-starred restaurant "first floor" (see p127), which boasts an award-winning wine list and where chef Matthias Diether serves modern, light European food such as pigeon with beetroot and caramelized nuts. Hotel staff are unobtrusive and very helpful.

Kempinski Hotel Bristol Berlin

MAP P4 ▪ Kurfürstendamm 27 ▪ (030) 88 43 40 ▪ www.kempinskiberlin.de ▪ €€

One of Berlin's most famous hotels, the Bristol has it all – a magnificent, cosmopolitan blend of elegance and modern amenities. Among them is a luxury spa, a 2-hour health check at a private partner clinic, and the Kempinski for Kids programme, which arranges

babysitting services and even child-sized robes and slippers. Its international reputation has attracted a host of famous guests, from Fidel Castro to Tina Turner.

SAS Radisson Blu

MAP K5 ▪ Karl-Liebknecht-Str. 3 ▪ (030) 23 82 80 ▪ www.radissonblu.com/hotel-berlin ▪ €€

Conveniently located on the banks of the Spree between Alexanderplatz and the Museumsinsel, this modern hotel is ideal for exploring city centre sights. The centrepiece of the hotel is the AquaDom, the world's largest freestanding cylindrical aquarium (see p65). A ticket to the adjacent Sea Life Berlin lets guests take a lift ride through the centre of the AquaDom. The hotel's bright rooms offer views of either the aquarium or the Berliner Dom. Its chic restaurant HEat (see p109) is a bastion of Asian fusion cuisine. In the warmer months, you can enjoy alfresco dining on the elegant terrace, watching the boats go by.

Sofitel Berlin Gendarmenmarkt

MAP L4 ▪ Charlottenstr. 50–52 ▪ (030) 20 37 50 ▪ www.sofitel.com ▪ €€

Relatively inexpensive and the smallest of the first-class hotels with just 70 rooms and 22 suites, the Sofitel is probably also one of the most attractive, with excellent views of the pretty Gendarmenmarkt. The classic Aigner (see p93) offers traditional Viennese cuisine.

Hotel de Rome

MAP K4 ■ Behrenstr. 37 ■ (030) 460 60 90 ■ www. hotelderome.com ■ €€€
Located off Bebelplatz near the State Opera, just steps away from Unter den Linden, Hotel de Rome is sited within the historic 19th-century Dresdner Bank building. After World War II, the GDR State Bank used the structure. The interior is now a vision of postmodern ideas, while the Italian restaurant, the Opera Court café (see p93) and the spa area live up to the expectations of a hotel geared towards the international jet-set crowd.

The Mandala Hotel Potsdamer Platz

MAP L2 ■ Potsdamer Str. 3 ■ (030) 590 050 000 ■ www.themandala.com ■ €€€
This apartment hotel, in a great spot at Potsdamer Platz, has suites of varying sizes between 35–200 sq m (375–2,153 sq ft), each equipped with a kitchenette, fitness area, sauna, stereo, daily newspapers and anything else you could possibly wish for. The Michelin-starred, light-filled restaurant Facil (see p71) is a peaceful haven from the hubbub of Potsdamer Platz.

Soho House

MAP H2 ■ Torstr. 1 ■ (030) 405 04 40 ■ www.soho houseberlin.com ■ €€€
This six-storey Bauhaus monument started life as a Jewish-owned department store before eventually housing the archives of the East German Communist Party. The heated rooftop pool, fancy art and a private cinema

seem at home alongside exposed cement walls. An excellent spot for celebrity sightings.

Westin Grand Hotel

MAP K4 ■ Friedrichstr. 158–164 ■ (030) 202 70 ■ www.westin-berlin.com ■ €€€
This Westin hotel offers luxury accommodation in a historic spot at the corner of Friedrichstraße and Unter den Linden, with large, elegant rooms and US-style service. The lobby and the grand stairs are breathtaking. There's also a café and a bar.

Designer Hotels

art'otel berlin-mitte

MAP L6 ■ Wallstr. 70–73 ■ (030) 24 06 20 ■ www. artotels.com ■ €€
This designer hotel emphasizes every detail and has styled everything, from the furniture to the soap in the bathroom. Blending architectural style with art-inspired interiors, each art'otel focuses on a contemporary artist. The historic building is decorated with paintings by the Neo-Expressionist postmodern artist Georg Baselitz. The hotel is centrally located, close to Nikolaiviertel.

Casa Camper

MAP J5 ■ Weinmeisterstr. 1 ■ (030) 20 00 34 10 ■ www.casacamper.com/ berlin ■ €€
This modern hotel near Hackescher Markt in the hip part of Mitte is beautifully appointed. It offers excellent service and free Wi-Fi and iPod docking stations in every room. The small spa and snacks and breakfast in the 24-7

rooftop bar are included in the price. Rooms on the upper floors have great views over the city.

Dormero Hotel Berlin Ku'damm

MAP P4 ■ Eislebener Str. 14 ■ (030) 21 40 50 ■ www.dormero.de ■ €€
With a design that strikes a balance between classical and modern, this boutique hotel mimics the city itself. Set in a historic building, the Dormero Hotel Berlin Ku'damm is located just a few steps from the shopping street Kurfürstendamm. The Quadriga restaurant (see p127) serves up creative French cuisine.

Hecker's Hotel

MAP B5 ■ Grolmanstr. 35 ■ (030) 889 00 ■ www. heckers-hotel.com ■ €€
The plain façade of this modern four-star business hotel, set in a side street just off Ku'damm, belies the much more sophisticated interior – you'll be greeted by modern art, cool minimalism, clever lighting and first-class service.

Ku'Damm 101

MAP G1 ■ Kurfürstendamm 101 ■ (030) 520 05 50 ■ www.kudamm101. com ■ €€
This minimalist hotel, one of the few based on the Bauhaus design principles of Le Corbusier, caters to an art-oriented, mostly European clientele, who appreciate the simple, comfortable rooms and large bathrooms, the stylish, modern interiors and the great views from the breakfast room. Prices are highly competitive.

Lux Eleven

MAP J6 ■ Rosa-Luxemburg-Str. 9–13 ■ (030) 936 28 00 ■ www.lux-eleven.com ■ €€
This stylish, modern apartment hotel is a designer's dream come true. Old townhouses have been converted into mostly white, sleek rooms with all the gadgets of a business hotel. The Luchs restaurant and bar, with its understated elegance, adds to the upmarket flair of the hotel.

Maritim proArte Hotel Berlin

MAP K4 ■ Friedrichstr. 151 ■ (030) 203 35 ■ www.maritim.de ■ €€
Predominantly styled in tones of green and blue, this modern business hotel boasts almost 300 modern paintings decorating its rooms.

nhow Hotel

Stralauer Allee 3 ■ (030) 290 29 90 ■ www.nhow-hotels.com ■ €€
A former warehouse on the Spree River is now a "music and lifestyle" hotel, complete with recording studio. Cutting-edge facilities in rooms include a flat-screen TV that doubles as a mirror.

Park Plaza Wallstreet Berlin Mitte

MAP L6 ■ Wallstr. 23–24 ■ (030) 847 11 70 ■ www.parkplaza.com/berlinde_wallstrasse ■ €€
The New York Stock Exchange is the theme here, with dollar-bill carpets and murals of stock-brokers' and business maxims all around the building. A pleasant hotel in a central location.

Q!

MAP P3 ■ Knesebeckstr. 67 ■ (030) 810 06 60 ■ www.hotel-q.com ■ €€
Stylish and discreet, this is a favourite among Hollywood stars. Its rooms are designed as "living landscapes" with furniture integrated into the walls.

Quirky Hotels and Guesthouses

Almodóvar Hotel

Boxhagener Str. 83 ■ (030) 692 097 080 ■ www.almodovarhotel.de ■ €
Berlin's first biohotel flaunts its pedigree with flourish. The in-house Bardot bistro serves organic vegetarian dishes, as well as lactose- and gluten-free and vegan. Every room comes with its own yoga mat. Guests can also relax in the top-level spa and admire the Berlin panorama.

Eastern Comfort

Mühlenstr. 73–77 ■ (030) 66 76 38 06 ■ www.eastern-comfort.com ■ €
Moored on the Spree near the pretty Oberbaum bridge, this popular boat-hotel draws visitors aiming at the hard-partying districts of Kreuzberg and Friedrichshain. Some 24 snug berths are spread over two decks. White sandy beach and bits of old Berlin Wall nearby.

Michelberger Hotel

Warschauer Str. 39 ■ (030) 29 77 85 90 ■ www.michelbergerhotel.com ■ €
Set right in the heart of the Friedrichshain entertainment district, the Michelberger Hotel offers guests quirky urban

sophistication and a young, fun dynamic. Amenities include free Wi-Fi and a cool lounge area strewn with books and magazines.

Ostel

Wriezener Karree 5 ■ (030) 25 76 86 60 ■ www.ostel.eu ■ €
Located in Berlin's trendy Mitte district, Ostel is designed to look like a communist-era hotel. The choice of rooms includes doubles with shared or private bathrooms, rooms with double- or triple-decker bunk beds and apartments that can sleep up to six people.

Scube Park

Columbiadamm 160 ■ (030) 69 80 78 41 ■ scubepark.berlin ■ €
These smartly-furnished wooden units in cool Scandinavian design have all the amenities. Located on the grounds of a swimming pool near Tempelhofer Park, each cabin can take up to four guests, year-round. An affordable hybrid of hotel and campsite.

25hours Hotel Bikini

MAP N5 ■ Budapester Str. 40 ■ (030) 26 36 95 94 ■ www.25hours-hotels.com ■ €€
Part of the new Bikini shopping mall, this smart 10-storey hotel offers guests the Monkey Bar, a rooftop restaurant with a 360º panorama and a ringside view of the primate enclosure and elephant house at the city's Zoologischer Garten (see pp42–3). The "jungle sauna" has windows overlooking the green expanse of the Tiergarten.

Arte Luise Kunsthotel

MAP J3 ■ Luisenstr. 19 ■ (030) 28 44 80 ■ www. luise-berlin.com ■ €€

This charming hotel has 50 rooms all individually and imaginatively decorated by local artists, with themes that range from loud pop art to classic Modernism. Near Unter den Linden and the Hauptbahnhof.

Hollywood Media Hotel

MAP P3 ■ Kurfürstendamm 202 ■ (030) 88 91 00 ■ www.filmhotel.de ■ €€

Located right on glitzy Kurfürstendamm, this hotel has loads of cinematic knick-knacks including props, movie posters and photos of stars. Each of the 182 rooms is dedicated to a film legend. The owner is Artur Brauner, an esteemed Polish-born film producer.

Propeller Island City Lodge

MAP B5 ■ Albrecht-Achilles Str. 58 ■ (030) 891 90 16 ■ www.propeller-island.de ■ No credit cards ■ €€

If you're staying at this unusual lodge, you will share it with the German audio-visual artist Lars Stroschen, who designed all the rooms himself, each in a unique style.

Riverside City

MAP J4 ■ Friedrichstr. 106 ■ (030) 28 49 00 ■ www. tolles-hotel.de ■ €€

Housed in a former GDR car dealership, this small hotel combines Baroque features, a spa and an excellent location on the Spree. The interior decor and the excellent service make it a popular choice.

Cozy Hotels

Midi Inn City West Kurfürstendamm

MAP P2 ■ Wielandstr. 26 ■ (030) 881 64 85 ■ www. kudamm-de.midi-inn.de ■ €

This is Berlin's best small guesthouse close to Ku'damm – a handful of atmospheric rooms, retrofitted in a non-fussy, mock 1920s style. Free Wi-Fi and flatscreen TVs.

Nürnberger Eck

MAP P5 ■ Nürnberger Str. 24A ■ (030) 235 17 80 ■ www.nuernberger-eck.de ■ €

A 5-minute stroll from Ku'damm, this handsome edifice has been a guesthouse since the 1920s. The eight rooms are a time capsule of furnishings. A highlight is the early 20th-century bridal suite, with pink rose wallpaper, carved wooden bedstead and bird motifs.

Pension Kreuzberg

MAP F5 ■ Großbeerenstr. 64 ■ (030) 251 13 62 ■ www.pension-kreuzberg. de ■ No credit cards ■ €

Clean and friendly, with an excellent atmosphere. The landlady takes great care of her guests and is happy to pass on tips for nightlife and culture. All rooms have showers.

Pension Peters

MAP N3 ■ Kantstr. 146 ■ (030) 312 22 78 ■ www.pension-peters-berlin.de ■ €

Located just off café-filled Savignyplatz, this friendly little pension run by a German-Swedish crew is thoughtfully furnished, with Belle Epoque details even in the marble fittings and frescoes. Rooms are large and bright – make sure you ask for one overlooking the peaceful rear courtyard.

Ackselhaus, Blue Home and Club del Mar

MAP H2 ■ Belforter Str. 21 ■ (030) 44 33 76 33 ■ www.ackselhaus.de ■ No credit cards ■ €€

Stylish themed rooms are offered in this small boutique hotel with a Mediterranean garden. It is located near Kollwitzplatz, a popular area with bustling bars and cafés.

Derag Livinghotel Henriette

MAP L6 ■ Neue Roßstr. 13 ■ (030) 24 60 09 00 ■ www.deraghotels.de ■ €€

A stylish hotel with classic decoration – warm oak-panelled walls and thick carpets and curtains adorn the rooms, which are arranged around an inner courtyard. Few hotels in town are better than this, and the service is very friendly.

Hotel Gendarm Nouveau

MAP L4 ■ Charlottenstr. 61 ■ (030) 206 06 60 ■ www.hotel-gendarm-berlin.de ■ €€

This small hotel on Gendarmenmarkt hotel is based in a venerable town residence. The designer-appointed rooms exude sophistication and elegance, although the lack of air conditioning could be an issue for some guests during the hotter summer months.

For a key to hotel price categories see p172

Hotel Johann
MAP G5 ■ Johanniterstr. 8 ■ (030) 225 07 40 ■ www.hotel-johann-berlin.de ■ €€
This small hotel with friendly staff offers moderately priced comfort. It is located in a quiet street a 10-minute walk from the Jüdisches Museum, near an open-air swimming pool complex.

Hotel-Pension Funk
MAP P4 ■ Fasanenstr. 69 ■ (030) 882 71 93 ■ www.hotel-pensionfunk.de ■ €€
Slightly antiquated, venerable guesthouse close to Ku'damm, based in the apartment of the silent-film star Asta Nielsen. The rates are unbeatable, while furnishings and service are personal and friendly. There are only 15 rooms, however, so it is advisable to book in advance.

Myer's Hotel
MAP H2 ■ Metzer Str. 26 ■ (030) 44 01 40 ■ www.myershotel.de ■ €€
A family-run hotel in the centre of Prenzlauer Berg ideal for families or couples. The rooms are elegantly decorated and the hotel is located in an historic part of town. The service is attentive and the atmosphere relaxed.

Hotels in Green Surroundings

Das Andere Haus VIII
Erich Müller Str. 12 ■ (030) 55 44 03 31 ■ dasanderehaus8.de ■ €
After the fall of the Wall, Communist leaders were interned in this comely 19th-century ensemble. The five guest rooms are, in fact, converted prison cells but surprisingly comfortable, with buffed wood floors and sleek modern bathrooms. The Rummelsburger Bucht, a bucolic arm of the Spree, flows past nearby.

Haus La Garde
Bergengrünstr. 16 ■ (030) 801 30 09 ■ www.haus-la-garde.de ■ €
This tiny guesthouse with only four rooms is hidden in a romantic villa on the Schlachtensee. If lakes aren't your thing, you can relax in the gardens. This is a non-smoking property.

Penta Hotel Berlin-Köpenick
Grünauer Str. 1 ■ (030) 65 47 90 ■ www.penta hotels.com/en/berlin-koepenick ■ €
The slightly sterile and impersonal atmosphere of this hotel is more than made up for by its location. It is right in the centre of the southeastern district of Köpenick, on the banks of the Dahme River, and Müggelsee is not far away. BER airport is only a few minutes' drive away by car or S-Bahn.

Spreeidyll-Hotel am Yachthafen
Müggelseedamm 70 ■ (030) 641 94 00 ■ hotel-spree-idyll.berlin ■ €
A small family-run house on the Müggelspree, not far from a bathing beach and a boat-hire booth – the ideal place to relax and forget all about the hustle and bustle of the big city, which is, however, only a short distance to the northwest. Come here to relax and take part in all kinds of watersports.

Forsthaus Paulsborn
Hüttenweg 90 ■ (030) 818 19 10 ■ www.forsthaus-paulsborn.de ■ €€
Sited in the southwestern Grunewald forest, this hotel is housed in a beautiful 1871 hunting lodge used by Kaiser Wilhelm II. There is a restaurant (see p155) and lakeside terrace, as well as riding stables nearby.

Hotel Bayrisches Haus
Im Wildpark/Elisenweg 2, Potsdam ■ (0331) 550 50 ■ www.bayrisches-haus.de ■ €€
Nestled in a former game reserve outside Potsdam, this deluxe take on Bavarian country living has marbled bathrooms, gorgeous linens, the Michelin-starred Friedrich Wilhelm restaurant (see p161) and an indoor pool.

Hotel Müggelsee Berlin
Müggelheimer Damm 145 ■ (030) 65 88 20 ■ www.hotel-mueggelsee-berlin.de ■ €€
A comfortable hotel on the Müggelsee, combining near-unspoilt nature and closeness to the city. There are tennis courts, boat and bicycle hire and plenty of leisure activities.

Hotel Seehof am Lietzensee
MAP A4 ■ Lietzenseeufer 11 ■ (030) 32 00 20 ■ www.hotel-seehof-berlin.de ■ €€
Centrally located in Charlottenburg, not far from the Messegelände, in a picturesque spot on the Lietzensee. The well-run hotel has a beautiful indoor pool as well as a delightful sun terrace.

Landhaus Schlachtensee

Bogotastr. 9 ▪ (030) 809 94 70 ▪ www.hotel-landhaus-schlachtensee.de ▪ €€

A 20-minute walk from the Schlachtensee (see p61) and Krumme Lanke, this villa oozes the charm of old rural Berlin. The furnishings in its rooms are a little old-fashioned, but the service is personable. The lovely beach at Strandbad Wannsee is just 4 km (2.5 miles away).

Schlossparkhotel

MAP A/B3 ▪ Heubnerweg 2A ▪ (030) 326 90 30 ▪ www.schloss parkhotel.de ▪ €€

The only hotel near Schloss Charlottenburg, next to the Schlosspark, this is just a few minutes from the west of the city centre. The facilities are good and service is impeccable.There are only 40 rooms.

Medium-Priced Hotels

Bleibtreu-Hotel

MAP P3 ▪ Bleibtreustr. 31 ▪ (030) 88 47 40 ▪ www.bleibtreu.com ▪ €€

The hotel's stylish inner courtyard – reminiscent of Tuscany – and bright, tasteful rooms are an oasis of tranquillity. The international clientele is equally stylish. The hotel has its own restaurant, pool and sauna.

Derag Livinghotel Großer Kurfürst

MAP L6 ▪ Neue Roßstr. 11–12 ▪ (030) 24 60 00 ▪ www.deraghotels.de ▪ €€

Close to the Spree south of the Museumsinsel, the hotel offers guests rooms as well as fully furnished apartments. It also has useful extras, such as a gym, sauna and bike hire.

Ellington Hotel Berlin

MAP P5 ▪ Nürnberger Str. 50–55 ▪ (030) 68 31 50 ▪ www.ellingtonhotel.de ▪ €€

This distinctive hotel is a beacon of modern design set within listed 1920s Bauhaus architecture. It has a conveniently central location close to the KaDeWe, Ku'damm and the zoo, offering a stylish alternative to a young, international clientele.

Hackescher Markt

MAP J5 ▪ Große Präsidentenstr. 8 ▪ (030) 28 00 30 ▪ www.classik-hotel-collection.com ▪ €€

A charming hotel in an unbeatable location right opposite Hackesche Höfe. Its large, bright, elegantly furnished rooms, friendly service, excellent restaurant and attractive patio guarantee a pleasant stay.

Honigmond Garden Hotel

MAP F2 ▪ Invalidenstr. 122 ▪ (030) 28 44 55 77 ▪ www.honigmond-berlin.de ▪ €€

Seeping nostalgia with a hint of luxury, this hotel is set within a listed 1845 building and has original antiques, stucco ceilings and a pretty courtyard with a Japanese fishpond.

Hotel Amano

MAP G2 ▪ Auguststr. 43 ▪ (030) 809 41 50 ▪ www.amanogroup.com ▪ €€

In a narrow street lined with galleries, this chic hotel is an excellent base from which to explore the Hackescher Markt area, Scheunenviertel and the Museumsinsel. Rooms and fully serviced apartments are available. Open bathrooms make this a better choice for couples. The view from the roof terrace is spectacular, and extras such as bike hire, pedestrian navigation systems and iPod walking tours help make your stay a great one.

Hotel Mani

MAP G2 ▪ Torstr. 136 ▪ (030) 53 02 80 80 ▪ www.amanogroup.de ▪ €€

A heartbeat from lively Rosenthaler Platz, this stylish hotel is a favourite with fashion models and weekend-breakers set to party. Its rooms are compact but beautifully appointed, with parquet floors and ultramodern, open-plan bathrooms.

Hotel-Pension Kastanienhof

MAP G2 ▪ Kastanienallee 65 ▪ (030) 44 30 50 ▪ www.kastanienhof.biz ▪ €€

A charming hotel set in a turn-of-the-20th-century building. The rooms are basic but well equipped. An ideal base for exploring Prenzlauer Berg.

Hotel Residenz Berlin

MAP P4 ▪ Meinekestr. 9 ▪ (030) 88 44 30 ▪ www.hotel-residenz.com ▪ €€

Bsed in one of the most beautiful old Berlin townhouses near Ku'damm, this hotel offers guests an intimate, characterful atmosphere. The late-19th-century rooms are tastefully furnished, and the restaurant has outdoor seating in summer.

For a key to hotel price categories see p172

Riehmers Hofgarten

MAP F6 ■ Yorckstr. 83
■ (030) 78 09 88 00 ■ www.
riehmers-hofgarten.de
■ €€

Here you can live the life of a Prussian officer. This remarkable hotel is part of a large complex of 19th-century Neo-Gothic buildings – old Kreuzberg apartments, with sombre rooms and elegant bath-rooms, are the perfect setting for trying out the 19th-century lifestyle. The hotel has free Wi-Fi and docking stations in every room. The restaurant has contemporary variations of traditional dishes.

Hotels for Business Travellers

Leonardo Airport Hotel Berlin Brandenburg

Schwalbenweg 18 ■ (030) 67 90 20 ■ www.
leonardo-hotels.com ■ €
Conveniently situated near Berlin Brandenburg Airport in Schönefeld, this hotel is ideal for brief business trips or for visi-tors on a budget. Service is efficient and friendly.

Arcotel John F

MAP K5 ■ Werdescher Markt 11 ■ (030) 405 04 60 ■ www.arcotelhotels.
com/JohnF ■ €€
Very conveniently located within walking distance of Unter den Linden and the stores of Friedrichstraße, and midway between the Museumsinsel and Gendarmenmarkt, this is a smart, modern hotel with a wealth of business and conference facilities. The breakfast is superb, and includes their exclu-sive sparkling wine and vegan food options.

Estrel Residence Congress Hotel

Sonnenallee 225 ■ (030) 683 10 ■ www.estrel.com
■ €€

With more than 1,000 rooms, this hotel is one of Europe's largest, offering three- to four-star service at moderate prices. Its numerous conference rooms and the latest technological equipment make it the perfect venue for international business meetings. The hotel is equally ready to cater for the needs of the individual business traveller.

Hilton Berlin

MAP L4 ■ Mohrenstr. 30
■ (030) 20 23 00 ■ www.
hilton.de ■ €€
Executives favour this luxury hotel because of its central location, the views across the beautiful Gendarmenmarkt and the Französischer and Berliner Doms, an excellent breakfast and specially designed exe-cutive rooms. There is a business centre, and a full secretarial service is included. The hotel also offers pet services, such as baskets and water and food bowls.

The Mandala Suites

MAP L4 ■ Friedrichstr. 185–190 ■ (030) 20 29 20 ■ www.themandalasuites.
de ■ €€
Sister establishment of the Mandala Hotel in Potsdamer Platz, this is also a central apartment hotel with suites between 40–100 sq m (430–1,076 sq ft) elegantly equipped as offices and offering a secretarial service. A maid service is available and newspapers are delivered each morning.

NH Berlin Friedrichstraße

MAP K4 ■ Friedrichstr. 96
■ (030) 206 26 60
■ www.nh-hotels.de ■ €€
Apart from its prime east Berlin location on Friedrichstraße, this luxury hotel boasts spa-cious rooms, a large lobby and inviting bar, furnished with the best materials.

NH Berlin Heinrich Heine

MAP H4 ■ Heinrich-Heine-Platz 11 ■ (030) 27 80 40 ■ www.nh-hotels.
com ■ €€
This hotel is the best choice if your business requires a longer stay in town. Not far from the Museumsinsel and the Nikolaiviertel quarter, the apartments are equipped with desks and kitchens. Staff are specially trained to cater for the needs of business travellers.

Pullman Berlin Schweizerhof

MAP N5 ■ Budapester Str. 25 ■ (030) 269 60 ■ www.
pullmanhotels.com ■ €€
One of Berlin's top luxury hotels right in the centre of western Berlin, the Schweizerhof features clean lines, precious woods and a large, well-designed fitness area.

Wyndham Berlin Excelsior Hotel

MAP N4 ■ Hardenbergstr. 14 ■ (030) 315 50 ■ www.
hotel-excelsior.de ■ €€
Part of the prestigious World Hotels First Class Collection, the Excelsior is elegantly decorated in a restrained style. Moderate prices, friendly staff, busi-ness services, a gym and a brasserie make this a top choice.

Sofitel Berlin Kurfürstendamm

MAP P4 ▪ Augsburger Str. 41 ▪ (030) 800 99 90 ▪ www.sofitel.com ▪ €€€

Designed by star architect Jan Kleiheus, this hotel boasts the largest rooms in Berlin and spectacular views over Ku'damm. Other perks include free Wi-Fi, friendly and efficient service and a helpful concierge desk.

Budget Hotels and Hostels

BaxPax Kreuzberg

MAP H5 ▪ Skalitzerstr. 104 ▪ (030) 69 51 83 22 ▪ www.baxpax.de ▪ €

Much better than a youth hostel yet much cheaper than a guesthouse at under €20 per night, this refurbished factory is an unusual place to stay – you may be sleeping in a decommissioned VW Beetle. Plus you'll meet friendly young people from around the world. BaxPax is in Kreuzberg, and less suitable for those over 30.

BaxPax Mitte

MAP F2 ▪ Chausseestr. 102 ▪ (030) 28 39 09 65 ▪ www.baxpax.de ▪ €

Find 20 funky themed rooms at this cool hostel close to Mitte's hotspots, complete with Internet café and laundry service.

Bed and Breakfast Ring

www.bandb-ring.de ▪ No credit cards ▪ €

Bed and Breakfast Ring arranges shared accommodation in private homes all over town, at low prices. You'll normally have your own room with one or two beds or an apartment to yourself. Quality varies considerably, but the rooms are mostly priced moderately, from €25 per person.

The Circus Hotel

MAP G2 ▪ Weinbergsweg 1A ▪ (030) 20 00 39 39 ▪ www.circus-berlin.de ▪ €

Near Alexanderplatz, this hostel offers great value accommodation close to many sights. Dorm beds and single, double and triple rooms are available as well as a rooftop apartment with good views. There is a restaurant, a garden courtyard, and bike and scooter rental.

EastSeven Berlin Hostel

MAP H2 ▪ Schwedter Str. 7 ▪ (030) 93 62 22 40 ▪ www.eastseven.de ▪ €

In a lively Prenzlauer Berg neighbourhood brimming with bars and cafés, this friendly hostel is also just a 20-minute walk from Alexanderplatz and the Museumsinsel. There is a garden and free Wi-Fi.

die fabrik

Schlesische Str. 18 ▪ (030) 611 71 16 ▪ www.diefabrik.com ▪ No credit cards ▪ €

This hotel, whose name means "the factory", is a guesthouse, youth hostel and an alternative youth and arts centre in deepest Kreuzberg. It attracts backpackers from around the world, hoping to meet locals and other travellers.

Gay Hostel

MAP D5 ▪ Motzstr. 28 ▪ (030) 21 00 57 09 ▪ www.gay-hostel.de ▪ €

Located in the heart of Schöneberg's gay quarter, this clean, hospitable and well-equipped hostel plugs visitors into the local scene with a booklet of local discounts. There are shared and private rooms on offer, and all have lockers, flatscreen TVs, coffee and free Wi-Fi.

Grand Hostel Berlin

MAP F5 ▪ Tempelhofer Ufer 14 ▪ (030) 20 09 54 50 ▪ www.grandhostel-berlin.de ▪ €

Housed in a 1874 building, this friendly hostel is in a central location in trendy Kreuzberg. It offers safe, clean, spacious dorms and private rooms, some with their own bathrooms. There is also a lounge with computer terminals, free Wi-Fi, bike rental and a large buffet for breakfast. The staff are friendly and helpful.

Hotel Transit

MAP F6 ▪ Hagelberger Straße 53–4 ▪ (030) 789 04 70 ▪ www.hotel-transit.de ▪ €

Housed on two floors of a former factory, this international youth hostel is located in a lively area close to the town centre. It has 50 large loft-style rooms, including singles, doubles and dorms.

Hüttenpalast

MAP H6 ▪ Hobrechtstr. 66 ▪ (030) 37 30 58 06 ▪ www.huettenpalast.de ▪ €

Tucked away in an old Neukölln vacuum-cleaner factory, this unique boutique hotel lets you slumber in designer caravans and Alpine huts placed inside the factory. Relax on the indoor swing, ponder the fake indoor trees, and dine organic in the streetside café.

For a key to hotel price categories see p172

General Index

Acknowledgments

Author
Historian Jürgen Scheunemann has published several documentary and photographic books on Berlin and other destinations. His award-winning articles are published in travel magazines and daily newspapers in Germany and the US, and have appeared in the Berlin daily *Tagesspiegel*, among others.

Additional contributor
Jeremy Gray

Publishing Director Georgina Dee

Publisher Vivien Antwi

Design Director Phil Ormerod

Editorial Ankita Awasthi-Tröger, Michelle Crane, Rachel Fox, Freddie Marriage, Fíodhna Ní Ghríofa, Scarlett O'Hara, Sally Schafer, Avijit Sengupta, Christine Stroyan

Design Richard Czapnik, Sunita Gahir

Picture Research Phoebe Lowndes, Susie Peachey, Ellen Root, Oran Tarjan

Cartography Dominic Beddow, Simonetta Giori, Mohammad Hassan, Suresh Kumar, Casper Morris

DTP Jason Little, George Nimmo, Azeem Siddiqui

Production Linda Dare

Factchecker Petra Falkenberg

Proofreader Anna Streiffert

Indexer Hilary Bird

Illustrator www.chrisorr.com
First edition created by DK Verlag, Munich

Commissioned Photography
Dorota Jarymowicz and Mariusz Jarymowicz, Britta Jaschinski, Rough Guides/Tim Draper, Rough Guides/Diana Jarvis, Rough Guides/ Roger d'Olivere Mapp, Rough Guides/Roger Norum

Picture Credits
The publisher would like to thank the following for their kind permission to reproduce their photographs:

(**Key:** a-above; b-below/bottom; c-center; f-far; l-left; r-right; t-top)

4Corners: SIME/Giovanni Simeone 2tr, 44-5.
Alamy Images: AA World Travel Library 13br; A. Astes 62bl; B.O'Kane 26tl; Pat Behnke 130cra; Bildagentur-online/Schickert 136tl, 139bl; Bildarchiv Monheim GmbH 89cla; Agencja Fotograficzna Caro 2tl, 8-9, 16cl, 20crb, 69cr, 125tl, 140tr; 153cl; David Davies 33cra; dpa picture alliance 88br, 115crb; dpics 11ca; Reiner Elsen 13tl; epa european pressphoto agency b.v. 63bc; FineArt 40br; Hemis 57cr, 125br, 138tl; Peter Horree 32br, 59tl; imageBROKER 34bl, 36crb, 42cla, 47br, 89bc, 139tl; imageBROKER/Ingo

Schulz 120t; INTERFOTO 37tl, 37b; Keystone Pictures USA 158bl; LOOK Die Bildagentur der Fotografen GmbH 14br; MARKA 48; Iain Masterton 25tr, 39tl, 146tc; Nature Picture Library 43cra; Novarc Images 137br; Stefano Paterna 42bl; Roussel Photography 121bl; Riccardo Sala 35crb; John Stark 99cla; travelstock44 107tl; VPC Travel Photo 150tl; Werner Otto 33cl; Westend61 GmbH 21bc; Julie G Woodhouse 23cl, 123clb; World History Archive 46br.

Ankerklause: olfgang Borrs 134tl.

Becketts Kopf: 72cr.

Berlinale: Andreas Teich 80tl.

Berliner Kaffeerösterei: 126cl.

Borchardt: 71cl.

Clärchens Ballhaus: Bernd Schoenberger 75crb.

Corbis: Bettmann 47tl; Eye Ubiquitous/Stephen Rafferty 88tl; Gemaldegalerie, Berlin, Germany / *Virgin and Child with Eight Angels* by Sandro Botticelli 1477. Tempera on poplar panel. 135 cm. 40cb, /*The Glass of Wine* by Johannes Vermeer, Circa 1661. Oil on canvas. 79.6 x 67.7 cm (31.3 x 26.7 in). 52tl; Hemis/Borgese Maurizio 116cra, / Ludovic Maisant © 2015 The Andy Warhol Foundation for the Visual Arts, Inc./Artists Rights Society (ARS), New York and DACS, London 2015 53tl; Hulton-Deutsch Collection 49tc; incamerastock/Iain Masterton 38-9; Ocean/John Harper 110-1; Reuters/Fabrizio Bensch 27tl; Reuters/Tobias Schwarz 152t; Schoening 16bl, 119tr.

DDR Museum: 90tl.

Deutches Technikmuseum/ © SDTB: C. Kirchner 64tl.

Deutsche Kinemathek: Hans Scherhaufer 22tl, Marian Stefanowski 20clb, 22crb.

Deutsche Oper: Marcus Lieberenz 66tr.

Deutsches Historisches Museum, Berlin: 18tr, 18bl.

Dreamstime.com: Rostislav Ageev 11cr; Albo 27b; Andreykr 128tl; Atosan 15cr; David Beaulieu 1, 4cra; Michal Bednarek 96tr; Goran Bogicevic 21tl, 96tr; Gunold Brunbauer 107cb; Buschmen 33br, 118tl, 122bl; Carolannefreeling 15tl, 144tl; Ccat82 103t,113t; Claudiodivizia 7tl, 10bl; 11clb, 24br, 39bc, 41tl; Mikael Damkier 10clb; Digitalsignal 95tr; Matthew Dixon 10br, 32-3c; Dennis Dolkens 129cr; Christian Draghici 4crb, 46t, 55t, 79bl, 102tl, 151t, 159bl; Elenabum 86t, 104bl; Elxeneize 16-7c, 158cra; Alexandre Fagundes De Fagundes 16crb,17tl, 52crb; Joerg Franzen 55bc; Kevin George 61c, 84tl, 147cla; Simone Gobbo 11tl; Gudmund1 14cl; Jorg Hackemann 4clb; Hai Huy Ton That 133br; Hel080808 12bl, 87cl; Hugoht 146b; Juliane Jacobs 130bl; Dragan Jovanovic 13clb; Junede 122-3t; Tom K 58tl, 85tr; Katatonia82 98tl; Sergey Kelin 4b, 11crb, 17cb, 35c, 60bl; Jan Kranendonk 6cla; Axel Lauer 94tl; Miroslav Liska 34-5cla; Locha79 7cr; Markwaters 15bl, 56br, 114bl, 136cl; Mateuszolszowy 41b; Matteocozzi 114tr; Lucian Milasan 12cl; Mishkacz 96bl; Luciano Mortula 51tc, 129tr, 145t; Kalin Nedkov 3tr, 162-3; Noppasinw 56cl, 79tr; Olena Buyskykh 25clb; Andrey Omelyanchuk 61tr; Sean Pavone 24-5c,

157tr; Petarneychev 78tl; Andrey Popov 12-3c; Peter Probst 60cr; Rhombur 81tr; Ricochet69 132cl; Romangorielov 10cra; Rudi1976 3tl,4t, 82-3; Mario Savoia 30cl; Spongecake 156tl; Petr Švec 124t; Svenwerk 154bl; Totalpics 142-3; Anibal Trejo 59b, 98cb,112tl; Ferenc Ungor 138c; Mirko Vitali 80bc; Vojtech Vlk 145br; Vvoevale 7tr, 24cl, 26bc, 53bc, 76tl; Jannis Werner 152br; Jeff Whyte 54cla; Anastasiia Ylitko 11br, 43tl; Alex Zarubin 116bc.

Facil Restaurant: Lukas Roth 71tr.

©Filmpark Babelsberg: 65bl.

Restaurant Florian: 127tr.

Friedrichstadt-Palast: Götz Schleser 67tr.

Brauhaus Georgbrau: 108bl.

Getty Images: 48crb; DeAgostini 51bc; John Freeman 31cra; Sean Gallup 68clb; Heritage Images 19bc, /The Merchant Georg Gisze, 1532 by Hans Holbein, the Younger (1497-1543) collection of the Staatliche Museen, Berlin 40cla; Lonely Planet 36tl; Andreas Rentz 63ca; Travelstock44 - Juergen Held 20-1c; ullstein bild 132br.

Gugelhof: 141cl.

Restaurant & Café Heider: 161crb.

Hotel Adlon Kempinski: Restaurant Quarrè 117tr

Klunkerkranich: Julian Nelken 134br.

Kulturforum Berlin: © Philipp Eder 4cla, 38cl, 38crb, 38bl.

Kunst-Werke: 99br.

Labyrinth Kindermuseum: 64bl.

La Lavanderia Vecchia: 135tr.

James MacDonald: 73bl.

Matrix: 148bl.

Museum für Naturkunde: A. Dittmann 64cr.

Nola's: 101tr.

Oxymoron: 100br.

Paulsborn am Grunewaldsee: 155tr.

Ratskeller Kopenick: 149cl.

Refugium: 93tl.

Reinstoff: 70tl.

Riva Bar: 100tl.

Robert Harding Picture Library: Hubertus Blume 31tl; Siegfried Grassegger 20bc; Jurgen Henkelmann 30-1c; Karl Johaentges 42-3c; Thomas Robbin 30clb; Ingo Schulz 28-9, 33tl; Urs Schweitzer 43br; Lothar Steiner 23b.

Schwules Museum: Tobias Wille 69b.

Theodor Tucher: 92bl.

Victoria Bar: 73t.

Weekend: 74b.

Zillestube: 109tr.

Zoologischer Garten, Berlin: 42crb.

Zur Letzten Instanz: 108tc.

Jacket

Front and spine – **Dreamstime.com:** Ccat82.
Back – **AWL Images:** Jon Arnold.

Pull out map cover

Dreamstime.com: Ccat8.

All other images are: © Dorling Kindersley. For further information see www.dkimages.com.

Penguin Random House

Printed and bound in China

First American Edition, 2002
Published in the United States by
DK Publishing, 345 Hudson Street,
New York, New York 10014

Copyright 2002, 2016 © Dorling
Kindersley Limited

A Penguin Random House Company

16 17 18 19 20 10 9 8 7 6 5 4 3 2 1

Reprinted with revisions 2004, 2006, 2007, 2008, 2009, 2010, 2011, 2012, 2013, 2014, 2016

All rights reserved. Without limiting the rights under the copyright reserved above, no part of this publication may be reproduced, stored in or introduced into a retrieval system, or transmitted, in any form, or by any means (electronic, mechanical, photocopying, recording, or otherwise), without the prior written permission of the copyright owner.

Published in Great Britain by Dorling Kindersley Limited.

A catalog record for this book is available from the Library of Congress.

ISSN 1479-344X
ISBN 978-1-4654-4090-7

MIX
Paper from
responsible sources
FSC™ C018179

SPECIAL EDITIONS OF DK TRAVEL GUIDES

DK Travel Guides can be purchased in bulk quantities at discounted prices for use in promotions or as premiums. We are also able to offer special editions and personalized jackets, corporate imprints, and excerpts from all of our books, tailored specifically to meet your own needs.

To find out more, please contact:

in the US
specialsales@dk.com

in the UK
travelguides@uk.dk.com

in Canada
specialmarkets@dk.com

in Australia
**penguincorporatesales@
penguinrandomhouse.com.au**

Phrase Book

In an Emergency

Where is the telephone?	**Wo ist das Telefon?**	*voh ist duss tel-e-fone?*
Help!	**Hilfe!**	*hilf-uh*
Please call a doctor	**Bitte rufen Sie einen Arzt**	*bitt-uh roof'n zee ine-en artst*
Please call the police	**Bitte rufen Sie die Polizei**	*bitt-uh roof'n zee dee poli-tsy*
Please call the fire brigade	**Bitte rufen Sie die Feuerwehr**	*bitt-uh roof'n zee dee foyer-vayr*
Stop!	**Halt!**	*hult*

Communication Essentials

Yes	**Ja**	*yah*
No	**Nein**	*nine*
Please	**Bitte**	*bitt-uh*
Thank you	**Danke**	*dunk-uh*
Excuse me	**Verzeihung**	*fair-tsy-hoong*
Hello	**Guten Tag**	*goot-en tahk*
Goodbye	**Auf Wiedersehen**	*owf-veed-er-zay-ern*
Good evening	**Gute Abend**	*goot'n-ahb'nt*
Good night	**Gute Nacht**	*goot-uh nukht*
Until tomorrow	**Bis morgen**	*biss morg'n*
See you	**Tschüss**	*chooss*
What is that?	**Was ist das?**	*voss ist duss*
Why?	**Warum?**	*var-room*
Where?	**Wo?**	*voh*
When?	**Wann?**	*vunn*
today	**heute**	*hoyt-uh*
tomorrow	**morgen**	*morg'n*
month	**Monat**	*mohn-aht*
night	**Nacht**	*nukht*
afternoon	**Nachmittag**	*nahkh-mit-tahk*
morning	**Morgen**	*morg'n*
year	**Jahr**	*yar*
there	**dort**	*dort*
here	**hier**	*hear*
week	**Woche**	*vokh-uh*
yesterday	**gestern**	*gest'n*
evening	**Abend**	*ahb'nt*

Useful Phrases

How are you? (informal)	**Wie geht's?**	*vee gayts*
Fine, thanks	**Danke, es geht mir gut**	*dunk-uh, es gayt meer goot*
Where is/are?	**Wo ist/sind…?**	*voh ist/sind*
How far is it to…?	**Wie weit ist es…?**	*vee vite ist ess*
Do you speak English?	**Sprechen Sie Englisch?**	*shpresh'n zee eng-glish*
I don't understand	**Ich verstehe nicht**	*ish fair-shtay-uh nisht*
Could you speak more slowly?	**Könnten Sie langsamer sprechen?**	*kurnt-en zee langsamer shpresh'n*

Useful Words

large	**gross**	*grohss*
small	**klein**	*kline*
hot	**heiss**	*hyce*
cold	**kalt**	*kult*
good	**gut**	*goot*
bad	**böse/schlech**	*burss-uh/shlesht*
open	**geöffnet**	*g'urff-nett*
closed	**geschlossen**	*g'shloss'n*
left	**links**	*links*
right	**rechts**	*reshts*
straight ahead	**geradeaus**	*g'rah-der-owss*

Making a Telephone Call

I would like to make a phone call	**Ich möchte telefonieren**	*ish mer-shtuh tel-e-fon-eer'n*
I'll try again later	**Ich versuche noch ein mal später**	*ish fair-zookh-uh nokh ine-mull shpay-ter*
Can I leave a message?	**Kann ich eine Nachricht hinterlassen?**	*kan ish ine-uh nakh-risht hint-er-lahss-en*
answer phone	**Anrufbeantworter**	*an-roof-be-ahnt-vort-er*
telephone card	**Telefonkarte**	*tel-e-fohn-kart-uh*
receiver	**Hörer**	*hur-er*
mobile	**Handi**	*han-dee*
engaged (busy)	**besetzt**	*b'zetst*
wrong number	**Falsche Verbindung**	*falsh-uh fair-bin-doong*

Sightseeing

library	**Bibliothek**	*bib-leo-tek*
entrance ticket	**Eintrittskarte**	*ine-tritz-kart-uh*
cemetery	**Friedhof**	*freed-hofe*
train station	**Bahnhof**	*barn-hofe*
gallery	**Galerie**	*gall-er-ree*
information	**Auskunft**	*owss-koonft*
church	**Kirche**	*keersh-un*
garden	**Garten**	*gart'n*
palace/castle	**Palast/Schloss**	*pallast/shloss*
place (square)	**Platz**	*plats*
bus stop	**Haltestelle**	*hal-te-shtel-uh*
national holiday	**Nationalfeiertag**	*nats-yon-ahl-fire-tahk*
theatre	**Theater**	*tay-aht-er*
free admission	**Eintritt frei**	*ine-tritt fry*

Shopping

Do you have/ Is there…?	**Gibt es…?**	*geept ess*
How much does it cost?	**Was kostet das?**	*voss kost't duss?*
When do you open/ close	**Wann öffnen Sie? schliessen Sie?**	*vunn off'n zee shlees'n zee*
this	**das**	*duss*
expensive	**teuer**	*toy-er*
cheap	**preiswert**	*price-vurt*
size	**Grösse**	*gruhs-uh*
number	**Nummer**	*noom-er*
colour	**Farbe**	*farb-uh*
brown	**braun**	*brown*
black	**schwarz**	*shvarts*
red	**rot**	*roht*
blue	**blau**	*blau*
green	**grün**	*groon*
yellow	**gelb**	*gelp*

Types of Shop

antique shop	**Antiquariat**	*antik-var-yat*

chemist (pharmacy)	**Apotheke**	*appo-tay-kuh*
bank	**Bank**	*bunk*
market	**Markt**	*markt*
travel agency	**Reisebüro**	*rye-zer-boo-roe*
department store	**Warenhaus**	*vahr'n-hows*
chemist's drugstore	**Drogerie**	*droog-er-ree*
hairdresser	**Friseur**	*freezz-er*
newspaper kiosk	**Zeitungskiosk**	*tsytoongs-kee-osk*
bookshop	**Buchhandlung**	*bookh-hant-loong*
bakery	**Bäckerei**	*beck-er-eye*
post office	**Post**	*posst*
shop/store	**Geschäft/Laden**	*gush-eft/lard'n*
film processing shop	**Photogeschäft**	*fo-to-gush-eft*
self-service shop	**Selbstbedie-nungsladen**	*selpst-bed-ee-nungs-lard'n*
shoe shop	**Schuhladen**	*shoo-lard'n*
clothes shop store	**Kleiderladen Boutique**	*klyder-lard'n boo-teek-uh*
food shop	**Lebensmittel-geschäft**	*lay-bens-mittel-gush-eft*
glass, porcelain	**Glas, Porzellan**	*glars, Port-sellahn*

Staying in a Hotel

Do you have any vacancies?	**Haben Sie noch Zimmer frei?**	*harb'n zee nokh tsimm-er-fry*
with twin beds?	**mit zwei Betten?**	*mitt tsvy bett'n*
with a double bed?	**mit einem Doppelbett?**	*mitt ine'm dopp'lbet*
with a bath?	**mit Bad?**	*mitt bart*
with a shower?	**mit Dusche?**	*mitt doosh-uh*
I have a reservation	**Ich habe eine Reservierung**	*ish harb-uh ine-uh rez-er-veer-oong*
key	**Schlüssel**	*shlooss'l*
porter	**Pförtner**	*pfert-ner*

Eating Out

Do you have a table for …?	**Haben Sie einen Tisch für…?**	*harb'n zee ine-uhn Tisch für…?*
I would like to reserve a table	**Ich möchte eine Reservierung machen**	*ish mer-shtuh ine-uh rezer-veer-oong makh'n*
I'm a vegetarian	**Ich bin Vegetarier**	*ish bin veg-er-tah-ree-er*
Waiter!	**Herr Ober!**	*hair oh-bare!*
The bill (check), please	**Die Rechnung, bitte**	*dee resh-noong bitt-uh*
breakfast	**Frühstück**	*froo-shtock*
lunch	**Mittagessen**	*mit-targ-ess'n*
dinner	**Abendessen**	*arb'nt-ess'n*
bottle	**Flasche**	*flush-uh*
dish of the day	**Tagesgericht**	*tahg-es-gur-isht*
main dish	**Hauptgericht**	*howpt-gur-isht*
dessert	**Nachtisch**	*nahkh-tish*
cup	**Tasse**	*tass-uh*
wine list	**Weinkarte**	*vine-kart-uh*
tankard	**Krug**	*khroog*
glass	**Glas**	*glars*

spoon	**Löffel**	*lerff'l*
teaspoon	**Teelöffel**	*tay-lerff'l*
tip	**Trinkgeld**	*trink-gelt*
knife	**Messer**	*mess-er*
starter (appetizer)	**Vorspeise**	*for-shpize-uh*
the bill	**Rechnung**	*resh-noong*
plate	**Teller**	*tell-er*
fork	**Gabel**	*gahb'l*

Menu Decoder

Aa		
Aal	*arl*	eel
Apfel	*upf'l*	apple
Apfelschorle	*upf'l-shoorl-uh*	apple juice with sparkling mineral water
Apfelsine	*upf'l-seen-uh*	orange
Aprikose	*upri-kawz-uh*	apricot
Artischocke	*arti-shokh-uh -*	artichoke
Aubergine	*or-ber-jeen-uh*	aubergine (eggplant)
Banane	*bar-narn-uh*	banana
Beefsteack	*beef-stayk*	steak
Bier	*beer*	beer
Bockwurst	*bokh-voorst*	a type of sausage
Bohnensuppe	*burn-en-zoop-uh*	bean soup
Branntwein	*brant-vine*	spirits
Bratkartoffeln	*brat-kar-toff'ln*	fried potatoes
Bratwurst	*brat-voorst*	fried sausage
Brötchen	*bret-tchen*	bread roll
Brot	*brot*	bread
Brühe	*bruh-uh*	broth
Butter	*boot-ter*	butter
Champignon	*shum-pin-yong*	mushroom
Currywurst	*kha-ree-voorst*	sausage with curry sauce
Dill	*dill*	dill
Ei	*eye*	egg
Eis	*ice*	ice/ ice cream
Ente	*ent-uh*	duck
Erdbeeren	*ayrt-beer'n*	strawberries
Fisch	*fish*	fish
Forelle	*for-ell-uh*	trout
Frikadelle	*Frika-dayl-uh*	rissole/ hamburger
Gans	*ganns*	goose
Garnele	*gar-nayl-uh*	prawn/shrimp
gebraten	*g'braat'n*	fried
gegrillt	*g'grilt*	grilled
gekocht	*g'kokht*	boiled
geräuchert	*g'rowk-ert*	smoked
Geflügel	*g'floog'l*	poultry
Gemüse	*g'mooz-uh*	vegetables
Grütze	*grurt-ser*	groats, gruel
Gulasch	*goo-lush*	goulash
Gurke	*goork-uh*	gherkin
Hammelbraten	*hamm'l-braat'n*	roast mutton
Hähnchen	*haynsh'n*	chicken
Hering	*hair-ing*	herring
Himbeeren	*him-beer'n*	raspberries
Honig	*hoe-nikh*	honey
Kaffee	*kaf-fay*	coffee
Kalbfleisch	*kalp-flysh*	veal
Kaninchen	*ka-neensh'n*	rabbit
Karpfen	*karpf'n*	carp
Kartoffelpüree	*kar-toff'l-poor-ay*	mashed potatoes

Käse	*kayz-uh*	cheese
Kaviar	*kar-vee-ar*	caviar
Knoblauch	*k'nob-lowkh*	garlic
Knödel	*k'nerd'l*	noodle
Kohl	*koal*	cabbage
Kopfsalat	*kopf-zal-aat*	lettuce
Krebs	*krayps*	crab
Kuchen	*kookh'n*	cake
Lachs	*lahkhs*	salmon
Leber	*lay-ber*	liver
mariniert	*mari-neert*	marinated
Marmelade	*marmer-lard-uh*	marmalade, jam
Meerrettich	*may-re-tish*	horseradish
Milch	*milsh*	milk
Mineral-wasser	*minn-er-arl-vuss-er*	mineral water
Möhre	*mer-uh*	carrot
Nuss	*nooss*	nut
Öl	*erl*	oil
Olive	*o-leev-uh*	olive
Petersilie	*payt-er-zee-li-uh*	parsley
Pfeffer	*pfeff-er*	pepper
Pfirsich	*pfir-zish*	peach
Pflaumen	*pflow-men*	plum
Pommes frites	*pomm-fritt*	chips/ French fries
Quark	*kvark*	soft cheese
Radieschen	*ra-deesh'n*	radish
Rinderbraten	*rind-er-brat'n*	joint of beef
Rinderroulade	*rind-er-roo-lard-uh*	beef olive
Rindfleisch	*rint-flysh*	beef
Rippchen	*rip-sh'n*	cured pork rib
Rotkohl	*roht-koal*	red cabbage
Rüben	*rhoob'n*	turnip
Rührei	*rhoo-er-eye*	scrambled eggs
Saft	*zuft*	juice
Salat	*zal-aat*	salad
Salz	*zults*	salt
Salzkartoffeln	*zults-kar-toff'l*	boiled potatoes
Sauerkirschen	*zow-er-keersh'n*	cherries
Sauerkraut	*zow-er-krowt*	sauerkraut
Sekt	*zekt*	sparkling wine
Senf	*zenf*	mustard
scharf	*sharf*	spicy
Schaschlik	*shash-lik*	kebab
Schlagsahne	*shlahgg-zarn-uh*	whipped cream
Schnittlauch	*shnit-lowhkh*	chives
Schnitzel	*shnitz'l*	veal or pork cutlet
Schweinefleisch	*shvine-flysh*	pork
Spargel	*sharg'l*	asparagus
Spiegelei	*shpeeg'l-eye*	fried egg
Spinat	*shpin-art*	spinach
Tee	*tay*	tea
Tomate	*tom-art-uh*	tomato
Wassermelone	*vuss-er-me-lohn-uh*	watermelon
Wein	*vine*	wine
Weintrauben	*vine-trowb'n*	grapes
Wiener Würstchen	*veen-er voorst-sh'n*	frankfurter
Zander	*tsan-der*	pike-perch
Zitrone	*tsi-trohn-uh*	lemon
Zucker	*tsook-er*	sugar
Zwieback	*tsvee-ba*	rusk
Zwiebel	*tsveeb'l*	onion

Numbers

0	null	*nool*
1	eins	*eye'ns*
2	zwei	*tsvy*
3	drei	*dry*
4	vier	*feer*
5	fünf	*foonf*
6	sechs	*zex*
7	sieben	*zeeb'n*
8	acht	*uhkht*
9	neun	*noyn*
10	zehn	*tsayn*
11	elf	*elf*
12	zwölf	*tserlf*
13	dreizehn	*dry-tsayn*
14	vierzehn	*feer-tsayn*
15	fünfzehn	*foonf-tsayn*
16	sechzehn	*zex-tsayn*
17	siebzehn	*zeep-tsayn*
18	achtzehn	*uhkht-tsayn*
19	neunzehn	*noyn-tsayn*
20	zwanzig	*tsvunn-tsig*
21	einundzwanzig	*ine-oont-tsvunn-tsig*
30	dreissig	*dry-sig*
40	vierzig	*feer-sig*
40	vierzig	*feer-sig*
50	fünfzig	*foonf-tsig*
60	sechzig	*zex-tsig*
70	siebzig	*zeep-tsig*
80	achtzig	*uhkht-tsig*
90	neunzig	*noyn-tsig*
100	hundert	*hoond't*
1000	tausend	*towz'nt*
1,000,000	eine Million	*ine-uh mill-yon*

Time

one minute	eine Minute	*ine-uh min-oot-uh*
one hour	eine Stunde	*ine-uh shtoond-uh*
half an hour	eine halbe Stunde	*ine-uh hullb-uh shtoond-uh*
Monday	Montag	*mohn-targ*
Tuesday	Dienstag	*deens-targ*
Wednesday	Mittwoch	*mitt-vokh*
Thursday	Donnerstag	*donn-ers-targ*
Friday	Freitag	*fry-targ*
Saturday	Samstag/ Sonnabend	*zums-targ zonn-ah-bent*
Sunday	Sonntag	*zon-targ*
January	Januar	*yan-ooar*
February	Februar	*fay-brooar*
March	März	*mairts*
April	April	*april*
May	Mai	*my*
June	Juni	*yoo-ni*
July	Juli	*yoo-lee*
August	August	*ow-goost*
September	September	*zep-tem-ber*
October	Oktober	*ok-toh-ber*
November	November	*no-vem-ber*
December	Dezember	*day-tsem-ber*
spring	Frühling	*froo-ling*
summer	Sommer	*zomm-er*
autumn (fall)	Herbst	*hairpst*
winter	Winter	*vint-er*